Praise for *Black Lives Matter to Jesus*

"With the surplus of studies on Luke-Acts, it is hard to imagine there is more to consider, but Jerkins has accomplished the task of inviting fresh consideration. Resourcing the history and imperatives of the Black Lives Matter movement, he provides a fresh view of Luke-Acts. Jerkins courageously reconfigures interpretive strategy, positioning Black life in America as an entryway for interpreting Luke-Acts. I commend this monograph to anyone seeking a fresh reading of Luke-Acts that resources contemporary social movements for the exegetical and hermeneutical tasks."

—Shively T. J. Smith, assistant professor
of New Testament, Boston University

"Jerkins argues that an 'I don't see color' attitude toward race and ethnicity is not a biblical perspective, certainly not reflective of Luke's Gospel and the book of Acts. Luke highlighted the gospel's impact on Black people to demonstrate Christ's victory over sin and the hope of redemption, which looks like a many-colored kingdom. This book offers fresh insight on how Black lives matter both then and now."

—Nijay K. Gupta, professor of New Testament,
Northern Seminary

"The years 2020–2021 have presented extraordinary challenges. In addition to a global pandemic that has already killed more than three million people, the brutal murder of George Floyd—and other acts of violence toward persons of color—stirred social unrest and protests grounded in a heightened awareness of the insidious structural racism that continues to prove devastatingly harmful—and too often lethal—to our Black and brown brothers and sisters. With *Black Lives Matter to Jesus*, Marcus Jerkins has provided biblical warrant for understanding the pivotal role that a Black-skinned person, the eunuch of Ethiopia, played in Luke's account of God's plan of salvation for humankind. *Black Lives Matter to Jesus* is as significant in its content as it is timely in its release—take up and read, and do it now!"

—Mikeal C. Parsons, professor and Macon Chair
in Religion, Baylor University

Black Lives Matter to Jesus

Black Lives Matter to Jesus

The Salvation of Black Life
and All Life in Luke and Acts

MARCUS JERKINS

FORTRESS PRESS
Minneapolis

CONTENTS

PREFACE

If you are reading this book, you matter. Yes, you matter. You matter because you are a member of God's creation. You matter because God ordained for you to live. Such talk may sound ridiculous to some. But their possible rejection does not at all diminish the truth contained in the claim.

The title of this book may elicit an unfounded charge that it is about Black supremacy. Not at all. This book is about the inclusion of all of the peoples of the world. All belong to the human family because God made this so. It is up to the members of the human family to recognize this truth and treat all members this way. My hope is that people of every variation of color will read this book and confront the biases that we have toward one another.

In particular, as a Black Christian, I believe we must confront the systemic issues that have precluded unity in America and around the world. There can be no reconciliation, however, without justice. True reconciliation is only possible once the truth has been spoken. And once the truth is known, then, and only then, can solutions be found for the problems of race and racism. The great violation of racism, the standardization of a particular phenotype and complexion in the human family, can only be overcome and rebuked when justice reigns. But justice cannot reign as long as we keep ourselves blind to the existence of the violation.

With the history presented in this book, it should become more apparent how the wickedness of racism was possible in America and around the world and took hold of the human imagination and executed in law. The contextualization offered to us by history can equip us to better understand why some thought it was natural to harm others on the basis of color. Historical contextualization provides the means to evaluate the faux analysis of physical differences. Instead of honoring our diversity, we have used our variety as a mechanism for stratification, for making caste systems. But proper engagement with Christian Scripture demands more of us.

When we look to the past, we discover that Scripture has already said this. Jesus came into the world to make all things new, to make all of the peoples of the world right with God. Jesus's work to make all things right meant that every kind of wrong is to be addressed. Among them, as will be explained hereafter, is the issue that we know as racism. And to combat an early form of racism in his day, Luke tells us that God's desire to save all the nations through Jesus was demonstrated through the salvation of Black people. To say that the lives of the world mattered to God, Luke showed us that Black lives mattered to God. I hope to convince you of this truth; I hope, being convinced, that you will lift up your voice in agreement with God about this issue. And as a consequence, you will join the kingdom of God in the fight for justice and against the degradation of Black life. For when Black life is degraded, all life is degraded.

ACKNOWLEDGMENTS

This book would not be possible without the love and care of my parents, Mark and Devora Jerkins. But also to my grandmother Juanita Fails, who encouraged me to read the Bible, to write as a scholar, to become someone who can make a difference in the world. And I am grateful for the love of my family, who helped me along the way.

Allow me to say that I would not have been able to write this book were it not for the love of my life, my wife. Thank you, Dr. Courtney Jerkins, for loving me, supporting me, and caring for me so that I could write this book. To my wonderful babies, thank you for motivating your dad to write this book. My desire for you to live in a better world than I impressed upon me the need to write it. And thanks to my Mother in Love whose support makes our lives so much better.

To my professors at Emory and Baylor, thank you for your support. Thanks to Carl Holladay, Steven Kraftchick, Carol Newsom, and Luke Timothy Johnson, who pushed me to pursue scholarship at my lowest moments, when I was ready to give up on my studies. Mikeal Parsons, my Doktorvater, was more than just that; he has become a father to me. Both he and Beverly Gaventa helped me write comfortably in my own black skin. Dr. Steven Reid served as a model of rich black scholarship. In word and example, he pushed me to go higher and achieve more. I am also grateful for the other member of my committee, Kelly Iverson, who was a tremendous source of affirmation during my doctoral studies. And to N. T. Wright, whom I have never personally met but whose scholarship has helped shape my worldview since I was a freshman in college, thank you.

There are many other scholars who have encouraged me, inspired me, and blazed the trail in front of me. Thank you, Doctors Thomas Slater, Jamal Hopkins, Dianne Stewart, Teresa Fry-Brown, Mark Sanders, Robert Brown, Michael Awkward, Dwight Andrews. All of you gave me extra time in your office and gave me the talk about what it means to be a transformative Black scholar. I am beyond grateful for the significant investment you made in me. I intend to honor the kindness and care you have granted me.

To my pastors, thank you for encouraging, supporting, and blessing this young pastor-scholar to use my voice as a vehicle for change. Without Pastor Stanley Smith, I would not know how to speak. Without Pastor William Dwight McKissic, I would not know how to speak boldly. Without Pastor Ralph West, I would not know what to say.

And thanks to Fortress and Carey Newman for believing in this project. I hope we are able to make a difference in the world through it.

CHAPTER I

BLACK LIVES MATTER, JESUS, AND HISTORY

Black lives matter. This statement is true. Indeed, it is categorically and universally true. Its truth transcends the affirmations of those who proclaim it, in their many ways. Its truth overcomes those who deny it. Black lives matter. The lives of those who are a little bit browner than others, most of whom have their biological ancestry in Africa, matter. Although history has not always recognized this truth, eternity has.

The record has been well established in human history, especially within the Western telling: the narrative has been unkind to Black life, especially in recent centuries. It must be understood that the saying "Black lives matter" is a response to the notion that they do not. Of course "all lives matter"; that is the point of saying "Black lives matter." If all lives do not matter, Black lives do not matter either. We say this not to declare that Black lives matter more but because in a large portion of human history, they really have not mattered at all.

I am placing my cards on the table. I do not write this work as a full supporter of the overtly nontheistic and anti-Christian leanings of the official Black Lives Matter movement. I offer them my respect and praise for the efforts they have wrought on behalf of Black and oppressed people around the world. But I am not an advocate of their complete ideological platform. This work, then, is not an attempt to provide biblical justification for all of their beliefs.

Rather, I am writing as a Christian, a follower of Jesus Christ. I am writing as a biblical scholar who has investigated biblical texts historically and exegetically. I am writing this book as a pastor concerned about the preaching of the gospel, which entails the dignification of Black life and the reconciliation of the nations to God. And as a consequence, I am advancing a position that rehearses the slogan "Black lives matter" but has a uniquely Christian take on this phrase. The reason is simple. If Black lives do not matter to God, do they really matter? But since they do matter to God, the one who has been revealed in Jesus, then we can boldly proclaim that they matter.

Some might ask, What kind of Christian take could one have on this phrase? It has been argued that this phrase is anti-Christian at its core. This book is an attempt to argue quite the opposite. Jesus, the resurrected Lord, believes that Black lives matter. They matter to him.

This is the message we hear from the author of Luke and Acts. When he wrote his Gospel, he portrayed Jesus as the savior of the children of Adam, those who were made in the image of God, the children of God (Luke 3:38; see Gen 1–2; 5:1–5). To express the explosion of the mission to save all of the children of Adam contained in Luke's second book, Acts of the Apostles, Luke discusses the salvation of Black life (Acts 8:26–40; 13:1). Luke mentions the presence of African peoples as a demonstration of the reach of Jesus's salvation. This salvation is of the Jews (Acts 2:10; see Isa 19:25). And most pivotally, when Luke wanted to express the extension of the gospel of Jesus to all of the world, he described the salvation of a person who was recognized in the ancient world as a black-skinned African (Acts 8:26–40). For Luke, Black lives mattered and continue to matter to Jesus.

A Proposal for a Biblical View of Blackness

It has been difficult for people to agree with this reading of the evidence.[1] For many centuries, white supremacist theology has blinded the minds of many who have looked at the biblical text.[2] As a rule, white supremacy invests the white reader with the notion that she stands at the center of all of history and eternity. Whether such a reader is cognizant of this lens or not, for this person, God may (rarely) be invisible but Jesus is most assuredly white.[3] He is not a brown-skinned Jew from first-century Judea, reared in the territory of Galilee. He, in the least, may have been the only white-skinned Jew in that area, if he were a Jew at all. The point is that the white supremacist reading is always colored white. One could understand this reading given that each color group images their god in some way like unto themselves. But it has had particularly devastating consequences for a proper reading of the New Testament and the spread of Christianity around the world.

We must be clear: Jesus certainly had a color. The typical response of many that Jesus's color did not matter is fundamentally wrong. It is interesting that many of these people have only been concerned about proclaiming that Jesus had no color, or that his color did not matter, in response to those who say Jesus looked like everyone else in Nazareth of Galilee. They had no problem with Jesus's color while he was imaged as white for centuries. But now there is a problem with Jesus having a color.

Color-blind theology will not do with a historical reading of the biblical texts.[4] The ancients would have recognized that Jesus had a color. Many Jews considered themselves to be the ideal color, which makes sense of the fact that they believed they were God's chosen.[5] But we do ourselves a disservice and we misread the biblical narratives if we suggest that skin complexion never mattered in the Bible. It mattered then and it matters now.

Yes, geography and culture also mattered. But we must be honest when we recognize that aesthetics and physicality also matter in the calculus of moral perception. Among those with ancient Mediterranean perspectives, in particular, skin color was part of the calculus for adjudication of one's personality and worth. This is what we call physiognomy, the determination of someone's character based on some aspect of his physicality.[6]

Again, we must be clear about this. Many ancients were concerned about how everyone looked. Aristotle and other ancients believed that people took on black skin complexion and features related to a black phenotype because of their location in Africa.[7] His view, as I will demonstrate, was not marginal. Moreover, it was also common to believe that people's character matched their appearance. And these descriptions might bring with them a negative assessment.[8]

Interestingly, we receive a decidedly different perspective in the New Testament. This point is not new. It has been established that the New Testament participates in the conventions in which it was birthed, discussing people in a way where one would expect to infer a conclusion about someone based on his physical appearance.[9] But the New Testament does so to subvert and overturn said conventions. I am doing this as I write this book. I was born being told by both white and Black people that I am Black, even though the color designation is not particularly accurate. I accept this, however, not to prop up a racist system but to affirm antiracism and engage in the conversation about how we disrupt the faulty ideologies that gave rise to the devaluation of people with dark brown skin.

But white supremacist perspectives are not the only ones that affirm the white supremacist attempt to ignore the testimony of Christian Scripture. Opposing the white supremacist view, though coming to the same conclusion, are those who profess that Jesus and the Bible have never valued Black life.[10] Many believe that Christianity is "the white man's religion." Oftentimes, Black conspiracy theorists accept white supremacist readings and argue that there is a white Jesus. And hence my enslaved ancestors accepted a white religion, devalued themselves, and wanted to please white people in the process. Again, this analysis is an unhistorical and problematic reading that equally does not do justice to the New Testament and the portrayal of Black life in the Bible.[11] When we read Jewish scripture and the New Testament, we see a different picture emerge. The God of Scripture has always loved and valued Black life. And in particular, Luke wanted his readers to know that Jesus saw the salvation of Black life as essential to the spread of the gospel around the world.

Here is what I would like to argue. It will sound completely unfamiliar to most Christians, though it is the story that Luke is telling us. When we go back to the New Testament, when we look at the writings of Luke and Acts, we see the following case being made. Jesus is the savior of the entire world (Luke 24:47). The world needed saving because Israel and the nations were sinful. Adam and his descendants, all of the nations of the world, were made in God's image and likeness. As such, they were children of God (Acts 17:26–31). But their status as God's children was in question because of the disconnection humans had with God. God planned to have Israel become the nation that resembled him, to exemplify what it meant to be God's child. To make this so—because sin taints every human—and bring divine childship (the status of being considered God's child) into fulfillment, God sent his own Son, Jesus.[12] Through Jesus, Israel realizes its own place as God's child and will be used as a reconciling agent, bringing the whole world back to God, restoring all peoples to their status as God's children. Through Jesus, the image of God is restored to its rightful appearance; humans reflect God as they are meant to. The children reflect their divine parent, their Father.

The further implementation of this soteriological project occurs through Jesus's work through the redeemed Israel, the church in Acts.[13] The symbolic redemption of all of Israel occurs at Pentecost, the cause of the Messiah grows, and Jews from around the Diaspora return to the God of Israel through Jesus and the work of the Holy Spirit. This was, in part, confirmed by the presence of African Jews and proselytes at Pentecost.

The salvation of the non-Jewish nations is symbolized by the presence of Christian black-skinned Africans (Acts 8:26–40; 13:1). Luke wanted his audience to know that these people were Black. The Ethiopian eunuch was certainly Black—indeed the blackest of all Black people in the eyes of the ancients.[14] And Simeon, who laid hands on Paul and Barnabas on the commencement of their apostolic journeys, is called "Black." The point is that Luke wanted his readership to recognize these key individuals as black-skinned.

Luke, a writer aware that color mattered to the ancients, highlighted blackness because it was despised, rejected, and considered a bad omen by many other ancients.[15] But for the cause of the Messiah to be completed, the redemption of the nations meant the rejection of aesthetic bias. Though despised by many ancients, Black was beautiful to the Messiah of Israel. He came to save every child of God. And just like a God who shows complete disrepute for the foolish prejudices of people, a God who loves the things humans despise (1 Cor 1:27), God arranged for the first non-Jewish recipient of the gospel to be a black-skinned African.

The implications of such a representation in Luke not only matter for the New Testament; they also matter for all of Christianity. What Luke gives us in narrative demonstrates the intentionality of God to demonstrate acceptance of all people regardless of external appearance. God accepts all colors. God does not exalt white over black, black over brown, brown over yellow. Whatever one's complexion, whatever one's phenotype, we all come from the same God. We all are linked together genetically. We all must endeavor to reject the sinful tendency to associate the appearance and the culture of an entire group with wickedness and indignity. We are all made in God's image and called to be God's children (Gen 1:26–31). My hope is that at the end of this work, the reader will have a listening ear, recognizing what biases they may have in seeing the reflection of God in a different color.

Where Do We Go from Here?

Rev. Dr. Martin Luther King Jr. asked this question with regard to racial justice in America.[16] I believe it is appropriate in our proposal for the case being made in Luke/Acts and its implications. Chapter 2 will be an evaluation of the various studies that have treated divine childship and blackness in ancient writings. What we will discover is that scholarly views, on the whole, have treated these topics in isolation. They make the most sense when seen as part of the same argument in Luke's narratives.

In order to make the case for this work, I will offer an investigation of Jewish and Greco-Roman concepts of divine childship. My focus will be how humans are described as the children of God. Chapter 3 allows us to better understand the ways in which the nations could be perceived as God's children.

Chapter 4 will describe how Luke explores divine childship in his Gospel and Acts. In this chapter, I will sketch how divine childship is the nexus for a multiethnic soteriology—that is, how the restoration of the children of God is described in terms of God's mission to reclaim all ethnicities. This chapter provides the foundation for an analysis of the multivalent implications of the stories of the Ethiopian eunuch and Simeon Niger.

Chapter 5 will make the case for how the salvation of the world, the reclamation of all of God's children, can be symbolized in the participation of black-skinned Africans in the church. In Acts, when we look with ancient perspectives of race, we discover that salvation had physiognomic consequences. The Ethiopian eunuch's story is told in such a way not only to speak of the salvation of a gentile but also to subvert popular views regarding the shamefulness of black skin.

In the conclusion, I will engage what implications our study has for racial thinking for the ancients and bring the project to conclusion. This will allow us to attempt to understand what we may learn theologically about race.[17] Even though there is no one concept of race in the ancient world, what we can learn from the theology of Jesus and the early church on it is inestimable. What we will see is that color blindness is wrongheaded. Yes, I believe Luke's history agrees with Paul that there is neither Jew nor Greek in Christ (Gal 3:28). But this call for unity does not at all destroy the diversity inherent in their histories and even their practices in Christ.[18]

CHAPTER 2

DIVINE CHILDSHIP AND ITS RELEVANCE TO BLACK LIVES IN LUKE/ACTS

In Luke/Acts, humanity's connection to the divine family is interwoven into the church's mission for black-skinned and other gentiles.[1] The two works frame the mission for Israel and the nations as the reclamation of God's lost children (Luke 6:35–36; 20:36; 15:11–32; Acts 17:26–31). In this mission, the reclamation of God's Black African children epitomizes and ensures the success of the total mission for the whole world (Luke 24:47; Acts 8:26–40; 13:1; 26:20).

The case for the importance of blackness in Luke/Acts is rooted in a reevaluation of the worth of humanity. Human dignity is tied to the conception of salvation through Jesus Christ. Through Jesus, humans of every nation are redeemed and restored in the image of the one who created them. Luke describes this redemption in divine childship terms—that is, God's claim that Israel, first, and the rest of the nations become his children through Jesus. Through Jesus, the human is recognized as God's child; there is no higher honor for a human than to be a child of God. One of the major lacunas in scholarship is that most have not seen this case being made in Luke/Acts.[2] This language is primarily treated in isolation and not considered foundational for how Luke perceives the function of Jesus's salvation for Israel and the nations.

Since this theological perspective is primarily unaddressed or underemphasized, it plays typically no role in interpretations of God's pursuit of all of human beings in Luke/Acts. That is, Luke establishes in his Gospel that the children of God are returning to be restored by God through Jesus. Then, in Acts, Luke maps out how Israel and the nations are being restored. And to accentuate the return of the non-Jewish nations to God, Luke draws upon the stories of black-skinned Africans who are part of the church. These Black lives symbolize that for Luke, Christ has assuredly come to rescue every nation that has descended from Adam.

Jesus, his followers, and Adam are all called God's children in various ways. And if Adam is called God's child, his status should say something about the status of all people. The overlap of language suggests some explication is necessary to better understand Luke's theology. Part of making the case for the dignification of blackness is an examination of the concept of divine childship. What will emerge in the analysis is that all of the nations are, in some sense, considered God's children.[3] As a consequence, the salvation wrought through Jesus brings all of the children of God back to God, their Father.

The Children of God in Luke/Acts

Emphasis on the nature and significance of being God's children occurs in Pauline studies.[4] Paul refers to the people of God as God's children (e.g., Rom 8:16). Trying to analyze Paul's explanation of divine childship, one interpretation argues that divine childship status, being God's child, in the corpus of biblical and postbiblical Jewish literature denotes three senses.[5] It could speak to one's identity as a divine/heavenly being (e.g., Gen 6:4). It could suggest that one is a royal figure (e.g., Ps 2:7). It could also suggest that one is an Israelite (e.g., Deut 14:1).[6] This interpretation concludes that human-divine childship status is rooted in Jesus's sonship.[7] Through Jesus, the revelation that humans are God's children occurs at the resurrection.

Divine childship may also signify an "angelomorphic" status.[8] The use of this language is meant primarily to denote that human beings are like the angels.[9] One understands this interpretation of the language given in Luke 20:36. But Luke 6:35–36 suggests Jesus's followers are not like the angels but like God. The angel comparison is not Luke's central point.

Luke's usage of divine childship language is not limited to Jesus and followers of Jesus. It pertains to Adam as well (Luke 3:38). That Adam is God's child has meant that Jesus's identity as Son of God can be a way of speaking of him as a second Adam,[10] though this has been refuted as a good interpretation of Adam's divine childship.[11]

Luke could also signify Jesus as a kind of Adam.[12] In this reading, Luke departs from Paul in a few ways. In Luke, Jesus is not the "last Adam," but he is the "second" Son of God.[13] As God breathed and created Adam, so did God breathe by the Spirit and bring forth Jesus (Luke 1:35).[14] Jesus's sonship is related to Adam's also because Jesus reverses the closure of "paradise" to humans.[15] In this view, Testament of Levi 18:10–12 and Testament of Dan 5:9–12 both suggest that God's chosen leader will reopen the gates to Eden when the end of the age mirrors the beginning. Jesus does this symbolically on the cross when he offers the thief entrance into paradise (Luke 23:43).

This particular view, or its phrasing, is in the minority. As it is framed, "the Second Son of God" has a vocation deeply connected to the mission of the church.[16] The bestowal and confirmation of the Spirit are evidence for this connection. This view suggests "the Holy Spirit plays an important role in Acts in verifying the authenticity of gentile conversion." Jesus's vocation involved passing on the Spirit to others: "Having been generated by the Spirit, having been filled with the Spirit, and having never lost the Spirit through disobedience, Jesus is able, in cooperation with his Father, to impart the Spirit as a gift to all who obey the Gospel."[17] Luke 10:17–20 is used as evidence for this Christological identity for Jesus. The seventy could possibly represent the seventy nations of Genesis 10. Jesus's sending of the seventy is symbolic of the mission for the whole world. And further, Jesus grants them "authority and power" (Luke 10:1, 19) over serpents, scorpions, and satanic powers. In this way, the disciples share in the very authority of the Christ who utilizes the authority of Adam (Gen 1:26–28).[18]

Their Spirit-given authority extends to their ability to mimic Jesus during times of temptation.[19] The argument is made that Luke changes some of the language from the Synoptic tradition to emphasize endurance during times of temptation from the devil. Also, unique to Luke is Jesus's warning to Peter about Satan's desire to "sift" him (Luke 22:31–32).

This view also holds that Jesus was able to pass along the Spirit and "generate more 'sons of God.'" The study cites the two foundational passages for divine childship language, Luke 6:35 and 20:36. The former may not express a unique Lukan idea. The latter text definitely expresses a unique idea: "Adam the first son of God sinned and died, but Jesus, the second Son of God, obeyed and lived (as seen in his resurrection). Those who believe in Jesus will follow his steps, no longer subject to death, as sons of God and sons of the resurrection." This view argues that "the Adam/Jesus typology, when understood properly against Luke's pneumatology, sheds light on the evangelist's Christology and on a problem with which he grapples throughout his two-volume work: the Gentile question." Adam affects every human and so, too, does Jesus.[20] Jesus, however, brings life to every nation, whereas Adam brought death.

Besides the language—"second Son of God"—this description makes sense of the evidence. There are two notable omissions in this study's articulation of Luke's approach to the gentile mission, however. First, there is no discussion of *why* this Adam/Christ typology mandates the gentile mission. Luke tells us that God has a penchant for reclaiming God's children (Luke 15:11–32; 19:10). Second, there is no discussion of the conversion of the first gentile in Acts, the Ethiopian eunuch. It is odd that this story is omitted in the analysis given the prominence of the Spirit in this narrative (Acts 8:29, 39). The Spirit-led conversion of a black-skinned African serves as an essential beginning for the reclamation and conversion of all of the nations of the world. This conversion is part of the restoration of all of God's children on the one hand and the dignification of black skin on the other. It is an essential part of Luke's story.

Drawing from Greco-Roman and Jewish perspectives, another study has investigated "son of God" language in the New Testament. Luke/Acts features minimally in this analysis. In this view, Paul and John provide "ideal types" of "divine sonship."[21] The study differentiates the motifs of begetting and making (adoption) of God's children as principal in the New Testament.

It argues that Luke says both of Jesus. For humans, Paul discusses adoptive sonship and John's sonship is by begetting. The study concludes, "In the end, divine sonship is an image that unites Christ with Christians more than it separates them."[22]

This study's argument is helpful in that it draws from both Greco-Roman and Jewish concepts of divine sonship. Greco-Roman resonances are essential to how Luke makes his case for the success of the Christological mission. It would be understood that the Ethiopian eunuch represented the "ends of the earth" (Acts 1:8). Also, the rhetorical value of divine childship language is brought into focus. It is not enough to say that calling humans "God's children" is meant to describe an anthropological perspective. It is meant to describe the desire and intentionality of divine relationship as well.

So what does it mean for humans to be God's children in Luke/Acts? Why is Adam called a child of God in the genealogy of *the* child of God, Jesus? And more, what does any of this have to do with the salvation of Israel and the nations? Discussing the nations for Luke/Acts involves the significances of race and black-skinned people in Luke/Acts. But arguments made about the Ethiopian, again, have been treated in isolation and have not connected the Ethiopian's story to the importance of his being a child of God. There even has not been much attention paid to the importance of his blackness.

RACE, BLACK SKIN, AND LUKE/ACTS

If it is true that divine childship is related to God's desire to save the peoples of diverse ethnicities, is this reflected in views about ethnicity in Luke/Acts? Many arguments made in scholarship struggle to discover the theological meaning of an Ethiopian as the first gentile convert and Simeon Niger's inclusion among the prophets and teachers. Their ethnographic origin and skin color have not been considered essential in the history of scholarship.[23] There may be three approaches to discussions of the Ethiopian's skin color and ethnography. First, there is "uncertainty," as one scholar notes that the "ethnic origin is strictly undetermined."[24] In another view, it is said that "what made his conversion to be remembered and told as a legend was neither his African provenance nor his black skin (it is quite possible he was black but that is never said)."[25] A second approach is to admit that the Ethiopian is from Nubia but pay scant attention to the ethnographic significance. Finally, views also approach the text emphasizing the ethnographic origins of the Ethiopian. Scholarly tendencies have changed. Recent Acts views have brought great attention to the Ethiopian's racial identity.[26] But even where there is emphasis on the Ethiopian's racial identity, there is more emphasis on his being a eunuch rather than his being a black-skinned African.[27]

Placing emphasis on the Ethiopian's ethnographic identity, his blackness is most helpful for understanding the importance of the text.[28] But even then, in most cases, the connection to Simeon Niger and the possibility that Luke may be focusing on blackness have not been readily seen. Many studies show that Luke is concerned with a universalistic gospel, but most scholars do not give attention to the Ethiopian's blackness to express this universalism. In other words, how does an Ethiopian, in particular, make Luke's universalistic case for him? How does the Lukan dignification of black skin as a means overturn cultural perspectives?

A groundbreaking dissertation from an African American scholar on the Ethiopian eunuch discussed his ethnic identity in novel ways.[29] During the writing of this dissertation, scholarship had missed the gravity of the Ethiopian's import. But this argument suggested that the Ethiopian had a central function for Luke's universalistic goals because the Ethiopian recalls Acts 1:8, the promise that the gospel would reach the end of the world. In a later study, it is argued that "partial fulfilment" of Acts 1:8 and "the Ethiopian's geographical provenance uniquely qualifies him to represent this fulfillment." The study argues that "the conversion of an 'Ethiopian' eunuch provides a graphic illustration and symbol of the diverse persons who will constitute the Church of the Risen Christ."[30] In the dissertation, the Ethiopian's conversion is analyzed in literary terms: "Luke's use of the pericope to foreshadow the drama of the mission to the gentiles fulfills one of the chief aims of foreshadowing: the creation of suspense about what will unfold within the narrative action. The reader has already been induced to wonder 'how' the Christian mission will expand beyond, Jerusalem to Judea and Samaria, and finally to the 'end of the earth.' The question was never what would happen, but 'how' it would happen."[31] The salvation of the Ethiopian marks the expansion of the gospel to the whole world.[32]

Another study discusses how Luke initially signaled the Ethiopian as the beginning of the gentile mission but later changed his position to please his Roman benefactor.[33] In the study, it is argued that the earlier accounts of Christianity are more celebratory of ancient darker peoples from Jerusalem and the Afro-Asiatic world. The Romanization of the Christian movement led to a kind of whitening of the mission of the church. The suspicion of Luke disallows the study to perceive the ways in which Luke subverts Greco-Roman aesthetic conceptions and physiognomic readings of black-skinned people in Acts.

Another study offers a rhetorical analysis of the Ethiopian's conversion. This study argues that the Ethiopian is included in Luke's motif of imperial submission. That is, those who had great authority—like centurions (e.g., Luke 7:2–10; Acts 10:1–8) and the Ethiopian eunuch—would have perceived the Ethiopian's conversion as a sign of the gospel's overwhelming power.[34]

These studies note the blackness of the Ethiopian and the importance of his provenance but still do not resolve the question of the necessity of his inclusion. To do so, one would have to see the larger task that Luke is attempting by including Black African figures into his narrative—one, in particular, at the beginning of the gentile mission.[35] Since their skin color would have been central to their identity in the Greco-Roman world, it is necessary to analyze what Luke might be suggesting in including black-skinned people.[36] Thus it is necessary to attend closely not merely to the ethnographic origin but also to their skin color.

Another study examines black skin and blackness as a rhetorical mechanism in the ancient world. It argues that black-skinned people were used symbolically in rhetorical and poetic contexts in the ancient world. It also suggests there are four primary ways Christians symbolically discussed black-skinned people: "(1) geopolitical identification, (2) moral-spiritual characterization, (3) descriptive differentiation, and (4) Christian self-definition." This study calls these "ethno-political rhetorics." This study proposes that these rhetorics are "discursive elements within texts that refer to 'ethnic' identities or geographical locations and function as political invective." It supports this analysis by primarily mining Greco-Roman references and tropes about black-skinned people. Being an Ethiopian/Egyptian/Black African in non-Christian and Christian use, in the Greco-Roman context, suggests more than merely identifying a person's provenance. It could provide one a method of comparison, a tool of denigration of *the other*, or a means of describing the problem of sin.[37]

In the case of the Ethiopian eunuch, this study argues that he is an example of how Christians used Ethiopians as an "ideal model" of conversion. It is suggested that "in these conversion stories, the ethnicity and color of the Ethiopian served as an important literary feature that enabled the authors to establish certain virtuous characteristics within the Christian community."[38]

The study also cites several different functions for the narrative. The study concedes that in earlier scholarship, the Ethiopian fulfilled the gospel's potential to reach the end of the world. The Ethiopian also served to show that Christianity could reach even those who were a threat to the empire, under the reign of the Candace. This is "political theater."[39] Moreover, the study suggests that the conversion allowed Luke to undermine cultural assumptions. The study focuses on the account's emphasis on the man as a eunuch to make this point. As a eunuch, he is considered an "outsider." The combination of Ethiopian and eunuch is meant to doubly accentuate his identity as "other."

As an "other," the Ethiopian serves "Luke's rhetorical strategy." He is silent and humble, which speaks to his "ascetic virtue." This virtue connects with stories from the Gospel where people are rewarded for being silent and humble (Luke 8:47–48; 18:13–14). In this way, the Ethiopian exemplifies Luke's system of values: even though he was reading out loud, Philip's appearance "effectively renders him 'silent' and 'humbled.'" Philip interprets Isaiah for him, and the implication of the story is that Jesus was both silent and humble in his suffering.

Ultimately, the meaning of the Ethiopian eunuch in "ethno-political rhetoric" can only be understood when placed alongside Cornelius (Acts 10:1–48). This argument suggests that Cornelius serves to round off the Ethiopian's story. God is truly impartial, if God allows both a Roman and an Ethiopian to be baptized. With the added significance of virtue in the eunuch's story, Luke demonstrates through him, "Christianity can extend to every nation—*even* Ethiopia." The study further concludes that this story would have been a fundamental "transgression of socio-political and cultural boundaries."[40]

The study is correct to identify the "ethno-political rhetorics" as part of Luke's strategy. The study is accurate to assume that Luke has a rhetorical strategy meant to upset boundary markers within his community. The major concern is that the study abandons "the color analysis" too quickly. The study places the weight of its argument on the Ethiopian's geographical origins and his condition as a eunuch. It does not examine a subversive resonance in which Luke undermines tropes not just about eunuchs but also about black-skinned people. They were considered cowards and humiliated because of their skin color (Ps. Aristotle, *Physiogn.* 812a–b; Philo, *Leg.* 1.68). Without focusing on skin color, Simeon Niger can more easily escape her analysis.

This lack of emphasis on skin color in Luke/Acts in scholarship does not necessarily equate to a lack of analysis on race and ethnicity. Another study provides one of the few monograph-length treatments of race/ethnicity in Acts.[41] Focusing on the Ethiopian in this study is an "exegetical dead-end": noting how black-skinned people have been excluded in the analysis of Acts does not further our understanding of race/ethnicity.[42] Race/ethnicity is best understood through the skirmishes around communal boundaries. To understand how the ancients construed the notion of ethnicity/race, it is important to see how more than one ethnicity clashed. The episode of the Ethiopian does not detail contested identity and, therefore, does not offer the best material for an evaluation of race/ethnicity. In these clashes, Luke/Acts, it is proposed, promotes a universal evangelistic agenda because of Luke's understanding of the importance of race/ethnicity.[43] The study concludes that Luke's presentation "does not imagine a church stripped of ethnic distinctives but a movement that embraces such differences as endemic to the cultures of antiquity and the ambiguities surrounding ethnic reasoning as a valuable discursive space within which to portray a movement that invites all peoples."[44]

Another study prioritizes emphasis on the bodily description of the Ethiopian as a eunuch. But this evaluation of the Ethiopian eunuch in terms of ancient physiognomic beliefs demonstrates it is incorrect that the Ethiopian is a "dead end" for our understanding of race and ethnicity.[45] In this study, Luke was intending to overturn "ethnographic" beliefs, among others, by inclusion of the Ethiopian's story. Dominant narratives that denigrate black-skinned people were being rebuffed in Luke's presentation.[46] Recognizing the points of conflict to better ascertain the worth of race and ethnicity is an essential contribution to the study of the theology of Luke/Acts. But not perceiving how the Ethiopian eunuch and other black-skinned people in the narrative deepen our understanding of ethnicity/race disallows us from seeing exactly how multifaceted Luke's universalism was.

WE HAVE WORK TO DO

These views show progress in study of the Ethiopian eunuch. But what is also true is that the studies show that divine childship and its relationship to blackness require further study. My hope in this work is to convince the reader that when we lay the foundation of human worth based on divine childship, we will better understand the essentiality of Black life in God's mission for the world. And when we accomplish this, we will better appreciate not only Black life but also every color God has made. To accomplish this, however, we must continue to lay the groundwork for understanding how divine childship language functioned in the world of the first century, when Luke told his story about Jesus and the early church. To accomplish this goal, we will explore the significance of divine childship within the cultures in which Luke's story was written.

CHAPTER 3

GOD'S CHILDREN IN THE BIBLICAL WORLD

An investigation of Luke/Acts must ascertain what divine childship meant. There are numerous investigations of divine childship language in Jewish scripture and the New Testament.[1] But many studies do not discuss what Luke meant by it.[2]

What does it mean for people to be the children of God? Divine childship among humans could indicate a special relationship status. Evidence from the ancient world suggests that many people thought that the gods were the source of all of creation. But what did it mean to be considered by the gods to be their children? This attribution could evince a higher claim of ontology than other creatures, the animals. But then there is also a sense in which divine childship could mean that a particular group or person is in better standing with a god than others.

Determining the significance of this language, then, provides insight into how Luke discusses Jesus's message. In two moments in which Jesus refers to his disciples as God's children, Luke discusses their childship in terms that imitate Jesus himself. First, Jesus is called "Son of the Most High" (Luke 1:32) and then "Son of God" (1:35). In similar order, the disciples are called "children of the Most High" (6:35) and then "children of God" (20:36). Second, as "children of the Most High," the followers of Jesus take on Jesus's practices. They take on love, forgiveness, and mercy, the bedrock of Jesus's ministry (e.g., 4:18–19; 5:20–24; 6:27; 6:36–37; 7:47–49; 10:37; 11:4; 12:10; 24:47). Though the disciples are not called God's children in joining Jesus in his suffering (9:23; 14:26–27), they are described as "children of God" in their worthiness to participate in the resurrection (20:36).

Thus in assigning the disciples the language first used of Jesus—the very first attributions used by God to identify him as the savior of Israel (Luke 1:32, 35; 3:22)—it is probable that the reader is to infer that an implicit link between his sonship and their childship is formed. The implicit link that is formed between Jesus and his followers suggests that a kind of transformation is involved, especially if following Jesus's teachings is necessary to obtain these attributions. Those who follow Jesus are like him in their praxis (love of enemies, mercy, etc.) and being (the resurrection). When the follower refers to God as "Father," this is a way of demonstrating that she has been included into the divine family with Jesus (Luke 8:19–21). Her status in the world has changed; she is now like God's elect Son, Jesus Christ (Luke 9:35).

To better understand the use of divine childship language in Luke/Acts and the implications it would have for Luke's audience, we must first investigate the background of this kind of talk. The language of divine childship in Luke/Acts can only be understood when the world in which it was spoken and was used is understood.

Was every human a child of God? This is a necessary question, since Israel lays claim to this language for themselves as a nation (Exod 4:22–23) and for the king of Israel individually (Ps 2:7). But did this status only apply to Israel alone, in the biblical texts?

This investigation looks at Jewish, Greek, and Roman usage of divine childship attributions. These three cultural streams are those in which Christianity began as a movement in the first century. They provide the most probable basis on which to determine what divine childship could have meant in Luke/Acts. Divine childship discourse was essential in Luke/Acts in part because such language resounded in Greco-Roman culture, especially with respect to the gods and the emperor. Luke "reaches out to Jew and gentile."[3] It is important, therefore, to explore how Jews, Greeks, and Romans may have heard this language.

DIVINE CHILDSHIP IN ISRAEL'S SCRIPTURES

The texts that discuss divine childship in the Jewish scriptures present a range of possibilities for the phrase *child of God*. In Genesis 6:2, 4, the writer calls the creatures described as "sons of God,"[4] but these are other-worldly persons, not human beings.[5] While also using semantically equivalent language, Hosea 1:10[6] refers to the people of Israel as "children of the living God." This language could also be used to characterize a Davidic monarch, as it does in 2 Samuel 7:14: "I will be a father to him, and he shall be a son to me." Thus divine childship language has at least three significant uses in Israel's scriptures; it could refer to heavenly beings, Israel, or a Davidic royal Israelite.[7]

Though the sense of divine childship can speak of heavenly beings and the king of Israel, the focus of this work will be on what it means for Israel and its relationship to the nations. Luke uses the term in all three senses to refer to how the follower of Jesus is a child of God. But my focus will be on how "child of God" is a way for Israel to recognize its ethnic uniqueness as a nation that is privileged to hold covenant with the true and living God. The concept of divine childship in Jewish usage, then, offers an ethnic connotation. This being so, our evaluation of Israel's identity as God's child brings up the question of what this kind of discourse might mean for Adam, since Luke speaks of Adam as God's child. Since Adam is God's child, in a sense, we *may* be able to say all human beings are from a Jewish perspective. This we will explore in what follows.

ISRAEL AS CHILDREN OF GOD

Israel and "Firstborn" Status

God's children are God's chosen people.[8] As a chosen, select people, God cares for them in a unique way. In the narrative of the Torah, read synchronically, the first instance in the biblical text in which God calls Israel his child is in the Exodus narrative: "And the Lord said to Moses, 'When you go back to Egypt, see that you perform before Pharaoh all the wonders that I have put in your power; but I will harden his heart, so that he will not let the people go. Then you shall say to Pharaoh, "Thus says the Lord: Israel is my firstborn son. I said to you, 'Let my son go that he may worship me.' But you refused to let him go; now I will kill your firstborn son'" (Exod 4:21–23). Israel as a collective is God's child, and God fiercely protects his child. God challenges another "god," Pharaoh, threatening the life of his child, his "firstborn," if he refuses to let Israel go.[9]

The entire nation is recognized as the Lord's "firstborn."[10]

What guaranteed God's demonstrations of power through God's children was God's covenant with them. YHWH's care for Israel is also demonstrated in his faithfulness to the people *as his children*. Deuteronomy 14:1–2 offers the parameters of this covenantal relationship. Israel belongs to God: "You are children of the Lord your God.[11] You must not lacerate yourselves or shave your forelocks for the dead. For you are a people holy to the Lord your God; it is you the Lord has chosen out of all the peoples on earth to be his people, his treasured possession."[12] The uniqueness of their relationship not only provides divine protection but also requires certain behaviors.

God's Restoration of His "Sons and Daughters"

Continuing the strong divine childship theme, in "The Song of Moses" (Deut 32), the writer explores both the security and the danger associated with being God's children.[13] The first occurrence of this language is in Deuteronomy 32:5. The Hebrew for this verse is difficult to translate, shown by how varied translations are as it pertains to the status of Israel as God's child. The KJV has, "They have corrupted themselves, their spot is not the spot of his children: they are a perverse and crooked generation." The NIV translates it as, "They are corrupt and not his children; to their shame they are a warped and crooked generation." RSV seems to reflect this same translational decision. The NRSV agrees more with the KJV in terms of the status: "Yet his degenerate children have dealt falsely with him, a perverse and crooked generation." Space does not permit a thorough engagement with the grammar of this verse or how it might have been heard by its first readers or those of the New Testament period. Whatever the correct translation of 32:5 may be, the use of divine childship language later in Deuteronomy 32:18–19 cautions against inferring that the writer intended to suggest that Israel was no longer God's child. If the NIV and RSV are correct in their translations, then the denial of childship is probably for rhetorical purposes rather than a complete denial of the relationship.[14]

The verse (Deut 32:5) epitomizes the tone of the chapter. God had designated Israel to be his sons and daughters, but they had corrupted themselves and devalued their own status in the eyes of their creator. But they are God's children, in a way, even though they are discussed as having broken the covenant. This childship relationship prompts God's question in verse 6: "Is not he your father?" This verse suggests that God's unique connection was expressed through God's family relationship, God's creation of the nation, and God's providing security for the nation.

Verse 8 is of interest because of a possible use of divine childship language. But there is strong evidence that the writer does not use this language to speak of humans. Since this text is debated on both theological and textual grounds, a focus on the texts that are much clearer is warranted.[15]

Verses 10–13 offer a more metaphorical imaging of this childship discourse. There, God's relationship with Israel is discussed as the eagle caring for her young. The way in which the eagle protects her young is the same way in which God protected Israel. Moreover, the Lord not only made it possible for Israel to eat produce but also "nursed him with honey." The use of the nursing metaphor heightens the childship conception. God nurtured Israel as his children as a mother nurtures her own children.

Verses 18–20 provide the last occurrences of divine childship language from this chapter: "You were unmindful of the Rock that bore you; you forgot the God who gave you birth. The Lord saw it, and was jealous; he spurned his sons and daughters.[16] He said: I will hide my face from them, I will see what their end will be; for they are a perverse generation, children in whom there is no faithfulness." Continuing with the motherhood metaphor, YHWH "bore" them and birthed them. Their behavior resulted in the Lord rejecting his "sons and daughters."[17] God sees them as unfaithful "children."

Following the theme of the previous verses, childship language should be considered in a similar light. Despite the fact that the personal possessive is not used of God, it is most probable that the writer does not intend children to signify age or maturity.[18] He uses this language to continue the divine childship theme. These are *God's* children in whom faithfulness was not found.

Despite the damning discourse of this chapter (Deut 32), the conclusion ends on a high note. Though God plans to punish the people of Israel for their disobedience (32:20–41), God promises to return to redeem them and avenge their blood (32:43). The Masoretic Text (MT) calls for the "nations" to rejoice in light of YHWH's vengeance on Israel's behalf.[19] The Greek Old Testament signals to the "angels of God" to "rejoice," the "children of God" to "worship" God. Since the "heavens" are also called upon to rejoice at the meting out of divine vengeance, it is likely that this reference to divine childship concerns heavenly beings. This tradition notwithstanding, the point is made that these children still belong to God despite their sin, and God intends to return to them, restore them, and vindicate them. One scholar summarizes verse 43 in relation to the rest of the "song":

> This creates a concentric structure in the last part of the poem (v. 43bcde), with references to God's actions on behalf of "his children" (or "servants" in the LXX [Septuagint]) and "his people" framing God's actions against "his adversaries" and "those who hate him." It is because of these actions that the heavens are summoned to make glad "his people," the ones God has delivered from their adversaries. Similarly, it is because of such actions that those delivered, who are also "sons of God," are called to worship the Lord. Thus, the song that began on a highly critical note in relation to God's people ends on a highly positive note.[20]

The Isaianic traditions also explore this theme of divine childship. Isaiah 1:2 chastises Israel, God's "children," for rebelling against and not recognizing the Lord as the one who "reared" them.[21] Isaiah 63:8, following the theme in the chapter of YHWH's righteous deeds for Israel, recalls how God said these were his "children."[22] Isaiah 63:16, after a reflection on God's past faithfulness and Israel's request for a present manifestation, claims that God is both the "father" and the "redeemer" of Israel. This concept is repeated again in 64:8, where God is "father" and "potter" and where Israel is the "clay."[23]

This special attention that God gives Israel as his people and his chosen is accentuated in Isaiah 43. The language of Israel's creation connotes its distinction from the rest of the nations. Israel was a nation that was started by YHWH. The people are unique. Their uniqueness allows for YHWH to call them his children:

> But now thus says the Lord, he who created you, O Jacob, he who formed you, O Israel: Do not fear, for I have redeemed you; I have called you by name, you are mine. When you pass through the waters, I will be with you; and through the rivers, they shall not overwhelm you; when you walk through fire you shall not be burned, and the flame shall not consume you. For I am the Lord your God, the Holy One of Israel, your Savior. I give Egypt as your ransom, Ethiopia and Seba in exchange for you. Because you are precious in my sight, and honored, and I love you, I give people in return for you, nations in exchange for your life. Do not fear, for I am with you; I will bring your offspring from the east, and from the west I will gather you; I will say to the north, "Give them up," and to the south, "Do not withhold; bring my sons from far away and my daughters from the end of the earth—everyone who is called by my name, whom I created for my glory, whom I formed and made." (Isa 43:1–7)

The use of divine childship language echoes that of Exodus 4:22–23 and Deuteronomy 32. God demands that the regions release them so that they may return to the Lord their God, basically saying, as to Pharaoh, "Let my people go!" Unlike Exodus 4:22–23, there is use of the plural again, but there is a blending of the singular and plural, since Israel is one and many at the same time. God says to them that the time of exile for God's children has ended and now is the time of their return. God, speaking of them using "family categories," is reaching out to them as a benevolent Father.[24]

This return reverses the exile, which is also described in Deuteronomy 32. There, the nations were given power over Israel because of the people's disobedience, but Isaiah tells them that God wants his children to return. Also, the specification of both sons and daughters is similar to the language of Deuteronomy 32.

Divine childship in Isaiah 43 emphasizes Israel as God's creation and personal possession. The Lord declares that he has created Israel, and he tells the people, "You are mine" (v. 1). As God's possession, God guarantees their security, supported by the promises of protection (v. 2). God considers them so highly that other nations, those that do not belong to YHWH, will be given in exchange for God's precious people (v. 3). When God cries to his people to return home, he designates them as his children by use of the possessive "my" (v. 6). This prophetic oracle alerts the reader, in no uncertain terms, that YHWH "love[s]" (v. 4) Israel. They are God's people by creation, possession, and oversight.

God condemns Israel, saying, "You are not my people and I am not your God" (Hos 1:9). But then there is a dramatic shift in the oracle.[25] God declares, "Yet the number of the people of Israel shall be like the sand of the sea, which can be neither measured nor numbered; and in the place where it was said to them, 'You are not my people,' it shall be said to them, 'Children of the living God'" (Hos 1:10). The oracle rehearses the Abrahamic promise (Gen 15:5; 22:17) that Israel will be innumerable like the stars of the sky and the sand of the seashore. Moreover, though it had been said that they were not God's people, now they will receive a better label, the living God's children. The denunciation is outweighed by the approbation. These people are not merely associated with God but are declared to have divine childship.

Later in the book, reflecting on the exodus tradition, Hosea says, "When Israel was a child, I loved him, and out of Egypt I called my son. The more I called them, the more they went from me; they kept sacrificing to the Baals, and offering incense to idols" (Hos 11:1–2). It is suggested in these verses that "the first event in the life of young Israel worthy of report is that Yahweh loves him."[26] In this case, the use of this motif is meant to shame the people of Israel for leaving the one who loves them. God took care of Israel in its youth. When they were in bondage, God delivered them. But they continued worshipping false idols despite God's many gestures of fidelity.

Jeremiah vilifies Israel for misplaced devotion using this motif, though he doesn't directly call the people children of God (Jer 2:26–27). The leaders of Israel, instead of worshipping YHWH as Father and begetter, "say to a tree, 'You are my father,' and to a stone, 'You gave me birth'" (2:27). To their shame, Jeremiah argues, the devotion that their Lord was due was stolen by objects that could not save them. It is indirect, but the implication of Jeremiah's castigation is that Israel should only consider YHWH to be its "Father" and begetter. The only rightful divine childship relationship the people can have comes from him.

Lastly, in Jeremiah 31, the chapter that discusses God's promise to offer a new covenant, Jeremiah discusses God's intention to retrieve the northern tribes from exile. This promise, as can be seen in other examples, shows how divine childship language is deeply connected with the exodus and exile themes in the Hebrew Bible: "With weeping they shall come, and with consolations I will lead them back, I will let them walk by brooks of water, in a straight path in which they shall not stumble; for I have become[27] a father to Israel, and Ephraim is my firstborn" (Jer 31:9).[28] The NRSV translation appears to suggest that God had to "become" Israel's parent, but then Ephraim "is" God's "firstborn."[29] The RSV offers the translation "For I am a father to Israel, and Ephraim is my first-born" (Jer 31:9). The word the NRSV translates as "become" can also be translated "I am." The RSV translation fits better with the language of the book. It is in line with the theme—which is apparent from the evidence—to argue that the Lord *is* the Father of the seemingly dispossessed northern kingdom. As Father, he will retrieve them. As recipients of his grace of deliverance, they can be considered God's "firstborn" as Israel was in Egypt (Exod 4:21–22). When Israel breaks covenant with God, its status as God's child, as "firstborn," can be restored.

The Covenant and Other Nations?

The question of status restoration raises another question. If Israel can lose its favored status as God's child, even if God still refers to the people as God's children, can other nations gain the status of God's child? In Isaiah 56:5, Isaiah says, "I will give, in my house and within my walls, a monument and a name better than sons and daughters; I will give them an everlasting name that shall not be cut off." This verse is in the context of a larger call to the nations and the eunuchs to come to the temple (56:1–8).[30] God promises Israel that they will return along with "others" (56:8). Their return also marks a time when foreigners and eunuchs will be able to join them and receive a greater "name than sons and daughters."[31] In this text, the name of the foreigner who decides to join in the covenant, though not born as part of it, is better because of its longevity. The sense of "better" is not in terms of rank. These people are allowed to enter into the covenant alongside the children of God. They will never be forgotten as some of the other children have been.

Setting the call of the nations within the framework of the divine childship of Israel is peculiar to this text. But it solidifies the significance that not only Israel's trust in the Lord but any nation's trust will result in divine rescue. Those outside of Israel who hope in YHWH with Israel can partake in YHWH's covenant of faithfulness. In fact, their conversion to the God of Israel grants them a position that exceeds those who are the genetic descendants of Abraham. We are not told in what way their names are greater. It is possible to conclude that the drastic step of conversion from idolatry to worship of God yields a greater recognition of faithfulness than if one were born into the family of Israel.

Divine Childship in Second Temple Jewish Literature

Divine childship continued to be a strong theme in Second Temple Jewish literature written mostly right before the New Testament. Writers, oftentimes reflecting on biblical themes, accented the concept. This section focuses on the people of Israel as God's children. There is much that can be said regarding heavenly beings and heavenly human beings in Second Temple literature.[32] Not as much concerns the Davidic ruler as a child of God.[33] The favored sense of Israel as God's chosen child is on display in this literature.[34]

VINDICATION

Divine childship language is used to designate the people of Israel, to demonstrate they are God's special people[35] in Second Temple literature.[36] In some places, they are considered God's vindicated over against the unrighteous non-Jewish nations. Testament of Moses 10:3[37] depicts a scene where the "devil" is destroyed (10:1) and God metes out vengeance against the enemies of his people.[38] 2 Baruch 13:9[39] shares that YHWH, who punished "his own sons first," plans to execute wrath against the rest of the world.[40] In 1 Enoch,[41] God will hold court with the "kings, the governors, the high officials, and the landlords" of the nations (1 Enoch 62:1) and will openly shame and punish them through "the angels for punishments" because they were "oppressors of his children and his elect ones" (1 Enoch 62:11).[42]

In 4 Ezra 6:57–59,[43] Ezra looks to God to punish the nations for their mistreatment of his elect: "And now, O Lord, behold, these nations, which are reputed as nothing, domineer over us and devour us. But we, your people, whom you have called your first-born, only begotten, zealous for you, and most dear, have been given into their hands. If the world has indeed been created for us, why do we not possess our world as an inheritance? How long will this be so?"[44] Again, in this plea, it is clear that God's retribution against the nations, and his rescue of Israel, should be warranted because they are God's "first-born" and "only begotten."[45] This language alludes to Exodus 4:22, Deuteronomy 32:18, and Psalm 2:7. The other nations do not matter. The fact that Israel has violated its special relationship with God, a point that 4 Ezra makes,[46] does not at all nullify the fact that these are God's special people.[47]

In 3 Maccabees[48] 2:21; 5:6–7; 6:4, 8, God is frequently invoked as "father," as the one who brings divine vengeance and provides divine protection.[49] In a moment akin to Daniel 3:25–30, the writer of 3 Maccabees reports that the king of Egypt has a revelation about the Jews. Instead of attacking them as he had planned—his troops had been holding them captive for perceived insolence—he declares, "Release the children of the almighty and living God of heaven, who from the time of our ancestors until now has granted an unimpeded and notable stability to our government" (3 Macc 6:28). God's miraculous intervention changed the king's mind about the Jews. He had sent angels, whom only the Jews could see, to make the animals on which the king and his men rode trample them,[50] causing fear and dread in the army (3 Macc 6:18–21).[51]

Wisdom of Solomon is one of the most important texts in our discussion of usage of divine childship language.[52] The work is rife with use of this language. It is also essential to the motif[53] explored in this study. Throughout Wisdom of Solomon, divine childship is used to designate God's special people as those worthy of God's protection and their enemies as worthy of God's retribution. A full analysis is beyond the scope of this project.[54] A few references will suffice to summarize the theme.

Divine childship can speak of the righteous and the wicked without specific reference to their ethnic status. The wicked are portrayed as recognizing the divine childship status of the righteous: "He [the righteous] professes to have knowledge of God, and calls himself a child[55] of the Lord" (Wis 2:13).[56] The wicked person's description of the righteous imagines how the righteous perceives the wicked: "We are considered by him as something base, and he avoids our ways as unclean; he calls the last end of the righteous happy, and boasts that God is his father" (2:16). The wicked person, fed up with the righteous person's trust in God and belief in God's protection, intends to do him harm with the taunt, "For if the righteous man is God's child,[57] he will help him, and will deliver him from the hand of his adversaries" (2:18).[58] Interestingly, the wicked are surprised when the righteous are vindicated by God, when they are "numbered among the children of God" (5:5). The wicked person was absolutely correct: despite the wicked's attacks on the just, the righteous are God's chosen, and God will honor them. As God's children, they will receive favor in the face of the wicked, while the wicked are given over to punishment.[59]

The author changes the focus of the referents to divine childship later in the book. He makes it clear that he is referring to Israel and Israel's foreign enemies. The author does so by envisioning God's favor on his children through the lens of the wilderness narratives.[60] When discussing God's protective favor, likely echoing instead of referring to Numbers 21:6–8, the writer describes how God made a distinction between his children and the Egyptians, probably to symbolize all the non-Jewish enemies of Israel.

While condemning idolatrous behaviors (Wis 15:1–13), the writer shifts to talking about how idolaters oppressed the people of God (15:14), but their worship of idols bespoke their folly (15:15–19). Their folly was truly revealed when the very animals they made idols to commemorate turned on them (16:1). But God protected his people and provided for them in the wilderness, shaming others who trusted in idols (16:2–8). God punished idolaters through animal attacks, but he disciplined and healed his people through them: "For they were killed by the bites of locusts and flies, and no healing was found for them, because they deserved to be punished by such things. But your children were not conquered even by the fangs of venomous serpents, for your mercy came to their help and healed them. To remind them of your oracles they were bitten, and then were quickly delivered, so that they would not fall into deep forgetfulness and become unresponsive to your kindness" (16:9–11). Here the writer merges the plagues from Egypt (Exod 7–12) and the story of the fiery serpents (Num 21:6–8). The implication appears to be that the children of the true God were preserved in part because they were God's children. Their worship and devotion to the true God marked them as worthy of God's preservation, even when God was disciplining them.

Another discussion of the distinction God makes between the children and the idolaters draws upon the wilderness wanderings. The writer describes how the unrighteous could not escape God's righteous judgment (Wis 16:14–19), since God caused the cosmos to fight against them, but for God's people, "instead of these things you gave your people food of angels, and without their toil you supplied them from heaven with bread ready to eat, providing every pleasure and suited to every taste. For your sustenance manifested your sweetness toward your children; and the bread, ministering to the desire of the one who took it, was changed to suit everyone's liking" (16:20–21). It is clear that when the writer speaks of Israel and the nations, he implies that Israel is righteous before God, while the foreign nations are not. Additionally, the allusion to the giving of manna (Exod 16:11–36) is seen as a sign of God's wholly appropriate provision for his children. That this bread was called "angel's food" may imply that the reader is tying one type of child of God to another so that the earthly children of God are allowed to eat what the heavenly children of God ate.[61]

One last use of this motif occurs in the last chapter of the book. Describing the parting of the waters at the Red Sea as an act of new creation, the writer claims, "The whole creation in its nature was fashioned anew, complying with your commands, so that your children might be kept unharmed. The cloud was seen overshadowing the camp, and dry land emerging where water had stood before, an unhindered way out of the Red Sea, and a grassy plain out of the raging waves, where those protected by your hand passed through as one nation, after gazing on marvelous wonders" (Wis 19:6–8). Here the creation and the exodus are connected to demonstrate the strength of God's protection for his children. God's favor, as it did with the creatures, caused nature itself to create a pathway for the children of God. While the children of God experienced God's deliverance, with God's creation propelling them forward, the wicked (the Egyptians) were sentenced to death because they tried to destroy God's children (19:1–5).[62] For the writer of Wisdom of Solomon, all of God's power is brought to bear in defense of God's people. Those who belong to God have the forces of nature itself working to help them. This is how far God is willing to go to protect God's people; they are God's children indeed.

God's Correction of His Children

In another use of divine childship language, the language connotes God's mercy during times of discipline. Psalm of Solomon[63] 13:9–10 says, "For he will admonish the righteous as a beloved son and his discipline is as for a firstborn. For the Lord will spare his devout and he will wipe away their mistakes with discipline." In Psalm of Solomon 18:4–6, similarly, God marks Israel out as deserving of merciful discipline as his "firstborn son" and as his "only child" for their sins of ignorance. God disciplines them in this manner for their preparation for the anointed one. Tobit 13:4–5 refers to God as "father . . . forever" in the context of discipline for his people and return from exile: "He has shown you his greatness even there. Exalt him in the presence of every living being, because he is our Lord and he is our God; he is our Father and he is God forever. He will afflict you for your iniquities, but he will again show mercy on all of you. He will gather you from all the nations among whom you have been scattered."[64] What was true of the house of David now applies to all of Israel in these texts (2 Sam 7:14–15).

POWER WITH GOD

Favored divine childship status also suggests an elect position and ability to wield divine authority in the eyes of God.[65] In the writing of Pseudo-Philo 18:4–5,[66] the writer narrates that Jacob was God's "firstborn" with the authority to counsel God as Abraham had done. Testament of Levi says of Levi, "The Most High has given heed to your prayer that you should become a son to him, as minister and priest in his presence" (4:2). Later, God promises that "he shall grant his children the authority to trample on wicked spirits. And the Lord will rejoice in his children" (Testament of Levi 18:12–13). In Jubilees,[67] when God makes promises to Moses about Israel's return to covenant fidelity after the people's apostasy, God makes this decree, "I shall be a father to them, and they will be sons to me. And they will all be called 'sons of the living God.' And every angel and spirit will know and acknowledge that they are my sons and I am their father in uprightness and righteousness. And I shall love them" (Jubilees 1:25).[68] God's promise to Moses recalls the language of 2 Samuel 7, Jeremiah 31, Hosea 1, and Isaiah 43, all of which feature divine childship in a prominent way. Excluding 2 Samuel 7, the theme of each chapter is covenant renewal and God's reassurance of Israel in the face of oppressors.[69] These themes are essential in the context of Jubilees.[70]

OBEDIENCE AS EVIDENCE OF CHILDSHIP

Another major theme to consider in discussions of notions of divine childship is how obedience works with childship status. There is notion of divine childship on the basis of righteous obedience. In Sirach 4:10, the writer proposes that those who care for the orphans and widows will be "like a son of the Most High."[71]

Pseudo-Philo explores the story of Korah's rebellion. In his rendition, he describes how many of Korah's sons refuse to rebel with him. They, in effect, deny their ancestry, since Korah has rejected the law of Moses by rebelling. They say to their father, "Our father has not begotten us but the Most Powerful has formed us." They then claim divine ancestry: "And now if we walk in his ways, we will be his sons" (Liber antiquitatum biblicarum 16:15). These sons explain that their status as God's children is determined not simply by being created by God but by their obedience to God's commands.

It bears mentioning that these texts do not necessarily presume that there was a widespread belief that covenantal fidelity was determined solely by birth. Faithfulness to the covenant was always required for divine benefits (Deut 27–30). On the other hand, these texts do not assume in and of themselves that obedience alone affords access to God. They do not explicitly exclude non-Jews from practicing the tenets of YHWH's law to partake in Israel's covenant. But they also do not extend the call of God for faithfulness to other nations to be God's children through obedience either, openly at least.

This notion of divine childship may have some connection to Isaiah 56. There, the writer explains that non-Jews—mutilated eunuchs, no less—can claim membership in the special covenant if they come to the God of Israel (see Deut 23:1). Their obedience to God privileges them with a name "better" than the children of God. While it is not clear that either Sirach or Pseudo-Philo believes this, obedience is the means by which the divine childship is determined. Consideration as a child of God is not innate but a function of praxis.

CHILDREN OF GOD IN DEAD SEA SCROLLS

In the literature of Qumran, the Dead Sea Scrolls community, there is emphasis on the people of Israel as the children of God.[72] The Dead Sea Scroll document 4Q504 3:2–9 provides an important use of divine childship language as regards Israel's preferential treatment and how that affects divine discipline:

> Behold, all the peoples are [like not]hing in front of you; [as] chaos and nothing / [they] are reckoned / in your presence. We have [in]voked only your name; for your glory you have created us; you have established us as your sons in the sight of all the peoples. For you called [I]srael "my son, my first-born" and have corrected us as one corrects his son.[73] You have [created us] raised [Blank] us over the years of our generations . . . / evil / illnesses, famine, thirst, plague, the sword [. . . requi]tal of your covenant, for you chose us [to be your people amongst all] the earth. For that reason you have poured on us your rage [and] your [jealou]sy with all the intensity of your anger.[74]

God may have poured out his anger upon these people, yet they remain his "sons." It is precisely because of their childship status that God chose to discipline them the way God did. It is their childship status before God that halted God's hand, softening the blows of discipline. God has plans for this people beyond any other. They were chosen while considered to be "chaos and nothing."

DIVINE CHILDSHIP IN PHILO AND JOSEPHUS

Philo and Josephus are two key Jewish first-century writers who are also essential in our understanding of first-century perspectival diversity in Second Temple Judaism.[75] Josephus says that God is the "father and lord of all things" (*Ant.* 1.20; see also 1.229; 2.152) and also "of the Hebrew race" (*Ant.* 5.93).[76] Philo is a bit more complex, though he agrees with Josephus that God is the "father of creation" (*Ebr.* 1.30; *Sobr.* 1.56).[77] Philo can call the world a "younger son of God" (*Deus.* 1.31), younger than time. Isaac, as "laughter," can be considered "an adopted son of God" (*Mut.* 1.131). Philo also discusses sonship in relation to how Israel could be considered God's "firstborn" even if Jacob was, in historical fact, not (*Post.* 1.63).

These aforementioned citations represent the explicit uses of divine childship concepts. They show God's special relationship with Israel, God's children, and possibly non-Jews who want to adhere to Israel's covenant. Divine childship is implied, however, in the beginning of the Bible and is pivotal to our discussion. It is this implied childship that may explain why Josephus and Philo would affirm YHWH as the parent of all peoples, beyond the obvious Hellenistic parallels. Luke called Adam God's child (Luke 3:38) and thereby implied that all human beings were the descendants of God (Acts 17:26–29). The Bible and Second Temple literature affirm Luke's characterization.

ADAM AS DIVINE IMAGE AND CHILD OF GOD IN JEWISH THOUGHT

As indicated earlier, Adam is also perceived as a child of God in Jewish literature. Although the only explicit statement that Adam is a "son of God" is in Luke 3:38, Luke picks this notion up from Jewish configurations of Adam. Exploring the biblical and postbiblical traditions surrounding Adam is helpful in understanding why Luke would have understood him as God's son and Jesus's direct ancestor.

Genesis 1:26 is the first place "Adam"[78] is discussed in the Bible[79] in canonical order.[80] The Hebrew name itself can mean "man," "human," or "humankind" in principal usage.[81] It could be personal or generic. Adam is created on the sixth day:

> Then God said, "Let us make humankind [Adam] in our image, according to our likeness; and let them have dominion over the fish of the sea, and over the birds of the air, and over the cattle, and over all the wild animals of the earth, and over every creeping thing that creeps upon the earth." So God created humankind [Adam] in his image, in the image of God he created them; male and female he created them. God blessed them, and God said to them, "Be fruitful and multiply, and fill the earth and subdue it; and have dominion over the fish of the sea and over the birds of the air and over every living thing that moves upon the earth." (Gen 1:26–28)

In the next chapter, it is stated, "Then the Lord God formed man[82] from the dust of the ground, and breathed into his nostrils the breath of life; and the man became a living being. And the Lord God planted a garden in Eden, in the east; and there he put the man whom he had formed" (Gen 2:7–8).

Genesis 1 may speak of the generic sense, humankind, while Genesis 2 speaks of the personal sense, the man, Adam. In the context of the creation, humankind's creation is part of God's demonstration of dominion over the earth: "We capture the essence of the idea of creation in the Hebrew Bible with the word 'mastery.' The creation narratives, whatever their length, form, or context, are best seen as dramatic visualizations of the uncompromised master of YHWH, God of Israel, over all else. He alone is 'the Lord of all the earth,' and when the cosmogonic events are complete, his lordship is beyond all doubt."[83]

If all of creation is part of a demonstration of the lordship of YHWH, then when YHWH creates beings in his "image" and "likeness" (Gen 1:26), they will take on some of these traits.[84] Scholars have been puzzled by the significance of "image" and "likeness" for generations. What does it mean to be "made in the image of God?"[85]

Scholars note the use of cognate terms in Egyptian, Babylonian, and Assyrian contexts and argue that this language connotes regality. For

Egyptians, the king is the image of the deity.[86] The king is a manifestation of the god on earth—the deity rules through the king.[87] In one document, and this is unique in its articulation, the use of this language goes beyond the king to all human beings as kinds of manifestations of the deities.[88]

Scholars also note that in Babylonian and Assyrian usage, the "image" cognate is used for the idols that kings would make of themselves.[89] These images were not mere statues as moderns would imagine. In ancient Near Eastern (ANE) thought—as was the case with other Mediterranean peoples—people thought the gods became present through idols and kings.[90] The "image and likeness" of God is taken to be a way of talking about the extension of God's presence and reign through human beings.[91]

The human's place in the world was exalted: "The assumption is that he has appointed humanity to be his viceroy, the highest-ranking commoner, as it were, ruling with the authority of the king. The human race is YHWH's plenipotentiary, his stand-in."[92] Humanity's participation in YHWH's rule, expressed in YHWH's command to flourish and have dominion over the earth (Gen 1:26–28), is a way of portraying the meaning of being in God's image. As the idols of God, God's representatives, and YHWH's presence on earth, humans function as God's "vice-regents." One scholar proposes the "image of God" would have suggested in its original context that "when humans subdue and rule, they are identifying functions for the animals and determining what role they will play. This is part of the human role—to serve as vice-regents for God in continuing the process of bringing order." Psalm 8:3–9 explores this conception of humankind: God has indeed made humanity lower than the divine beings, but they are crowned with glory and honor and set over the works of God's hands, even all animal life. Humans, through their subjugation of creation and naming of the animals (Gen 2), are imitating God as creators in their own right.[93] One study offers a coherent summary of the view of Adam and Eve as the *imago Dei* in its original context: "Imago Dei refers to human rule, that is, the exercise of power on God's behalf in creation. This may be articulated in two different, but complementary, ways. Said one way, humans are like God in exercising royal power on earth. Said another way, the divine ruler delegated to humans a share in his rule on earth."[94]

Genesis 5:1–3 also indicates that Adam, in the personal sense, was God's child, and this is vital for our purposes. One scholar suggests "the language of image and likeness is sonship language":[95] "This is the list of the descendants of Adam. When God created humankind, he made them in the likeness of God. Male and female he created them, and he blessed them and named them ['Adam'] when they were created. When Adam had lived one hundred thirty years, he became the father of a son in his likeness, according to his image, and named him Seth" (Gen 5:1–3). One can easily infer, within the context of Genesis, that the early readers would have considered Adam to be God's son. If Seth, as Adam's son, is made in his "image and likeness," it makes sense to interpret that Adam is God's son, made in his "image and likeness." This understanding of divine childship reflects the Egyptian understanding of divine childship. The major difference is that the king was considered to be God's son and image. The Jewish conception not only expands the notion of dominion for all humanity, but also seems to extend this notion of divine childship to all humans through the first humans. If all humans are made in the image of God, then all humans are, in a general sense, also God's children.[96]

The importance of Adam's role, used in this individual/personal sense, is also exhibited in the tragedy of human sin. As the father of all human beings, the inclination towards sin comes from Adam. Genesis 3:16 promises pain in childbearing to Eve but foretells death to all of Adam's descendants through Adam (3:19). God curses the ground for Adam's sake, which, in effect, undoes the blessing God gave to Adam in Genesis 1:26–28. As is clear in Genesis 9, the narrative still holds that humans are made in the image of God after Adam's failure. But the narrative moves to explain how God intends to bring blessing to the world through the tribes of humanity described in Genesis 10 and in Genesis 12:1–3.[97]

Also in Second Temple literature, mostly using the personal sense of the term, Adam is hailed as a ruler. Wisdom of Solomon 10:1–2 states, "Wisdom protected the first-formed father of the world, when he alone had been created; she delivered him from his transgression, and gave him strength to rule all things."

In a statement introducing one of the community's discussions of the origin of evil, a Qumran writer claims, "He created man [Adam] to rule the world and placed within him two spirits so that he would walk with them until the moment of his visitation" (1QS 3:17–18). Fourth Ezra 6:54 magnifies the ruling power of Adam while, at the same time, claiming direct descent from Adam to the people of Israel: "You placed Adam as the ruler over all the works which you made: and from him we have all come, the people from whom you have chosen."[98] Sirach 49:16 echoes the belief that Israel saw Adam, the greatest of all people, as their ancestor.[99] In Testament of Abraham (Resc. A) 11:4–12, Adam judges on a throne, taking on the appearance of God. Adam's depiction makes sense in light of the fact that he is described as God's image.

Many texts are emphatic that Adam is to blame for all of human sin and corruption in creation.[100] In many of these texts, Adam is elevated as a world ruler, heightening the immensity of his failure, which bears world-wide implications. But Adam's failure directly affected Israel. This is especially so in 4 Ezra. Adam's sinfulness corrupted Israel in particular and created a situation where the people could not claim the "world" that had been "created" for them (4 Ezra 6:55). A fair inference from this conception of descent is that the writer sees Israel, in a unique way, as the image of God. As such, it would make sense that in both their Scripture and Second Temple literature, the people considered themselves to be the children of the Most High.

But Adam is not always to blame. Wisdom of Solomon assumes that Cain is to blame for the flood (Wis 10:3–5). In 1 Enoch, human sin is blamed on the teachings of the Watchers (1 Enoch 9:5–11).

Adam is also portrayed as a priest in Jubilees 3:27, offering a sacrifice after his expulsion from the garden.[101] It is no wonder, then, that the priestly community of Qumran saw the triumph of the community as the attainment of "the glory of Adam."[102] The community believed their call as God's chosen was to attain to Adam's glory. This glory is described as the elimination of "injustice" in 1QS 4:23. In each case, Adam's glory in the end of the age is termed "Adam's" because it is the time when the glory of God will dwell in Eden once again as it did in the creation.[103]

There are many debates surrounding both the dating and the provenance of the Life of Adam and Eve and the Apocalypse of Moses.[104] Reference to

Adam is important to how he was perceived in both works.[105] In the Apocalypse of Moses, after Adam's death, while Eve and Seth mourned, Eve speaks to him about the state of his father; this conversation is essential for our understanding of divine childship and image language (35:1–4). Eve says to Seth,

> Look up with your eyes and see the seven heavens opened, and see with your eyes how the body of your father lies on its face, and all he holy angels are with him, praying for him and saying, "Forgive him, O Father of all, for he is your image." So then, my child, Seth, what shall this be? When will he be given over into the hands of our unseen Father and God? And who are the two dark-skinned[106] persons assisting at the prayer for your father?' Seth said to his mother, "These are the sun and the moon, and they themselves fall down and pray for my father, Adam." And Eve said to him, "And where is their light, and why have they become dark?" Seth said to her, "They are not able to shine before the light of all, and this is why the light is hid from them." (35:2–36:3)

This the only time in the two documents when God is called "father." Both angels and humans speak of God as Father, and both can be thought of as children of God. The angels also ask God to have mercy on Adam because Adam is God's image. This mercy will be shown in its fullness when Adam attains his own throne (Apocalypse of Moses 39:1–3), displacing the "seducer" (39:3). In the meantime, Seth appears to have taken up his father's role as the image of God in the world.

These traditions suggest that Adam was considered the image of God and therefore the child of God. Adam provides an important corollary for discussions of David as an all-powerful ruler (Psalm 2). In Second Temple literature, Adam is an essential ancestor and eschatological hero. As the first human, he is armed with power and authority, reflecting also the traits of heavenly beings (Psalm 82). But he is the first human who ushered in death and corruption for all humans, especially Israel. In other traditions, Adam is not to be blamed at all. In Life of Adam and Eve and Apocalypse of

Moses, Adam is portrayed as making a comeback in the eschaton, retaking his throne and overcoming the power of Satan.

ADAM, ISRAEL, AND THE REST OF HUMANITY

Before concluding this exploration of Jewish conceptions of divine childship, it is necessary to draw these threads together to discuss the anthropology of the nations. Jews considered Israel God's "firstborn." This is true in Jewish scripture and in Second Temple texts. It is also correct that Israel received preferential treatment from God; the people were recipients of God's grace-filled covenant. God protected them and punished them in ways that made them distinct from the other nations. But where did the distinction end?

All human beings were the children of Adam; this is the view of the literary witness. And Adam was God's image and likeness. God could even extend this designation to Noah and speak of all humans in this way (Gen 9:1–11). But if image is a way of discussing childship, how do we understand the nations and their childship status with God?

Genesis 10 follows directly from the affirmation of God's blessing on all human beings after Noah. Humanity is made in God's image and the people are God's descendants. But implied in the call of Israel, beginning with Abraham (Gen 12:1–3), is that there is a disconnect. Abraham and his family were meant to be a blessing to all of the families of the earth. We can assume that the relational disconnect is manifest through idolatry. The nations were under the rule of other heavenly beings, but Israel belonged to God (Deut 32:8–9). Even though all people had been made in God's image, the people of the image had forgotten their true maker and substituted deities to which they had no resemblance (Sibylline Oracles 3:8–48).

Israel, however, had a strong relationship with the God of Adam. Israel worshiped the God of Adam, the one who created the heavens and the earth (Gen 1:1). In Jewish tradition, Adam typified the role of a priest prior to the establishment of the priesthood in Second Temple texts. Thus we come to understand that the covenant and its cult were prefigured in Adam.

Fourth Ezra takes the view that the nations are "spittle" before God. The entire world was created for Israel. The people's oppressed condition was not at all what God intended. This more negative view of the nations does not reflect the majority of the views. The people of Israel saw themselves as God's unique children among the diverse nations; Israel had been created by God while, at the same time, they were still punished for their sins.

Regardless of the status of the relationship—whether living in favor with God through right worship, even when placed in punishment, or in disfavor because of idolatry—the binding point for God to all humans was Adam. Adam exemplified what all humanity was meant to be. Corruption and the dominion of powerful beings over the nations disallow humans from living out their potential as God's ruling image in the world. Israel, through covenant, was able to manifest aspects of these expectations. Through the people's right worship, they were meant to be a light to the nations (Isa 42:6; 49:6; 60:3). The temple of Jerusalem would be the magnet of all of the world, attracting people back to the God in whose image they were made (Isa 2:1–4). The impetus for the call of humanity is that all of the nations belonged to God (Ps 24:1), all human beings were made in God's image, and God wanted all humans to walk with him as their primordial ancestor once did. The nations fell out of fellowship with God, but God wanted that fellowship with all nations, all ethnic groups around the world.

DIVINE CHILDSHIP AMONG THE GREEKS

Turning to Greek and Roman views allows a better grasp of how New Testament first-century readers would have perceived divine childship. In the *Iliad* and other Greek and Roman texts, Zeus is "both the father of humans and the gods" (1.544).[107] There are numerous references in Homeric literature of divine childship language, with Zeus or some other being as divine ancestor.[108] Later than Homeric usage, the Stoics would acclaim that Zeus was the father of all beings, gods and humans (Arrian, *Epict. diss.* 1.3; Stobaeus, *Ecl.* 1.1.12). The phrase *son of God*, however, is sparse in Greek and Roman usage.[109]

In the *Iliad*, while Zeus is wooing Hera, his divine wife, he narrates many of the mortal and divine children he has had: "Come; let us to bed and the delights of love. Never has such desire, for goddess or mortal overwhelmed my heart; no, not when I loved Ixiom's wife who bore Perithous, wise as the gods; or Danae of the slim ankles, daughter or Acrisius, who gave birth to Perseus, the greatest hero of his time; or the far-famed daughter of Phoenix, who bore me Minos and god-like Rhadamanthus; or Semele, or Alcmene in Thebes, whose son was lion-hearted Heracles, while Semele bore Dionysus, mankind's delight; or lady Demeter with her lovely hair, or incomparable Leto" (*Il.* 14.312–40).[110]

In Greek understanding, gods can have children with other gods and bear other gods. Gods can have children with other humans (see Gen 6:1–4). And as stated before, Zeus is hailed as the general father of all humans and many of the gods.[111]

The offspring of the unions between humans and gods are typically, at minimum, capable of wielding some element of divine power or demonstrating an uncanny heroism in the world. The "heroes" are the offspring of the unions of gods and mortals.[112] Heroes have transcendent capabilities, as Zeus explains in the above passage. In most cases, they are the male offspring of male gods and female humans. One study notes, "Most often we are dealing with an affair between a male god and a female human who becomes the mother of a male child."[113] The divinity of these offspring is in question, however. There is a tradition that Heracles experienced apotheosis, becoming a god after his death (Hesiod, *Theog.* 943–44, 950–55). Dionysus, although half-human, was born a god (Hesiod, *Theog.* 940–42).[114] The literature does not provide guidelines to determine which of the divine progeny would actually be understood as gods or just heroes. But a fair implication of the literature does suggest that there is a uniqueness to divine childship. Humans who are children of the gods wield godlike power and authority, as seen in their actions or wisdom.[115]

Aristophanes summarizes some of the perceived powers of heroes: "So then, men, be on your guard and reverence the heroes; for we are the guardians of evil and good. We examine the unjust, the thieves and robbers, and to some we send sickness: spleen trouble and coughs, and dropsy, catarrh, itchy scabs and gout, madness, and skin eruptions, lumps, chills and fevers" (frag. 322).[116] This passage indicates that heroes were understood as bearers of divine power. They shared in the power of the gods to an extent. As such, it was common for people to erect shrines to the heroes,[117] which seems to be one of the backgrounds of Aristophanes's play.[118]

Alexander the Great, in some traditions, is asserted to have divine childship.[119] It is said that he claimed to be known as a son of Zeus, who is equivalent to the Egyptian deity Ammon. Divine descent was common mythos as regards the ancestry of the Macedonian kings when Alexander ascended to the throne.[120] But divine childship did not necessarily mandate a right to kingship, even though it may have helped secure monarchial authority.[121] The Ptolemies and Seleucids began using divine childship language, some calling themselves "children of Helios." Their claims to godhood were claims for divine honors and to rightful rule.[122] Alexander's divine childship suggested his heroic prowess but did not necessarily indicate a divine right to royalty; this was not necessitated in Greek thought. It did provide a strong basis, however, for him to claim the right to kingship, which was indicated by the declaration that he was the son of Ammon, a deity. On the whole, it demonstrated his ability to exercise that kingship by conquering the nations around the Mediterranean.[123]

Among the Greeks, the children of the gods obtained inherited divinity from their divine ancestors in some shape or form. One may have been the child of a god-god union or the progeny of a god-human union. In either case, divinity from the deity was passed down to the child. For our purposes, as it pertains to the god-human unions, divinity was passed down to humans, in some cases making them deities from birth, as is the case of Dionysus. Or divinity could be passed down through the exercise of some divine ability, as is the case with Heracles. In his case, he obtained god status after his death, which shows that the gap between gods and humans was not impassable for the mortal children of the gods. These children were deemed heroes, capable of exercising divine power on earth.

The foundation laid by the heroes was exploited by Alexander the Great and his Hellenistic successors to legitimize their rule. Alexander used his divine descent as evidence that he not only had the ability to conquer but was given this ability by divine right. There is disagreement about whether Alexander claimed divine status because of his belief in divine descent. Some views hold that Alexander never understood himself as divine when he came to the East. Regardless, his successors understood themselves as divine figures because of their supposed divine descent. By the end of the fourth century BCE, ruler cults had been established for Alexander's successors. Hero cults and beliefs about divinity for children of the gods would be picked up by the Roman emperors.[124]

Divine Childship among the Romans

The Romans accepted the Greek and many other pantheons and believed that the gods have children. They had their own heroes who were children of the gods and heroes, some of whom became gods, such as Romulus, Remus, and Aeneas.[125] But the use of divine childship language, "child of God," in the first century primarily indicated the emperor among Romans.[126] In this sense, divine childship language implied that Caesar was a living god, the human manifestation of divine power and authority (*Res gest. divi Aug.* 34). Despite some scholarly objections, there is great evidence to suggest that the emperor obtained this divine childship status with all of its connotations in his own lifetime.[127] Caesar was worshipped, and he was considered by many in the empire not only as the son of a god but as a god:

> To the god Tiberius Caesar Augustus, son of the god Augustus, Emperor, Greatest High Priest, holding the tribunician power the 31st time. In the era of Lucius Axius Naso as proconsul, and Marcus Ertrilius Lupercus as legate, and Gaius Flavius Figulus as quaestor: Adrastus, son of Adrastus, friend of Caesar, the hereditary priest of the sanctuary and statue of Tiberius Caesar Augustus that was established in the gymnasium by him with his own funds the patriotic and all-virtuous, serving free of charge and voluntarily as gymnasiarch and priest of the gods in the gymnasium, did establish the sanctuary and the statue with his own funds for his god.[128]

This inscription from Cyprus says it was written on the occasion of Tiberius's birthday on the sixteenth of November in 29 CE. A study notes that this would have been during the lifetime of Jesus of Nazareth.[129]

Divine childship, then, in a Roman perspective would have signified that if one is able to wield divine power, one is a god or could authoritatively claim to be one.[130] As a child of a god, one stands in the lineage of the beings who bear all authority and power in the cosmos. As such, one shares in the authority and the power of the gods when one is their child. It is argued that Caesar Augustus, and many of his subjects, considered himself a child of divine Caesar, Julius, and the god Apollo, demonstrating his god-inherited authority:[131]

> In fact, Octavian wanted to have it both ways—he was a "son of god" by Caesar's adoption and a "son of Apollo" by divine begetting. In his competition with Antony for sole possession of Roman imperium, he used both aspects of his divine sonship: the childship connection to Caesar swayed the troops and much of the public, while the patronage of Apollo served to rival Antony's self-presentation as Dionysus or Hercules. Ultimately, though, the connection to Caesar proved most powerful, and it was this particular divine relationship—*divi filius*—that was propagated by adoption through the Julio-Claudian "dynasty."[132]

Both divine imperial ordination and manifest divine power were the implications of divine childship in a Roman perspective. As explained earlier, worship was only natural for one of these children of the gods. They were no different from the gods themselves in their ability to exercise power on earth. Like Zeus/Jupiter, it would have been believed that the emperor became "father of the whole human race."[133] In this case, the fatherhood did not denote biological origin, but it did signify the kind of reverence people were supposed to have for the emperor.

*   *   *

The purpose of this investigation has been to determine the prominent resonances that would have been heard when the phrase *child of God* was heard by a reader or hearer of Luke/Acts. In Jewish scripture, this language principally indicates three senses: heavenly beings, the king of Israel, and the people of Israel.

The children of Israel—God's elect, God's unique people—are also discussed as God's children. Their divine childship bespeaks several things. For one, it suggests that Israel is upheld by God above all of the other nations. God treats the people differently. They have a covenant with God that others do not have. This covenant allows God to be wrathful against them while, at the same time, planning their return to his favor. The texts of Jewish scripture set the stage for debates about whether Israel could lose its divine childship status. The evidence suggests that even when God makes a seemingly unalterable and irrevocable declaration—"You are not my people" (Hos 1:9)—there is still room for an even stronger embrace for Israel in the end.

This covenantal embrace is often expressed as God's special love for Israel. On more than one occasion, it is not a stretch to infer that the cause of this love, especially since Israel had been displeasing to God, is that these people are God's children. Other nations are devoted to other divine beings, but Israel belongs to YHWH. YHWH protects them. But they must also obey him.

Second Temple literature shows a development of the senses we have discussed. One principal notion of divine childship is the conception that God's children are special: they will be disciplined as God's special people, have access to God as God's special people, and be avenged for the maltreatment others have given them. There are also senses in which they are known to be the children of God if their behavior aligns with God as their Father.[134] Josephus and Philo, however, were willing to expand God's Fatherhood to all human beings. They use the language that often takes on a special sense to pertain to all of God's human creatures.

Adam is the image and child of God also. From our analysis, Adam is implied as God's child in biblical traditions against their ANE background.

Biblical writers describe Adam in similar terms that they would use to describe a ruler (see Ps 2; 8). In most Second Temple literature, Adam is not explicitly called God's child but is depicted as God's child. Adam as the ancestor of all humans bespeaks the notion—though not emphasized in the biblical texts—that both Israel and the nations are God's children. Israel, as the Lord's firstborn in both Scripture and Second Temple literature, may indicate that the other nations are considered children as well.

Divine childship conceptions are also present in non-Jewish contexts. What is common to Jewish, Greek, and Roman beliefs about divine childship is that transhuman divinity is present among the children of the God/gods. In these cultural streams, being children of the God/gods is seldom meant as mere metaphor.[135] The concept suggests that the children carry evidence of the divine presence. For Greeks and Romans, this language could suggest that one is worthy of honor—in the least, worthy of worship and divinely given the right to rule because of one's abilities. In all cultural streams that would serve to be the background and foundation of early Christianity, the children of God were understood to be God's descendants and, like God, were considered special.

When we read through Luke, then, we should keep these interpretations of divine childship in mind. From the other ideas we have associated with divine childship in Luke, it seems most likely that Luke is primarily using Jewish perspectives. Divine childship, in relation to Jesus, is most certainly associated with his divine abilities, somewhat mirroring Greeks and Romans. But divine abilities can also be seen in Second Temple literature. In the same chapter in which Jesus describes the feats of astonishing power and authority (Luke 10:17–20) that the disciples received from Jesus (see 9:1), the narrative moves quickly toward the argument that divine childship is solely mediated through Jesus as the true divine childship figure (10:21–22). In Luke 6:35–36, godlikeness merits being called a child of God. In Luke 20:36, the children of God are compared to and take on the immortal life of angels, also considered God's children, at the resurrection of the just (see Luke 14:14; Acts 24:15).

What must be determined is how the notion of divine childship as a sign of a chosen people—God's one, unique nation, Israel—develops into the call of all nations (Acts 17:28–29) and their inclusion in Israel's chosen status. Josephus and Philo, contemporaries of Luke, affirmed that all people were God's children, as they were his creation. But how do we get from the very specialized sense that construes Israel as a favored child among the nations to the notion that this favor is available to all nations (Luke 24:47)?

Although there was room within Judaism for non-Jews, there was no major thrust for evangelistic mission for non-Jews.[136] God wanted the nations' devotion, but we do not see the development of the mission to get it until the rise of Jesus and his movement.[137] The next chapter will explore the theology of this movement. We will discover that this movement saw the worth of humanity, since all humans were made in God's image, tied to the call for all people to return to the God who made them.

CHAPTER 4

JESUS AND THE SALVATION
OF GOD'S CHILDREN

In the previous chapter, we surveyed the uses of divine childship language in Jewish, Greek, and Roman traditions. Among Jews, the phrase *child of God* could mean that a creature was a nonhuman, heavenly being, an angel. It could also mean that a human was an Israelite, whether one's behavior pleased YHWH or not. Finally, it could mean that a person was God's royal representative of the house of David. In an implied sense, the concept could also be understood to speak of all of the nations. Such a view was echoed among Greek thinkers. Romans thought similarly but also placed emphasis on Caesar as a child of God. With this background, Luke/Acts becomes a lot clearer in its references to God's children. When speaking of human beings, it could mean that the child of God is special, marked out from among all people in the earth. It could also mean that the person is a bearer of God's image and likeness in creation.

WHO ARE THE CHILDREN OF GOD IN LUKE/ACTS?

In Luke/Acts, the referents of divine childship language are Jesus (Luke 1:32, 35), Adam (Luke 3:38), and Jesus's followers (Luke 6:35; 20:36). We have already explored the various resonances this language would have had with Luke's audience. The current task is to determine how Luke explores these resonances and what arguments he advances through them in his Gospel and Acts.

Divine childship is essential for Luke. On one level, this view involves anthropology, God's view of humanity. Luke speaks of divine childship in a favored sense (God's firstborn) and a general sense (humans in God's likeness). On another level, recognizing divine childship explains the reason for the evangelistic mission of Luke's stories. Bringing these senses together allows a better understanding of Luke's theology.

Seeing the restoration of divine childship as a major principle in Luke on these two levels allows a better understanding of the importance of the Ethiopian eunuch in Acts. Though this will be taken up in the next chapter, it is important to note at this point that this story is polyvalent, especially when coupled with that of Simeon Niger. It dignifies black skin and the humanity of all people. It also suggests that nations far and wide are returning to God and that the gospel of Jesus will be triumphant. For now, it is important to lay the biblical and theological foundation on which these claims are made.

ADAM, GOD'S CHILD, PROTOTYPE OF JESUS

To come to an understanding in Luke of divine childship for both Jesus and the disciples, it all begins with Adam, as in the creation of the world. Even though Jesus is the first referent of the title "Son of God" (Luke 1:35), Adam has a significant role to play in explaining exactly why this is so. Luke wants us to know that the story of Jesus as a human starts with God through Adam (Luke 3:38).[1]

Before the genealogy proper, Luke discusses the sonship of Jesus: "And Jesus was, himself, starting out at thirty years old, being the son of Joseph, as it was thought, who was the son of Eli" (Luke 3:23).[2] Instead of beginning with the ancestors and ending with Jesus, as Matthew does (Matt 1:1–16), Luke begins with Jesus and ends with "son of Adam, son of God" (Luke 3:38).[3] In the Greek, Luke shows that Adam is Jesus's father (3:38).[4] Luke 3:22 shows that Jesus is declared to be God's child. The reader should not ignore the fact that Jesus begins the genealogy, having been declared

God's Son, and God ends the genealogy, as Father of Adam. The genealogy is flanked by the Son and Father pair that will define the Gospel itself.[5] But the other pivotal child of God discussed in the genealogy is Adam.

It is noted that this is the only time Adam is mentioned by name[6] in the three Synoptic Gospels.[7] It has also been famously argued that the temptation narrative in Mark alluded to Adam.[8] But to what end does Luke explicitly reference Adam as God's son?[9]

Adam is the progenitor of humanity, considered the ideal human being, and also the one human who allows corruption to enter creation. It is not clear, however, that *all* Second Temple and subsequent Jewish writers agreed that death and corruption could be blamed on the sins of Adam.[10] While it is debated that Luke considered Adam as the source of human corruption, he most probably held this view.[11] The discussion of Adam also broadens the impact of sin to affect all of creation.[12]

While it is beyond the scope of this work to establish all of the contours of a possible Adam Christology in Luke,[13] arguments have been raised to do so in Synoptic Gospels.[14] The best reading of the evidence concludes that Jesus is a type of Adam, God's Son generated through the Spirit.[15] It is cogent that Luke argues that both Jesus and Adam are considered God's children[16] because both come into the world via the Spirit. Adam lived by the "wind" of God (Gen 2:7), and Jesus was called "holy" and "Son of God" through the Spirit (Luke 1:35).[17]

It could be argued that Adam was considered a disobedient son in Luke's genealogy.[18] Jesus plays the opposite role. He is the new man, the true image of God, God's obedient Son who is the model for all humanity.[19] The weight of Luke's association of Jesus with Adam is on Adam's sonship. But since Jesus as Son of God reverses the effects of Adam's sin, if Jesus is a direct descendant of Adam, as Son of God, it bears in mind that Jesus corrects Adam's failures. To be sure, this is implied in Luke/Acts (Luke 4:6; see also 2 Enoch 31–32; Testament of Levi 18:10).

One interpretation, contrary to my own, suggests that the unity of Luke/Acts seen in the Adam/Christ parallel is not a contrast between the disobedient and obedient sons of God (Adam and Jesus).[20] Luke/Acts emphasizes that Adam and Christ are presented to share their commonality, not their distinctions. Through both, God extends divine childship to all. There is no "original sin" in Luke attributive to Adam.[21] There is no "brokenness" in human history that has to be mended by the work of Christ, as it is in Paul. "Continuity is crucial," because Luke considers the Spirit a "gift," not a remedy for human failure.[22]

The problem with this argument is that Luke does tell his story to demonstrate brokenness and human failure.[23] The narrative portrays a disconnect caused by sin that Jesus—and through him, the church—repairs. First, the very opening of Luke, and elsewhere beyond this point, tells us that God was sending John to restore the lost connection Israel had with God and the patriarchs by remembering the covenant (Luke 1:16–17, 55, 71–72; see also Acts 3:25; 13:32–33; Deut 14:1–2; 32:5). If YHWH is to remember the covenant, surely there is a sense in which he is returning to what he had promised. Second, with the preparation John gives, Jesus comes as a "Savior" (Luke 2:11) whose task is to save Israel from its sin and enemies (Luke 1:50–54, 71, 74, 77–79; 3:3; 4:18–19; 13:34; 24:47; Acts 2:21, 38, 47; 4:12; 5:31; 10:43; 11:14; 13:38; 15:11; 16:30–31; 26:18). The power of evil, both internal and cosmic, has affected the entire generation to which Jesus had come (Luke 3:7;[24] 5:32; 7:31–33; 9:41; 11:4, 18–24, 29–36, 46–52; 13:1–5; 16:8; Acts 2:40).[25] Israel and, it is assumed, the rest of the nations are under the power of sin and the devil and are in need of divine rescue. This is why Jesus faces Satan himself (Luke 4:1–13; see also 22:3) and promises his defeat (10:18) and the rise of the people of God—because of his intervention (10:19; 22:31–32).

There is indeed a disconnect. When taken within the context of other literature, the focus on Adam suggests attribution of the disconnection to the view in Second Temple literature that Adam had a part to play (see 4 Ezra 3:21). Furthermore, the fact that Jesus is the harbinger of the coming age while Adam was the beginning of the present confirms this belief. Another point of confirmation is that Luke knew Paul and shares in his theology.[26]

In the writings of Luke, it seems that Adam as God's son prefigures Jesus as an ideal human being. He set the original human standard of human authority and righteousness. In some ways, Israel's calling as a nation resembles the blessedness described to the original Adam (Gen 12:1; 13:15–17;

15:18; Exod 12:25; 13:5; Deut 6:3; 19:8; 27:3). The restored Israel, through Jesus, certainly reflects Adamic traits (Luke 18:24–25; 22:29–30; Acts 1:7–8). These concepts are not overt in Luke, but the language of the kingdom and the fulfillment of the promises to David, God's son, to rule the world in Jesus (Acts 4:25–26; see also Ps 2:1–8; Luke 20:41–43) bespeak that we should think of Jesus, and Israel through Jesus, as reflecting Adam or God's original intent for Adam.

Adam's role, then, provides a way to understand Jesus as a harbinger of the age to come. Adam and Jesus mark the eons of human history. Adam and Jesus are unique human beings, the proprietors of the two ages (see Acts 17:26–31).[27] The new age is supposed to begin with Adam's restoration, according to the Testament of Levi 18:10–12.[28] Testament of Levi 18:12 is an example of recognition of the people of Israel as God's children. But the recognition of the people of God as the children of God is preceded by the restoration of Adam to his place in Eden and the opening of paradise (Testament of Levi 18:10).[29] This seems to be going on in Luke as well. In Luke/Acts, Jesus provides access to paradise, showing he is an Adamic figure (Luke 23:43).[30]

Before the rest of Israel can be discussed as God's children, Luke discusses Jesus as God's Son and takes this sonship back to Adam. Therefore, as Luke narrates, Jesus comes to dismiss the age of ignorance seen in the descendants of Adam (Acts 17:30). This age has been overcome by the "wisdom of the righteous" (Luke 1:17), which comes through Jesus, God's Son, who brings the new age.

To sum up Adam's role, first, Adam serves as prototype of Jesus as "son of God."[31] Again, there are arguments to the contrary; it is true that Jesus does not need to be Adam's child to be God's child.[32] Jesus is God's child from birth (Luke 1:32, 35). But Luke does not use a singular, coherent way to describe Jesus's identity as God's Son.[33] Jesus is affirmed as God's child throughout in his birth, baptism, and exaltation. Luke does not *need* to place Adam in this list to support his defense of Jesus's identity, but he certainly exploits it. And it furthers Luke's point to speak to Jesus's place as the transformative agent for all human beings. He is the true human, succeeding where all other humans failed.

Again, as noted in Second Temple literature, Adam was a ruler, a priest, and an eschatological hero. In the Testament of Abraham, Adam will be an eschatological judge, judging all of his seed. In many of these writings, Adam takes the throne occupied by Satan. Aspects of these traits are reflected in Luke's portrayal of Jesus (Luke 4:6–8; 10:17–20; 22:69).

A second way to understand Adam is that he shows the intent of God's creation of humanity to be God's children. In Jesus's discussion of the restored Israel's divine childship (e.g., Luke 6:35; 11:1–4, 13; 15:11–32; 20:36), Adam is part of this calculus. The traditions suggested that Israel was chosen by God to uphold the covenant to be God's child in the earth. Brokenness entered and all of humanity suffered under Satan's power (Luke 4:6; 10:17–20; Acts 10:38). All of the nations, including Israel, were lost, and this is why all nations are called to repentance (Luke 3:1–16; Acts 17:26–31).

Jesus's mission, as child of God, is necessary because Israel had failed to uphold the covenant (see Deut 14:1). Using the language from Deuteronomy 32, Jesus calls Israel to account. He calls the nation "faithless and perverse" (Luke 9:41),[34] which echoes LXX Deuteronomy 32:5.[35] *All* of the children of Adam are in trouble. Israel's unique status as God's child had been corrupted. The people were just like the rest of humanity. All were God's children (Acts 17:28–29). But that status had been lost. But only through the ministry of Jesus, when the status of Israel had been restored, would the rest of the world could have their divine childship status restored. On these grounds, we can conclude, "Through association with Jesus, all people can find the way of return to the Parent, for Jesus' mission is humanity."[36]

Luke describes Adam as the ancestor of humanity (Acts 17:26)—and, as such, the ancestor of Israel—but he also presents him as the ancestor of Jesus (Luke 3:38). Jesus sums up Israel and all of the nations. By looking at Jesus, Adam can be seen as the harbinger of the present age and a kingly, authoritative figure. He is a "son of God" like Jesus. Turning to who Jesus is, then, is the next logical place to continue this study.

JESUS THE MESSIAH: SON OF GOD AND
LORD OF HEAVEN AND EARTH

To understand divine childship in Luke/Acts, this study must now consider how Jesus is understood as God's Son.[37] For Luke, understanding Jesus's divine childship is essential to both Adam and the disciples.[38] Both Adam and Jesus's followers are children of God in a way that reflects Jesus's sonship in Lukan theology.

In this discussion, my focus is on what Luke means when he says Jesus is God's child (Luke 1:29–37; 3:21–22; 4:1–13; 4:41; 8:28; 9:35; 10:21–24; 11:1–13; 20:9–18; 22:29, 42, 70; 23:34, 46; 24:49; Acts 1:4–11; 9:20; 13:33).[39] All of these texts cannot be addressed in depth. But some analysis of a few of them will suffice for demonstrating the point that Jesus is the nexus for divine childship. The followers of Jesus, and even Adam himself, should be understood in light of Jesus, the Son of God.

Luke frames his Gospel around the sonship of Jesus.[40] Luke's birth narrative differs from Matthew's in that Luke emphasizes that Jesus is God's Son, who will be called "Son of the Most High" (Luke 1:32) and "Son of God" (1:35).[41] The question remains as to what Luke intended when he reported these declarations by Gabriel.[42] It has been argued that these declarations were meant to signify Jesus's Davidic lineage.[43] Other arguments promote this interpretation with the view that divinity is not to be inferred for Jesus from this title.[44] But there is suggestion that calling Jesus "God's Son" in Luke did mean divine incarnation.[45] When he is called "Son of the Most High" (1:32), the text follows with the promise that he will have an everlasting kingdom, always sitting on the throne (1:33). This could be understood to mean that this promise[46] indicates that Jesus is "indestructible." In the second instance, in which Jesus is declared to be "Son of God" (1:35), the description of his "holy" state at birth indicates that Jesus is in "God's sphere." Jesus is discussed as God's Son not just at his baptism, as in Mark, but at his birth.[47] Luke is even distinct from Matthew with the only reference to Jesus being God's child in the infancy narrative coming from Matthew's own reference to Hosea 11:1 (Matt 2:15). Luke is the only Gospel writer to refer to Jesus as God's Son by the narrative characters at his birth.

Whether one agrees with this interpretation of the Lukan birth narrative or not, it makes a persuasive point that would not have been missed by an ancient reader. Both Jews and non-Jews would have noted that Gabriel promised that Jesus would not have a human father (Luke 1:35). The Jew would be reminded of Genesis 6 and Second Temple speculations concerning the progeny of the heavenly beings. Even though there is no evidence of sexual intercourse between the Holy Spirit and Mary, the reader would expect that Jesus was more than a mere human.[48] The non-Jew would be reminded of the numerous accounts of the demigods who had divine fathers and mortal mothers.[49] Again, the demigods were not necessarily hailed or worshipped as gods. But the reader would have known that Jesus was no mere mortal, similar to any common person.

The birth narrative establishes from the beginning of Luke's treatises that Jesus is human but something more.[50] He is born "holy" and declared by the angel to be God's child from the womb.[51] Jesus is paralleled with John the Baptist.[52] John comes as "prophet of the Most High," while Jesus is "son of the Most High." Why speak of Jesus's sonship at all if it is to be understood in the normal human sense or only as the king of Israel? The significance appears to be that Jesus's sonship marks him out not only in the messianic sense, which was to be expected. It is meant to emphasize that Jesus transcends humanity. This is even demonstrated in Jesus's maturation. Luke tells us that he had an uncanny connection with the temple, a place he understood as a child that belonged to *his* Father (Luke 2:49).[53] Jesus inherits but also transcends his Davidic lineage.

In another interpretation, the birth narrative references Jesus's sonship to claim that Jesus is the Lord.[54] There is no doubt that Luke has a high Christology.[55] Even when scholarship disagrees and suggests Luke does not imply Jesus's preexistence, it can still conclude that Jesus was unique and possibly divine.[56] The well-supported conclusion from the evidence of Luke is that Luke intends the reader to consider Jesus as the embodiment of God.

This is the foundation Luke lays for his reading of Jesus, which suggests that Luke intends to communicate throughout his narrative that Jesus is not just human. When John arises, it becomes clearer exactly who Jesus is. John proclaims that he came to "prepare the way of the Lord" (Luke 3:4; see also

1:76).[57] After Luke tells us about the ministry of John, he then moves quickly to the beginning of the ministry of Jesus. Narratively, Jesus is the Lord whom John came to proclaim.

Jesus's baptism by John also sets Jesus apart in two ways.[58] It demonstrates that Jesus is the king and a true Israelite: "Now when all the people were baptized, and when Jesus also had been baptized and was praying, the heaven was opened, and the Holy Spirit descended upon him in bodily form like a dove. And a voice came from heaven, 'You are my Son, the Beloved; with you I am well pleased'" (3:21–22).[59] The Spirit's bestowal upon Jesus openly designates that he is the coming king (Isa 11:2; 61:1).[60] The Spirit had already taken part in Jesus's human existence at birth. Now the Spirit publicly demonstrates Jesus's identity as the king of Israel. The narrative leaves it ambiguous about which of the parties saw the dove land upon Jesus.[61] But the ambiguity allows the reader to surmise that what happened to Jesus is known to those present. The reader could have easily interpreted that God had restored his covenant with Israel somehow through Jesus (Ezek 36:25–27). Jesus partook in the powers of the new age; he had just come out of the water and received the Spirit of God, two essential aspects of the promise God made in Ezekiel 36.

There appears to be no ambiguity, however, with God's declaration about Jesus's sonship (see Luke 9:35; Matt 3:17; 17:5; Mark 1:11; 9:7; John 12:28; 2 Pet 1:17–18). At the baptism, God declares not only that Jesus is his Son, evoking Psalm 2:7, but that Jesus is "my Son, the Beloved;[62] with [whom] I am well pleased."[63] Jesus has found favor with God in a way that distinguishes him among the servants of the Most High. We have no record in the biblical accounts of public callings where God has spoken from heaven to identify with a servant. The closest we come is when God defends Moses against Miriam and Aaron (Num 12:1–16). But in that instance, the creation itself does not respond the way it did for Jesus. The heavens themselves "opened" for Jesus. This occurrence is unprecedented in Jewish scripture. Jesus is not anointed with oil as were David and the priests; Jesus is anointed with the Spirit and power (Acts 10:38). The revelation that Jesus is God's Son through the Spirit sets the stage for the public, communal anointing of the disciples as God's children (Acts 2:1–4).

As the Spirit-anointed true Israelite, Son of God,[64] Jesus was able to defeat Satan (Luke 4:1–13).[65] Luke, again, differs from Matthew in the way he arranges his temptation narrative. Luke ends the temptation narrative with Jerusalem based on the rhetorical aim of "recency."[66] The narrative picks up with the temple (Luke 1:5–9) and also has its high moment with the disciples going back and rejoicing in the temple after Jesus's ascension (24:53). Luke may be doing something else in addition to this. Luke also begins his temptation and ends it with Satan's challenge of Jesus's sonship,[67] which is also demonstrated in the essential beginning (1:32, 35) of the whole Gospel narrative and its essential closing moment (24:49).[68]

Within the temptation narrative itself, the primary discussion is not of the temple but of Jesus's divine childship.[69] Jesus's temptations by Satan indicate that "Jesus is Israel, God's son, who is called out of Egypt to complete Israel's exodus. . . . But Luke also casts this scene as a reversal of Adam's disobedience, in that sense filling out the allusions to Adam in Mark 1:12–13."[70] Jesus is both Israel and Adam; to speak of Israel and its execution of the covenant of God is to understand Israel fulfilling an Adamic role in the world. The temptation narrative demonstrates in no uncertain terms that Jesus stands above the rest of the children of God. He is the model child of God, outdoing both Israel and Adam in his obedience to God.[71] By vanquishing Satan, he wields authority like Adam (see Gen 1:26–28).[72] He has also, as the new David and representative of Israel, defeated the monster of chaos as the Davidic figure was said to have the power to do (Ps 89:10, 25).

In the Gospel, the only time human beings communicate that Jesus is God's Son is by the prompting of a heavenly, nonhuman figure.[73] The transfiguration scene serves as the only other time we have God speak on behalf of Jesus, declaring his identity. In this scene, Luke, as well as the other Synoptic writers, portrays Jesus's physical transformation in the likeness of other heavenly figures at the end of the Gospel (Luke 24:4) and Acts (1:10; see also Matt 17:5; Mark 9:7). Moreover, Luke also includes the appearance of Moses and Elijah, symbolic of the law and the prophets, as witnesses of Jesus's glorious appearance in Luke 9:28–36. God's interruption of Peter "while" he was speaking accentuates the seriousness of the moment. Peter has spoken out of a misunderstanding, placing Jesus alongside other "idealized human figures," but God is clear that Jesus alone should be heard. The transfiguration is multivalent; it points toward Jesus's suffering and his enthronement as Messiah.[74] It also shows that he is unique among the greatest of the children of Israel. He is not *just* an "elect" agent of YHWH; he is *the elect* agent of YHWH, the one who defines the role for all others.

If Jesus is the Lord who has been manifested as the child of David, then it makes sense that he would be the only means by which knowledge of the God of Israel was possible. After the disciples returned from vanquishing the demonic hosts, Jesus tells them not to rejoice in their victory but to rejoice because their "names are written in heaven" (Luke 10:19–20). In what is called a "bolt out of the Johannine blue," Jesus expresses his uniqueness in a way that verifies God's previous declaration about him:[75] "At that same hour Jesus rejoiced in the Holy Spirit and said, 'I thank you, Father, Lord of heaven and earth, because you have hidden these things from the wise and the intelligent and have revealed them to infants; yes, Father, for such was your gracious will. All things have been handed over to me by my Father;[76] and no one knows who the Son is except the Father, or who the Father is except the Son and anyone to whom the Son chooses to reveal him" (Luke 10:21–22).[77] Luke again departs from Matthew in his description of this event (Matt 11:25–27). Jesus is not merely making a declaration to his disciples. Luke emphasizes that Jesus is under the influence of the Holy Spirit when he declares his own unique status and victorious posture.[78] The magnitude of the Spirit's importance should be noted in Luke's Gospel:

> The possibility of this relational notion of identity—unity and distinction—depends on a third presence, the Holy Spirit. That the Spirit is mentioned as Jesus addresses the Father in prayer as [Lord] is of substantial importance. It recalls the Spirit's vital presence in the conception of Jesus and continued activity through his baptism, temptation, and programmatic scene in Nazareth. There is no moment in Jesus' life as [Son] or [Lord] when he exists apart from the Spirit, or when his relationship to the Father is not made possible by the Spirit. The Spirit is the Power between the Father and his Son that constitutes the Father-Son relation itself.[79]

Jesus begins by thanking God as his Father and as the one who is also "Lord of heaven and earth." This declaration sets God as the God of creation, the one who is in control of both heaven and earth. This uniqueness sets God apart from every other being.[80] The fact that Jesus identifies God as Lord of heaven and earth also sets the terms of what he means when he says "all things" in verse 22.[81] It makes sense to infer that he is speaking of "heaven and earth." Again, this sets Jesus apart from all others. Other people have been given rule and authority on earth, but Jesus is unique in that he alone has been given rule and authority in heaven and in earth. Both he and God are considered "Lord" in these verses. The epistemic symbiosis between God and Jesus that Luke relays is a way to place Jesus on the level of God. Their relationship is without precedent.

A "high human Christology" does not account for Jesus's uniqueness in this passage. Jesus is not merely *an agent* who discloses the identity of God; he is *the agent* who makes God known. Taken to its logical conclusion, Jesus's sonship becomes the mechanism for all divine childship connectivity with God, both past and present. Such a belief is not out of sync with early Christian theories of Jesus's divinity. Paul would proclaim that Jesus's exaltation makes sense in light that he was already "equal with God" (Phil 2:5–11; my translation). All things are given to Jesus by the Father as a human, we can argue, because Jesus had already had all things in the first place.

Pointing out the uniqueness of Jesus and God's relationship is not Luke's only point for giving us his version of this dominical statement. Jesus's proclamation of his own high sonship and understanding of the Father was not only for "eschatological significance" of this relationship for the disciples but so that his disciples might know God as "Father."[82] Jesus's relationship with God is described this way as a means to invite others to join their divine family.

Jesus, as the locus of God's divine identity on earth, also walks in the role of God as the one who appoints kings and rulers in the kingdom and initiates new creation. At the Passover feast, after Jesus explains how he will take on the role of the Passover lamb, he promises his disciples that they will be rulers in his kingdom: "You are those who have stood by me in my trials; and I confer on you, just as my Father has conferred on me, a kingdom, so that you may eat and drink at my table in my kingdom, and you will sit on thrones judging the twelve tribes of Israel" (Luke 22:28–30). Jesus, as Son, confers the kingdom to his disciples in the manner in which his Father did it to him.[83] He stands in the role of God giving the kingdom to those whom he chose.[84]

This conferral of the kingdom also connects with the expansion of the kingdom of God to the gentiles and access to paradise. Earlier in the narrative, Jesus makes the provocative claim that those who expected to enter the kingdom might not: "There will be weeping and gnashing of teeth when you see Abraham and Isaac and Jacob and all the prophets in the kingdom of God, and you yourselves thrown out. Then people will come from east and west, from north and south, and will eat in the kingdom of God" (Luke 13:28–29).[85] No table is mentioned, but it appears that Jesus's comment meant a table he will later discuss in Luke 22. Also, "kingdom" is not possessive. Jesus does not call this kingdom his, but we are not forced to conclude that this kingdom is not different from Jesus's kingdom. They are different ways of saying the same thing. Jesus will bring about the reign of God on earth, where he stands as king of kingdoms, fulfilling the promises made to David's family (Ps 2:7–8; Isa 11:1–12).

Jesus's kingdom also has worldwide implications because through it, entry into paradise is granted.[86] On three crosses, Luke reports, three men were condemned to die. One of those men, Jesus, was completely innocent (Luke 23:41, 47). One of the condemned caustically challenged Jesus to save all of them, if he were truly Messiah. The other condemned man defended Jesus (Luke 23:39–41). His defense of Jesus led to an unusual request from Jesus, which could be perceived as wishful at best. Jesus's response had eschatological implications: "Then [the condemned] said, 'Jesus, remember me when you come into your kingdom' He replied, 'Truly I tell you, today you will be with me in Paradise'" (Luke 23:42–43). Here Luke repeats the possessive form he used in 22:28–30. The kingdom of God is Jesus's kingdom. But Jesus's response concerning the kingdom he received from his Father has remarkable implications. Jesus states that he and the condemned will enter paradise together.[87] Jesus promises paradise to this man as part of his request to be remembered in the entrance of his kingdom. Luke's narration combines the notion of the kingdom—fulfilling the promises to Abraham and David—with the entrance into paradise, the eschatological Eden.[88]

Other texts inform us that we should view paradise as an eschatological abode. The messianic context of the statement suggests we should prefer Testament of Dan 5:10–13 and Testament of Levi 18:10–14 to inform our reading. In both of these texts, the restoration occurs within the framework of the rise of the Messiah (Luke 9:18–22; Acts 2:36), the restoration of Israel (Acts 1:7–8; 5:31), and the defeat of Satan (Luke 10:17–20). These are all major themes in Luke's Gospel, as we have discussed. Testament of Levi adds a further significance, which we have discussed: the opening of the kingdom of God to the nations (Luke 24:47–49).

Luke's portrayal of Jesus, however, goes beyond a merely human messianic figure. Jesus's conferral of the kingdom and the Spirit signifies that he is not just a human being. Jesus stands as the creator who confers the Spirit of God upon his disciples. John explains his mission as one of baptism with water, but Jesus will baptize with the Holy Spirit and fire (Luke 3:16). Jesus repeats this, excluding the fire element, in Acts 1:5.[89] The act of baptizing people in the Spirit of God—not simply as the agent of God but as the authorizer of the baptism itself—demonstrates that Luke understands Jesus to function in the role of God. As God was creator of Adam, who conferred the breath of life upon him, Jesus confers the Spirit of God, the breath of new creation, upon his followers. Jesus's final words in the Gospel should be seen in light of Peter's announcement of the source of the Spirit (Acts 2:33), indicating that Jesus has attained the very throne of God: "And see, I am sending upon you what my Father promised; so stay here in the city until you have been clothed with power from on high" (Luke 24:49).[90] For Luke, the arguments go hand in hand; the one who confers the kingdom is the same one who confers the Spirit of God. The coming of the Spirit upon the disciples (Acts 2:1–4), like Jesus, was a coronation (see Luke 3:21–22). When they receive the "power" (Acts 1:8) of the kingdom, they are proleptically sitting at Jesus's table, judging the tribes of Israel.

Integral to the divine Christological significance of these passages is the phrase *my Father*. This phrase only appears in Luke four times in reference to Jesus and God (Luke 2:49; 10:22; 22:29; 24:49). Each passage posits that

Jesus is unique in his identity as God's Son and his mission. Excluding the moment of Jesus's childhood (2:49), the passages involve a heavenly transfer from Jesus to his disciples. Jesus is mediating the relationship of God the Father to other children of God. In 10:22, Jesus mediates the revelation of God to others. In 22:29, Jesus mediates the kingdom of God. In 24:49, Jesus mediates the Spirit of God.

This understanding of Jesus makes sense not only of why his name has apotropaic qualities but also of why he can freely give his disciples power and authority (Luke 9:1; 10:19). In Luke, Jesus stands in the role of God granting the disciples dominion over the earth as God did for Adam (Gen 1:26–28). There is a similitude with the Genesis creation accounts. The God who gives authority in Genesis 1:26–28 also gives the breath of life in Genesis 2:7, while Jesus gives authority and then gives breath to the manifestation of the restored people, the disciples (Acts 1:7–8; 2:1–4).

As Jesus stands in this unique position, Adam as a prototypical figure only serves as a human precedent, providing a lens for us to understand Jesus's messianic identity. We must be clear that his divine identity and messianic identity are not at odds. They are mutually inclusive in Luke and the other Gospels. Jesus takes on the roles of Adam, Moses, Elijah, David, Solomon, and even Jonah not because he is imitating them (Luke 3:38; 9:33–35; 11:31–32; 20:41–44; Acts 7:37). As a human, it would appear this way. Luke frames his narrative in a way to demonstrate that in the end, these humans were reflecting Jesus the whole time (Luke 24:27).

Jesus's role as teacher mandates that his disciples imitate him (Luke 6:40). But this is not Luke's only proposal about Jesus. He beckons the reader to look deeper. The disciples imitate him and God in praxis (6:35–36) and will imitate Jesus's resurrection, their own divine childship exaltation (20:36). In both cases, Luke emphasizes that in the disciples' participation in both showing mercy to enemies (6:35) and the resurrection (20:36), they are revealed as the children of God. Jesus's divine childship is the defining divine childship status and operative mechanism for divine childship in the age to come. Jesus, in this way, provides the new way by which the children of Abraham, those who have taken up the divine childship status, may be defined (3:8). As John the Baptist stated, one cannot rest on one's genealogy to claim this status. Luke makes it clear that this status is only claimed through *the Son*, Jesus. Jesus's status provides the means to understand the divine childship of his followers. When they are imitating Jesus, they are imitating their Father, God. Said in another way, being made in the image of Jesus is the same as being made in the image of God. Again, this statement is not without precedent within early Christianity.[91]

Through the giving of the Spirit, then, Jesus is cementing the restitution of divine childship status. The Spirit is the medium through which Jesus manifests as a human being as God's Son.[92] The Spirit rests on Jesus identifying him as the messianic Son. While rejoicing in the Spirit, Jesus speaks of himself as the nexus of divine childship. The Spirit is critical to Jesus's divine childship status. The Spirit signifies the dawn of the age to come and the reinstatement of God's people to the covenant (Acts 2:39). Through Jesus and the Spirit, the children know the ancestors and the ancestors know the children (Luke 1:17). As such, the Spirit would also be an essential quality for Jesus's followers. The Spirit of God is the Spirit of divine childship. Those on whom the Spirit of God rests are also the children of God (see Rom 8:9, 14).

Jesus's task, that which he shared with his disciples, was to pick up the Adamic vocation himself and restore the children of God. If this is to happen in earnest, then the rest of the world must be reclaimed.[93] The true children of Abraham restore the other families of the earth (Luke 1:54–55; 2:32; 13:16; 13:28; 19:9; Acts 3:25; 13:26, 47).[94]

"The Children of the Most High": The Restoration of Divine Childship Status of Israel in Luke/Acts

If Jesus embodies true divine childship and is the means by which this status is understood, what does this mean for the other human children of God? John the Baptist clarified the status of Israel: a renewal had to occur for the people to be accounted worthy of the age to come (Luke 3:8), when the children of God would be revealed (20:35–36). Biological relationship with

Abraham no longer mattered to define the vocation and identity of the children of God.[95] But when did it stop being enough?[96] We are not told why the hearts of the children must be turned to the patriarchs (1:17), but it is clear that there is a disconnect. The reader is dropped right into the middle of a long tumultuous history and expected to fill in the blanks about why people were waiting for a messiah.[97] Jesus came to David's throne because it was vacant.[98] John was declaring Abrahamic heritage was no longer enough to escape God's wrath because the people of Israel failed in fulfilling their Abrahamic vocation. Their divine childship relationship with God was essentially like the rest of the world (see Isa 1:10; Jer 23:14; Ezek 16:46–48; Amos 9:7–8; Luke 10:10–16). Demons were wreaking havoc, creation was in chaos, and Satan's power had control of the house of God (Luke 11:24; 19:46; 22:53). The Messiah had come to restore order. God was starting the new age in the kingdom of God. To enter into it, Israel had to embrace God as its Messiah, Jesus. Following the divine child would make one a child of the divine one. This was the key to entrance into the kingdom of God. Jesus gave Israel its favored covenantal status back. And through Jesus, all of the descendants of God would enjoy the status of favor.

Luke 6:35–38 is the appropriate place to begin considering how divine childship for Jesus's followers is understood in Luke/Acts:

> But love your enemies, do good, and lend, expecting nothing in return. Your reward will be great, and you will be children of the Most High; for he is kind to the ungrateful and the wicked. Be merciful, just as your Father is merciful. "Do not judge, and you will not be judged; do not condemn, and you will not be condemned. Forgive, and you will be forgiven; give, and it will be given to you. A good measure, pressed down, shaken together, running over, will be put into your lap; for the measure you give will be the measure you get back." (Luke 6:35–38)

Obedience has already been discussed as a qualification for divine childship.[99] Jesus gives commands to take on a merciful paradigm similar to God's in order to be "children of God." In this context, to be a child of someone entails taking on that person's nature. In essence, this divine childship is not merely by virtue of birth but by the adoption of a way of being. This paradigm, as seen in Luke 6:35–38, amounts to the "imitation of God."[100] This way is the path of God and, as is clear from the crucifixion narrative, the way of Jesus himself.[101] Before the crucifixion, however, Jesus plainly tells them, "A disciple is not above his teacher, but everyone when he is fully trained will be like his teacher" (Luke 6:40; my translation). He is not telling them to do anything that he is not going to do.[102]

Through their attendance to the behavior of Christ, the way of God, the disciples become God's children; they partake in the family of God.[103] Jesus expresses this same sentiment in a different way in Luke 8:21. People report to Jesus that his family wants to see him (8:20), but he says to them, "My mother and my brothers are those who hear the word of God and do it" (8:21). In 11:27–28 NKJV, the woman's cry about the blessedness of Jesus's mother is met with the response, "Blessed *are* those who hear the word of God and keep it." The "word of God" is not a general word. This word is one of restoration and salvation, the word of the kingdom of God. He is telling people that they will be part of the family of God, become the children of God, if they obey God through him. In so doing, they are obeying him as the Messiah and Lord of the world.

This obedience entails sharing in Jesus's power and authority. Luke 9:1–2 says, "Then Jesus called the twelve together and gave them power and authority over all demons and to cure diseases, and he sent them out to proclaim the kingdom of God and to heal." The same work that Jesus did as Son of God, he sent the other children of God to do. Just as Jesus loved his enemies and forgave his detractors (Luke 6:37; 11:4; 17:3–4), indeed the sins of rebellious Israel, so to would Jesus allow the disciples to share in his power and authority to tame the chaos of this age, bringing in the new one.

This mission continues with more people when Jesus calls the seventy in Luke 10:1.[104] Jesus's initial summons does not include the discussion of the dispersal of power and authority, but it is assumed (10:17–20). It is apparent that the other fifty-eight have the same power and authority that the disciples have: "The seventy returned with joy, saying, 'Lord, in your name even the demons submit to us!'" (10:17). Their power and authority grant them the ability to vanquish demonic forces.

But this is not the reason to rejoice: "He said to them, 'I watched Satan fall from heaven like a flash of lightning. See, I have given you authority to tread on snakes and scorpions, and over all the power of the enemy; and nothing will hurt you. Nevertheless, do not rejoice at this, that the spirits submit to you, but rejoice that your names are written in heaven'" (Luke 10:18–20).[105] Jesus witnesses the fall of Satan, the prince of demons; the top enemy has fallen, and all his forces have essentially been defeated with him. Jesus does what Satan thought he could do; he gives power and authority to his disciples to rule against chaos (4:6). But the fall is not the occasion for rejoicing; the people of God are to be excited about their rise (see Isa 14:11–12). They are accounted among the luminaries; their names have been written in heaven. Satan and his forces have fallen, while the true children of God have risen. This record may be another way of saying that the Son of Man will mention the names of the faithful to the Father and the angels (Luke 9:26; 12:8–9).

The fall of Satan and his forces is only taking place through the Son, the restorer of divine childship. Luke 10:21–24 elucidates what is occurring in Jesus's sending of his disciples. Through following him, through their obedience to the Son, using his name to rescue people from chaos, they are coming to know the Father.[106] They are being revealed as the children of God in the age to come (Luke 6:35). The power and authority he has given them are evidence that the God of Israel is demonstrating his covenant faithfulness to Israel once again.[107] Their obedience to the mission allows them to be "children of the Most High" (Luke 6:35; see also Sir 4:10). God warned Pharaoh about the treatment of his children, his firstborn (Exod 4:21–23). Now the powers against the pharaoh of pharaohs, Satan, have manifested. The powers that they are showing, divine abilities that made demons admit that Jesus is God's Son (e.g., Luke 8:28), are the same powers that will expose Jesus's followers as God's children to the rest of the world.

Moreover, through Jesus, the disciples discover that they have a renewed covenant with God. The prayer Jesus gives them allows them to call God "Father" and ask for the coming of the kingdom, sustenance, forgiveness of sins, and deliverance from the power of Satan (Luke 11:1–4). The disciples will be revealed as God's children, but those who trust in Jesus's ministry in the present can call God "father."[108]

This covenant is reinforced through Jesus's promise that God, as loving Father, will "give the Holy Spirit to those who ask him" (Luke 11:13). The reader must remember, all of this is occurring in and through the ministry and person of Jesus as messiah. God is granting the restoration of the vocation of divine childship through Jesus.

To further the point, Luke 20:34–36 establishes the case that divine childship is essential through Jesus: "Jesus said to them, 'Those who belong to this age[109] marry and are given in marriage; but those who are considered worthy of a place in that age[110] and in the resurrection from the dead neither marry nor are given in marriage. Indeed they cannot die anymore, because they are like angels and are children of God,[111] being children of the resurrection." The NRSV translator has glossed verse 34, translating "children of this age" as "those who belong to this age." A literal translation brings out the contrast more sharply. Jesus speaks about the children of this age, those only defined by this age's Adam (see Luke 3:8; 21:36). This is not a commandment for abstention from marriage (see Luke 16:18).[112] Jesus refers to the future eschaton, when the dead will be raised. In that day, when the age to come has overtaken this present age, the worthy children of God will no longer participate in the customs of this present age. They will not have to procreate any longer because they will live forever. They will no longer be lower than the heavenly beings in their mortality. They will be equal to the angels. They will be on par with the heavenly beings, the otherworldly children of God.

This passage bolsters Luke's typology of divine childship.[113] The resurrection is the ultimate reclamation of divine childship status. In that moment, God will actualize the greatest act of covenant faithfulness to Israel (see Ezek 37:1–14). In that moment, the people of God will overcome the powers of death and sin present in the world.[114] Jesus-believing humanity will no longer be subject to death but live forever.[115]

Jesus's own resurrection confirms this interpretation. In Acts, Paul says, "He has fulfilled for us, their children, by raising Jesus; as also it is written in the second psalm, 'You are my Son; today I have begotten you'"

(Acts 13:33). We should note the context of Paul's argument. He is discussing the reconnection of the children to the fathers—the restoration of the Adamic/Abrahamic vocation (Luke 1:17)—to emphasize the accomplishment of Christ. Jesus's own divine childship was publicly confirmed in the resurrection. God demonstrated his power and his faithfulness on Jesus's behalf. The next verse reminds the reader of the "sure mercies of David" (Acts 13:34; my translation). The promises that God made to the Davidic ruler to protect him and demonstrate his power for him were now manifested again for Jesus. His messiahship, his status as the Son of God, the king, was confirmed in the resurrection.

The promise of the resurrection for the people of God functions as the appropriate parallel. God's faithfulness is evinced in the resurrection. Through Jesus, the people of God will live forever in the land, the world, which God had promised. The inheritance offers assurance to the believer that she is God's child (Ps 2). Through Jesus, God has restored his divine childship status for all of God's children.[116]

Before this day, the people of God will receive the sign of the age to come, the Spirit (Luke 3:16; Luke 24:49; Acts 1:4–11). The Son baptizes them with the breath of the age to come so that they may live as they will in its full manifestation. The followers of Jesus are, thereby, granted the powers of the age to come to be witnesses of the mediator of the new age, Jesus Christ (Acts 1:8). Through their faithfulness to the Son of God, they fulfill the task of being children of God. They receive accompanying signs that confirm their divine childship. They are charged with the responsibility of winning others to faithfulness to the Son of God, Jesus. God through Jesus and Jesus through his witnesses are rescuing the first human child of God, Adam, restoring him back to his divine childship status, first through Israel and then the nations.

The Restoration of the Children of God and God's Mission

Luke 15:11–32 and the Mission of Restored Childship

The restoration of divine childship (Luke 6:35; 8:21; 10:21–24; 11:1–13; 20:36; 24:49; Acts 1:4–5), then, necessarily entails the commission to evangelize. Luke's missiological agenda is interwoven in the restoration of the divine childship status in Israel through Jesus Christ. Luke 15:11–32 shows us that divine childship is about the mission to transform and save God's lost children.

What is normally called the parable of the "prodigal son" in Luke 15:11–32 is better understood as the parable of the "restored son."[117] A lengthy discussion of all of the history of interpretation is unnecessary at this juncture. But a cursory review of perspectives on the parable establishes that divine childship is a central theme in the Gospel.

Overall, interpreters tend toward generic readings of the parable without exploring how it fits within Luke's divine childship paradigm. It is seen as a defense of Jesus's ministry to the rejected.[118] The legal milieu and symbolism and multiple allusions to Israel's Scripture are considered as a way to say Jesus was defending his own missionary practices.[119] Another argument suggests that the parable fits within Luke's penchant for "prodigality" throughout his work.[120] In a highly generalized reading, all three parables of Luke 15 could be seen as a way to talk about God's relentless pursuit of reconciliation with humankind.[121] It is true, however, that the parable of the "restored son" stands to portray God himself as a loving Father with unconditional love, and this is part of Luke's salvation historical narrative.[122] Also, it is quite correct to note that the father's behavior directly contrasts with the behavior of the paterfamilias of Roman culture.[123] But, again, these assessments are too general.

Some arguments claim that the parable is more in line with the tumultuous history of Israel. One could see the parable as a way to illustrate Jesus's preaching concerning Israel's return from exile.[124] In this view, the parable is a retelling of Israel's narrative: the son—representing Israel, lost among the nations—has returned home. Another argument suggests the narrative of "exile and return" is appropriate for the parable but adds, more precisely, the celebration in the parable demonstrates "*restoration* from exile."[125] To speak of "return" is not quite correct; rather, a looser parallel between the story of Israel's exodus, exile, and return is necessary, since there is no one-to-one analog between the parable and the story of Israel.[126] The story follows the practice of adding new stories to ancient traditions among Jews. Jesus's parable is a "new story" that reclaims the story of Jacob and retells it in view of the history of Israel in exile (e.g., Egypt, Babylon, etc.).[127] Jesus's story alludes to Israel's suffering in a faraway place but finding its glorious restoration through Jesus himself. Jesus tells Israel's story with himself at the very center. These interpretations of the parable are groundbreaking and essential, but they still do not fully take into account the whole sweep of Luke's divine childship thrust.

Another approach to the parable rebuts many of these interpretations. This approach resists Luke's own treatment of the parable tradition.[128] Additionally, this view argues that it is tenuous at best to view the father in the parable as God.[129] It proposes that the parable defies stereotypical interpretation, that the father should have been vengeful toward his son, and that he shamed himself through running toward him and kissing him.[130] The history of interpretation, in view of this perspective, lends itself to a Marcionite perspective, one that causes the reader to polarize Jesus against the God, laws, and traditions of Israel.[131] Ultimately, this view claims that the parable, beyond Luke's own use, challenges us to be more perspicacious about our willingness to reconcile with loved ones who have done wrong.[132] The utility of this reading—the much-needed attack against the stereotyped and culturally biased interpretations that have proliferated in the West—is refreshing. There is a widespread misreading of ancient Judaism that envisions God as a compassionless, unemotional Father ready to smite his children. The weakness of this view is that it divorces the parable too readily from the Lukan context. This parable is very much at home in Luke's presentation of Jesus. It functions to advance his case that God is restoring God's family in profound ways through Jesus's ministry. Consequently, the integral tools of restoration, "repentance and forgiveness," should not be readily dismissed.[133]

These and other interpretive schemes are extremely close to what is most likely the function of the parable. Luke tells the story of a Messiah who is born God's Son. Through him, Israel is restored to its childship status with God. Jesus tells this parable to stress that the covenant status of Israel is being restored, echoing Deuteronomy 32, Hosea 1–2, Isaiah 43 and 63, and other texts. Israel is being brought back to its maker through the Messiah and is being restored to its authority as God's child. Jesus, then, retells the story of Israel's exile and courtship with sin as a way of rebutting the religious leaders who do not understand God's plan of restoration. Through him, and only him, Israel is being brought back from a state of lostness and death.[134]

Here are portions of the parable:

> Then Jesus said, "There was a man who had two sons. The younger of them said to his father, 'Father, give me the share of the property that will belong to me.' So he divided his property between them. A few days later the younger son gathered all he had and traveled to a distant country.[135] . . . When he had spent everything, a severe famine took place throughout that country, and he began to be in need. So he went and hired himself out to one of the citizens of that country. . . . But when he came to himself he said, 'How many of my father's hired hands have bread enough and to spare, but here I am dying of hunger! I will get up and go to my father, and I will say to him, "Father, I have sinned against heaven and before you; I am no longer worthy to be called your son; treat me like one of your hired hands."' So he set off and went to his father. But while he was still far off, his father saw him and was filled with compassion; he ran and put his arms around him and kissed him. Then the son said to him, 'Father, I have sinned against heaven and before you; I am no longer worthy to be called your son.' But the father said to his slaves, 'Quickly, bring out a robe—the best one—and put it on him; put a ring on his finger and sandals on his feet. And get the fatted calf and kill it, and let us eat and celebrate; for this son of mine was dead and is alive again; he was lost and is found!' And they began to celebrate. Now his elder son was in the field; and when he came and approached the house, he heard music

and dancing. He called one of the slaves and asked what was going on. He replied, 'Your brother has come, and your father has killed the fatted calf, because he has got him back safe and sound.' Then he became angry and refused to go in. His father came out and began to plead with him. But he answered his father, 'Listen! For all these years I have been working like a slave for you, and I have never disobeyed your command; yet you have never given me even a young goat so that I might celebrate with my friends. But when this son of yours came back, who has devoured your property with prostitutes, you killed the fatted calf for him!' Then the father said to him, 'Son, you are always with me, and all that is mine is yours. But we had to celebrate and rejoice, because this brother of yours was dead and has come to life; he was lost and has been found.'" (Luke 15:11–32)

A cogent reading is this: God, the Father, is welcoming people home through Jesus's ministry.[136] The Son of God is bringing other children of God back home. The sick, the demonized (Luke 4:41; Acts 10:38), the sinful tax collectors, and the like represent the younger son (Luke 5:30; 7:34; 15:1). The older brother represents the elites. They do not want to join in the celebration with the father and son. Their rejection of the celebration will result in their ultimate rejection (Luke 13:29). But in agreement with one view and against another,[137] the parable ends ambiguously with the door open for the elder brother's return. Indeed, this interpretation seems to be implied by Luke's emphasis on the inclusion of priests and Pharisees in the early church (Acts 6:7; 15:5).

In the context of the entire passage, Jesus is responding to Pharisees who question his ministry because he fellowships with tax collectors and sinners (Luke 15:1–2).[138] In response, Jesus gives three parables, all of which discuss something that is lost and has been found. In the first two, the main characters of the tales search for that which they lost (15:3–10). Both of the first two parables discuss the pursuit of the minority, the one lost out of the one hundred sheep and the ten coins (15:7, 10). The last parable is different. It details a son who became lost because of his wantonness (15:13). We should not be deaf to the allusions to Israel's current condition. They, like

Aholah and Aholibah (Ezek 23), have left from home and gone for foreign lands. The younger son's rebellion against his father caused him to lose his inheritance while he was in a foreign land (Luke 15:14–16). While far away, the unthinkable occurs; the younger son (15:17) comes "to himself." Before he ever makes his way home, he remembers who he is. He resolves to return home as a servant, but the father receives him as a son (15:23–24).

The father restores him. His repentance places him in line to receive this restoration from the father.[139] His confession that he was not "worthy" recalls Luke 3:8.[140] It also points forward to Jesus's comment about worthiness in 20:35. Repentance is the way to attain worthiness and new life.[141] Thereafter, the father places the best robe upon him and the ring of his house back on his hand. The son considered himself unworthy to ever be a son, but the father would not have it.[142] He has been renewed in his childship status in the home.

The occasion of renewal of childship status, in the father's view, demands a celebration (Luke 15:25–32). This celebration is not usual. The father kills the fatted cow and invites the community. To this, the older brother objects. To show the comparison, the older son rebuffs his father with the claim that he had never been celebrated in this way, not even with a goat.[143] Instead of the parable concluding as the previous two, with the declaration of the angels' celebration over the restored items, the father states, " 'For this son of mine was dead and is alive again; he was lost and is found!' And they began to celebrate" (15:24). The father continues, "But we had to celebrate and rejoice, because this brother of yours was dead and has come to life; he was lost and has been found" (15:32). The restoration of this son is designated as his resurrection and his being found.

The resurrection language affirms the thesis of this book (Luke 20:36). When the son is restored back to his former glory, the father says he is alive again.[144] The parable discusses the resurrection in a metaphorical and familial sense, but the point is still made.[145] A son who comes home, ending his rebellion against his father, is, in a real sense, alive again. Losing his status as a son killed him. But now that his status has been restored, he is alive again.

The other statement (Luke 15:32) we have only discussed indirectly. This comment should be expected given the previous two parables in 15:3–10.

The comment reflects what the reader will hear later in the Zacchaeus episode, "For the Son of Man came to seek out and to save the lost" (19:10). Jesus's statement of his missiological paradigm is justified by the notion that Zacchaeus was a child of "Abraham" too (19:9). His status as a child of Abraham was not sufficient in and of itself for entrance into the age to come, but Jesus's mission was to redeem Israel, Abraham's progeny (3:8). As Christ, he came to the children of Abraham to restore them to being true children of Abraham. The parable helps us understand this concept. The younger son was always a son, but he had lost his place in the home; he had lost his status. When he returned home, because he was a son, he could fill his role in the home once again. In the same way, Jesus's mission was to restore the children of God to their vocation and covenantal status (Luke 1:72; Acts 3:25). They were still God's children because of the ancestors. But their status as children had been lost. Jesus's coming was to provide a place for the children to come and be restored to the glory they had lost. Through Jesus, God remembers the childship that had been forgotten.[146]

It can assuredly be argued that the original audience would have perceived that this parable concerns the love of a father for the son.[147] The rhetorical "inflection" would have been the "lavish love" of the father for the son. This is an important idea to draw from the overall thrust of the parable. If the parable is what I am arguing, a means of understanding Luke's missiological agenda, then it is safe to infer that Luke intends his readership to perceive the driving force of the mission is God's love for God's lost children. This trait of Jesus's ministry is quite explicit in John (e.g., 3:16) but not so much in the Synoptic literature. It does, however, suggest itself in this parable.

The restoration of Israel in love and repentance (see Luke 6:35)—and more, the resurrection of Israel (see Luke 20:36)—through the ministry of Jesus was only the beginning. After Jesus's reaffirmation of his messianic identity through his death and resurrection (24:46), Jesus seamlessly commissions his disciples to preach repentance and forgiveness to all nations, starting in Jerusalem (24:47). His death and resurrection, the climax and revelation of his messianic identity, open the way for the kingdom to come near to all people, beginning with Israel. Again, the vocation of Israel was to bring blessing to all the families of the earth. Peter will explain in Acts 3:25–26 that God has done that through Jesus: "You are the descendants of the prophets and of the covenant that God gave to your ancestors, saying to Abraham, 'And in your descendants all the families of the earth shall be blessed.' When God raised up his servant, he sent him first to you, to bless you by turning each of you from your wicked ways." If we follow the narrative of Acts properly, however, it appears that the disciples did not necessarily understand the "blessing" to all people, which required them to evangelize non-Jews (Acts 10–11). This may be the reason Luke tells us that Philip was directed by the Spirit to preach to the Ethiopian eunuch (Acts 8:26–27).

Acts 17:24–31 and the Restoration of All of God's Children

This reading of the evidence is buttressed by evaluating it in light of Acts 17:24–31.[148] When taken within Luke's overall theological framework, the parable of the restored son is meant, ultimately, to speak about God's desire for the whole world:

> The God who made the world and everything in it, he who is Lord of heaven and earth, does not live in shrines made by human hands, nor is he served by human hands, as though he needed anything, since he himself gives to all mortals life and breath and all things. From one ancestor he made all nations to inhabit the whole earth, and he allotted the times of their existence and the boundaries of the places where they would live, so that they would search for God and perhaps grope for him and find him—though indeed he is not far from each one of us. For "In him we live and move and have our being"; as even some of your own poets have said, "For we too are his offspring." Since we are God's offspring, we ought not to think that the deity is like gold, or silver, or stone, an image formed by the art and imagination of mortals. While God has overlooked the times of human ignorance, now he commands all people everywhere to repent, because he has fixed a day on which he will have the world judged in righteousness by a man

whom he has appointed, and of this he has given assurance to all by raising him from the dead. (Acts 17:24–31)

This narrative attempts to describe the mission of God to save his creation from the beginning of creation to the present moment. Paul, frustrated with the idolatry he sees around him, preaches on the true source of humankind.[149] The God who is real is not the god who is made by human hands. Paul speaks of YHWH—the Lord of heaven and earth, alluding to Genesis 1— as the one who made people, and not the other way around. This God gave all humans life and breath (Gen 2:7).

Second, all humans come from one person, Adam (Acts 17:26).[150] This interpretation is confirmed, first, because of the Genesis allusions and, second, because he says all nations of "humans." Also, in the narrative, Paul echoes Deuteronomy 32:8 in the passage that speaks of the nations as the "children of Adam" who have been divided by God.[151]

It is certain that the "one" is Adam also because of the allusion to Genesis 1 and 10. The term *offspring*[152] echoes Luke's genealogy. Adam was "son of God" (Luke 3:38), and Luke would argue, as we have established, that all people are "God's offspring" through Adam (Acts 17:28–29). As such, he uses creation language to say that we are made in the "image" and "likeness" of God and that humans cannot make God from our imaginations (see Gen 1:26–28). In Genesis 10, we are told that these offspring of Adam divided up into nations.

A third reason we can be sure we are speaking of Adam is because Paul features Jesus, the new Adam. This, again, speaks to the new creation, the expected consequence of Jesus's triumph. In Luke's view, Jesus and Adam were both children of God.[153]

The argument here presented is consistent with the parable of the restored son. God is not far from us (Acts 17:27), and the younger son went into a far country (Luke 15:13). God gave human beings the capacity to look for God and find God (Acts 17:27). In Luke 15:24, 32, the younger son was lost and found. Distance language plays off well with the discussion of the marking out of the nations. God made the nations far and near, God knows where each one is, and God set a time when they are to repent of their

ignorance and return to him. But God is not far from any of us. In the parable of the restored son, the son goes far from home but returns and becomes
found. Luke's theology is quite consistent when viewed with the childship
theme as central.

Furthermore, the climax of this passage is with the designation of the
resurrected ruler. In the parable, the son's restoration is a resurrection. He is
alive again. His life begins anew in the home. In Acts 17, Paul says one
man began the process of life in the world (i.e., this time, this present age),
but another man, Jesus, would judge at the "appointed" time (17:31).[154]
One view concludes that Paul is speaking from "creation to consummation."
Indeed, "by situating human existence within God's creative purpose in
Adam and eschatological end in Jesus Christ, Luke enframes the totality of
human life."[155] Paul is speaking of the age to come in a veiled way, but the
point is the same. Jesus as resurrected ruler is the only human qualified to
judge all others because he is the mediator of the new age.[156] Jesus becomes
the qualifier for the whole world to be welcomed home.

Therefore, like the parable, the rationale for the nations to repent is
because they were lost but are now to return (Acts 17:28–29). Now God
is crying out through the new Adamic figure to bring "God's offspring"
home. Again, like the parable, the son was always the son, so too humans
were always God's offspring. Now obedience and repentance are necessary to
be restored. By forsaking their idols, the nations are allowed to be alive and
found. Though there is no mention of the Spirit, as would not be expected
in a speech where Paul does not even mention the name of Jesus (17:31),
the Spirit is assumed.[157] As in all of Acts, the Spirit is the restoring sign that
humans have been reconnected with God righteously, received by their repentance (2:38).

Their repentance, coming to the right God through the right Lord, Jesus,
is the means of restoration. In this way, the discussion of the resurrection of
Jesus is not only a way to talk about Easter. Jesus's resurrection is the criterion for
measuring all who will truly live as "God's offspring." His resurrection involves
the reclamation of all of Adam's children so that Adam's children may be
restored as God's children (see Acts 15:13–18).[158] And this restoration will
be confirmed when they, too, are raised from the dead.

The mission is accomplished *through* the children of God. Paul, a member of Israel, shedding God's light (Acts 13:47), represents the Son of God, Jesus. Through his witness, and certainly the witness of others, Israel and the nations will be redeemed. The Son of God, Jesus, produces other children of God through the Spirit, and they continue the process of replication.

Lukan anthropology is the identification of the people of God as the quintessential children of God. This anthropology is manifested through Jesus's mission. Thus the mission of God, Luke suggests, is the restoration that occurs through these restored children winning other children of God through the witness of Jesus. Those who are lost and dead will discover that God was always near and made known through repentance and dedication through the man God raised from the dead.

* * *

When viewed from this perspective, it can be said that divine childship in Luke/Acts narrates the renaissance of divine childship status in the world. Luke says in both documents that Jesus is an Adamic figure, restoring the childship of Israel and the rest of the world. Jesus's plan of restoration begins with Israel and extends to the nations (Acts 1:8).

If Jesus's mission is to rescue Adam and his children, all of God's children, by way of the witness of his death and resurrection, then why does Luke discuss the salvation of nations beginning with an Ethiopian eunuch? It makes sense for Luke to begin with Israel. Abraham's children had a covenant with the real God. But why is a black-skinned person the first to hear the message of God's restoration outside of Israel? This will be the subject of the next chapter.

CHAPTER 5

SAVING BLACK LIFE
AND SAVING THE WORLD

The death and resurrection of Jesus function as an explosive event that laid the foundation for the reclamation of all of God's children. Jesus is what Israel was supposed to be, the true child of God, so that Israel might become like Jesus, true children of God.[1] Through the sacrifice and triumph of the Son of God, the new age had dawned. All of the children of Adam were to be notified that the time of the dominion of their ignorance of God as Father had ended (Acts 17:30). Through the witnesses of Jesus (Luke 24:48; Acts 1:8), all were to be told that God had brought salvation to the world through the lordship of Jesus Christ (Acts 15:16–17).

Acts reiterates that the mission of reclamation was to begin with God's covenant people (Acts 1:7–8; 2:39). The children of Abraham, by covenant, were meant to be the first to receive the restoration (Luke 1:54–55, 72–73; Acts 2:35). God had redeemed Israel through the Son of God (Luke 2:30; 24:21; Acts 2:21). Through Jesus as the Passover (Luke 22:17–20), God's firstborn children, the people of Israel, would escape the oppression of Pharaoh (Exod 4:22), Satan and his allies, to serve the Lord Jesus as his witnesses (Luke 10:19). But this was only the beginning of the mission. The beginning of the new age, with restored childship for Israel, began the time when wisdom was to be proclaimed to all of the world (Luke 1:17; Acts 17:30). The children of Adam were being called to repentance, to recognition of the God of Adam through the new Adam, Jesus Christ.

Acts provides a missiological agenda in the very beginning. In Acts 1:8, we are told that the mission was to begin in Jerusalem and move to Judea, then to Samaria, then to the extent of the earth.[2] The narrative follows this agenda directly. The narrative starts in Jerusalem; the gospel seems to spread throughout Judea (Acts 2–8); and in Acts 8:4–25, we finally come to Samaria. After Israel, inclusive of the Samaritans, is reached, Philip preaches to the Ethiopian eunuch (8:26–40).

Many scholars agree that the ministry to the Ethiopian eunuch intimates that the gospel has reached an end of the earth, beginning the gentile mission.[3] There is disagreement about this, however, with arguments that Cornelius is the beginning of the gentile mission.[4] But if the itinerary of Acts 1:8 guides the geographical narrative sequence, then it makes sense that the Ethiopian eunuch's turn to the Way would be evidence that the witness of Jesus had reached the end of the earth.[5]

As is indicated in some arguments, Luke could have meant "end of the earth" in a general sense.[6] Luke could have excluded the Ethiopian's story and just spoke about how the ministry of the church was breaking ground throughout the world to signify that it would reach the limits of the world. Instead, choosing to demonstrate the truth of Jesus's mission statement, Luke provides a story of a nonapostle preaching to a person who was deemed an inhabitant of one of the ends of the earth. Of all the various peoples, not an Indian, but an Ethiopian, "the blackest and remotest" of the people in the world, was chosen.[7]

Indeed, it is because this man was both Black and from a remote place that Luke saw unique significance in him.[8] In addition to the fulfillment theme that was so important to Luke, it is also essential that Luke saw in this story an opportunity to exhibit the far-reaching implications of Jesus's death and resurrection.[9] When moving beyond the boundaries of Israel and the Diaspora Jews, Luke highlights that the gospel will be successful in part because it reaches someone who would have been vituperated by some Jews, Greeks, and Romans in the community.[10] Luke continues his story of the triumph of the gospel by establishing, from the very beginning of the gentile mission, that God is fulfilling his promise to bring salvation to all flesh (Luke 3:4) by bringing in a black-skinned child of Adam.

Skin color is important to Lukan anthropology. It is probable that Luke is attending to the implications of skin color because of Simeon Niger (Acts 13:1). If this man was a Black African, then this provides further rationale for Luke to focus on the blackness of the Ethiopian eunuch. It has been noted that Luke wanted to promote diversity in the leadership of the Antiochene church.[11] This can be said with more vigor if Luke wanted to accent complexional differences by demonstrating the desired diversity of the kingdom of God.

God's plans to bring about the unification of a multiethnic, multicolored people begin to come to fruition through the salvation of a black-skinned man. Especially with the Greco-Roman background, the presence of Simeon who is nicknamed "Black man" suggests that Luke tells his story not only to talk about the historical expansion of the church. Rather, the inclusion of black-skinned people *means* that God has rejected acrimony not only against them but against any who are deemed aesthetically displeasing based on faulty standards. God's desire to restore his children, to reclaim all of the children of Adam, rightly begins with those considered ugly ducklings among the nations of the world. To demonstrate why all of God's children matter, it is appropriate that the mission of God's reclamation of the entire human family begins with those considered to matter less because of their physical appearance.

The Spirit of Reclamation Moves into Action

The story uses different words but is a continuation of the same story in Acts. The theology is consistent. Luke speaks to his chief auditor, catching him up on where he left off in the previous missive:

> In the first book, Theophilus, I wrote about all that Jesus did and taught from the beginning until the day when he was taken up to heaven, after giving instructions through the Holy Spirit to the apostles

whom he had chosen. After his suffering he presented himself alive to them by many convincing proofs, appearing to them during forty days and speaking about the kingdom of God. While staying with them, he ordered them not to leave Jerusalem, but to wait there for the promise of the Father. "This," he said, "is what you have heard from me; for John baptized with water, but you will be baptized with the Holy Spirit not many days from now." So when they had come together, they asked him, "Lord, is this the time when you will restore the kingdom to Israel?" He replied, "It is not for you to know the times or periods that the Father has set by his own authority. But you will receive power when the Holy Spirit has come upon you; and you will be my witnesses in Jerusalem, in all Judea and Samaria, and to the ends of the earth." (Acts 1:1–8)

Luke foreshadows the ascension, telling his auditors that Jesus gave instructions to his disciples (Acts 1:1–2). These instructions were no mere declarations of a wise teacher; the disciples were given revelation. Jesus was speaking through the Spirit (1:2). It is appropriate that Jesus, through the Holy Spirit, would give these instructions over forty days (1:3). Jesus's ministry started with forty days when he, empowered with the Spirit, emerged as the conquering Son of God against Satan (Luke 4:1–13).[12] Now Jesus, confirming his own resurrection, proving his own sonship (see Acts 13:33–34), gave his disciples insight into the kingdom of God. These instructions were not only insight into what God was doing, apocalyptic wisdom, but also what God was about to do in and through the people of Jesus by the Spirit. This Spirit-led wisdom drives the scope of the narrative.

The disciples, by Jesus's mandate, were to stay in Jerusalem to receive the Father's promise (Acts 1:4–5). Jesus's command to his disciples impelled them to abide in Jerusalem until the Spirit came upon them (see Luke 3:21–22). Similar to Jesus, they were to have the Spirit *from the Father* come upon them. Through their baptism by Jesus, though Luke only implies this, they will be identified as the children of God. They have the same Spirit that fomented the heavenly declaration of Jesus's sonship. The divine childship status of the disciples will be affirmed by the coming of the Spirit upon them. It is clear, however, throughout Acts that this Spirit is for all who believe, whether Luke tells the reader about a specific Spirit encounter or not.[13]

The key to understanding the moment of the Spirit's coming, then, is not discovered in the reestablishment of the kingdom of Israel proper (Acts 1:6–7; Isa 11:11). Rather, the purpose is to testify of the coming of the Messiah and Lord, Jesus Christ. But this witness requires the equipping of the Spirit.[14] Jesus, in the fullness of the Spirit, returned to Nazareth, declaring war against oppressive powers (Luke 4:18–19).[15] It will take the same Spirit to enable the disciples to become witnesses of Jesus's salvation for the world.

The world mission, however, is to unfold a certain way. It begins with Jerusalem, goes to Judea, crosses into Samaria, and then concludes with the wide potentiality of "the ends of the earth" (Acts 1:8). The mission of restoration begins with Israel and then moves to the nations. The coming of the kingdom, through the power of the Spirit, necessitates the reclamation of Adam's children in Israel first (see Rom 1:16–17). Then and only then would the mission be released in fullness to go to the other nations.

But following the corollary with Jesus—the Son of God who brings others back to childship—the church would carry on his effort. Israel, filled with the Spirit, would be responsible for telling others about Jesus. Through disciples' testimony of his resurrection, his sonship, they would receive the childship indicator, the Spirit of God (Acts 2:38).[16] The Spirit is the mechanism of divine childship reactivation, the guiding source of their obedience to Jesus. People with the Spirit are able to have suprahuman authority and show God's power, are recipients of God's faithfulness, will be immortal in the resurrection, and so on.

In Acts, the prevailing idea is that the guiding power of God is not without human agency, although God and angels act directly at times. The primary means of God's action is *through* the people. God's intention was to work *through* God's people (Luke 6:35–36; 9–10; Acts 1:8). They are allowed to share in the authority of God on earth, just as Adam did in the garden of Eden.

The evidence suggests that Luke intends a strong allusion to Genesis in the baptism scene during Pentecost: "When the day of Pentecost had come, they were all together in one place. And suddenly from heaven there came a sound like the rush of a violent wind, and it filled the entire house where they were sitting. Divided tongues, as of fire, appeared among them, and a tongue rested on each of them. All of them were filled with the Holy Spirit and began to speak in other languages, as the Spirit gave them ability" (Acts 2:1–4). In this passage, there are resonances with Genesis 2:7 and 11:1–9.[17] The coming of the Spirit announced the renewal of humanity. Humans were given back the heavenly wind that made Adam live. Second, the Spirit granted humans the ability to speak in different languages. Instead of causing confusion, as in Genesis 11, the different tongues demonstrated their unity with God and one another.[18]

This communal call and baptism laid the groundwork of the mission to Israel and the rest of the world. The fact that the nations will be rescued through the Spirit's working is, again, foreshadowed through the listing of the Diaspora Jews present in Jerusalem for Pentecost (Acts 2:5–11). Luke tells us that Jews from "every nation under heaven" were "inhabiting" Jerusalem (2:5).[19] Acts 17:26 is linked to this verse by theme and the mention of dwelling. The assemblage of Israel mirrors the division and reunion of all the nations of the world with the God who made them.

Of particular note, here, are the African nations represented in Acts 2:10 (Egypt and Libya [Cyrene]).[20] Interestingly, Ethiopia is absent from this list of nations.[21] Israel, God's firstborn, had symbolically returned from exile. Part of the process of this return would be that those from African nations worship God (see Zeph 3:9–10). The ingathering of Diaspora Jews—by the same token—symbolized the return of the nations to God.[22] The destructive scattering of Israel had been converted to a way for God to reveal that all of the children of Adam were being called home to God through his firstborn Son, Jesus, the Spirit, and the Son's witnesses (Jer 49:36; see also Ezek 37:9).

Peter's speech serves to clarify the extent to which this witness will go (Acts 2:16–21). God's salvation is meant to be seen by "all flesh" (Luke 3:6), and the Spirit is to be poured "upon all flesh" (Acts 2:17). Peter's recitation of the Joel prophecy, again, reminds us that a new age has dawned. It is correct to infer, by implication, that this new age is that of a new Adam (Acts 17:30). Peter's recitation changes the words of Joel from "after this" (Joel 2:28–32) to "in the last days" (Acts 2:17). This is no mere sharing with the elders the Spirit that was on Moses (Num 11:16–30). This event is the emergence of a new time in which God has been revealed as the Spirit pourer for the children of God. Luke 24:49 and Acts 1:4–5 explain that God the Father is sending the promised Spirit through the Son. And Peter continues, "Being therefore exalted at the right hand of God, and having received from the Father the promise of the Holy Spirit, he has poured out this that you both see and hear" (Acts 2:33). Through Jesus's exaltation, he is revealed as God's Son; that revelation allowed for a new creative action of God, the giving of the Spirit (Acts 2:34–36).

The necessary response to the outpouring of the new age is repentance: "Peter said to them, 'Repent, and be baptized every one of you in the name of Jesus Christ so that your sins may be forgiven; and you will receive the gift of the Holy Spirit. For the promise is for you, for your children, and for all who are far away, everyone whom the Lord our God calls to him'" (Acts 2:38–39).[23] The restoration of the children of God, their hearts being turned back to the ancestors and vice versa (Luke 1:17), occurs in a similar manner to the disobedient son (Luke 15:11–32). Through repentance, the lost children have been found and the dead children have been raised.

This divine childship theme is confirmed by Peter's allusion to Deuteronomy 32:5 in Acts 2:40.[24] By being saved from "this crooked generation" (Acts 2:40, literally in Greek), through repentance and recognition of the Son of God, one becomes restored as a child of God, and her divine childship status is no longer in question. Thereby, the member of Israel or the nations has forsaken the generation that was twisted.

From this twisted generation, God's rescuing power designated witnesses to draw the nations. The grounds for their witness were found in the worldwide lordship of God's child, Jesus of Nazareth. To properly bear witness to Jesus's lordship, the Spirit of divine childship had to be functional within the testifying vessel (Luke 24:49; Acts 1:8).

God's mission for the world is accomplished through the children of God who pass along the Spirit to others. And this is how the Spirit reaches the nations (Acts 8:26–40; 10:34–48). The movement of the Spirit drives the mission to reclaim God's children (Acts 15:13–17; 17:26–31). In each of these citations, God has affirmed the pursuit of the nations, compelling

God's people to move to regions culturally and ethnically different from their own. Each passage reiterates the themes of Luke 15:11–32. In Acts 15:13–17, James discusses God's desire for all humans to seek the Lord. Again, this is a major theme for the lost son in Luke 15:11–32. Second, in Acts 17:26–31, Paul preaches that the nations must seek the Lord because God is not far—again, another major theme of Luke 15:11–32. The story that typifies and exemplifies this kind of missionary thinking is Acts 8:26–40.

THE NARRATIVE OF THE ETHIOPIAN EUNUCH: PRELIMINARY ISSUES

To discuss the launch of the mission to the nations outside of the boundaries of Israel, at least ethnically, Luke tells us about the salvation of an Ethiopian:

> Then an angel of the Lord said to Philip, "Get up and go toward the south to the road that goes down from Jerusalem to Gaza." (This is a wilderness road.) So he got up and went. Now there was an Ethiopian eunuch, a court official of the Candace, queen of the Ethiopians, in charge of her entire treasury. He had come to Jerusalem to worship and was returning home; seated in his chariot, he was reading the prophet Isaiah. Then the Spirit said to Philip, "Go over to this chariot and join it." So Philip ran up to it and heard him reading the prophet Isaiah. He asked, "Do you understand what you are reading?" He replied, "How can I, unless someone guides me?" And he invited Philip to get in and sit beside him. Now the passage of the scripture that he was reading was this: "Like a sheep he was led to the slaughter, and like a lamb silent before its shearer, so he does not open his mouth. In his humiliation justice was denied him. Who can describe his generation? For his life is taken away from the earth." The eunuch asked Philip, "About whom, may I ask you, does the prophet say this, about himself or about someone else?" Then Philip began to speak, and starting with this scripture, he proclaimed to him the good news about Jesus. As they

were going along the road, they came to some water; and the eunuch said, "Look, here is water! What is to prevent me from being baptized?"[25] He commanded the chariot to stop, and both of them, Philip and the eunuch, went down into the water, and Philip baptized him. When they came up out of the water, the Spirit of the Lord snatched Philip away; the eunuch saw him no more, and went on his way rejoicing. But Philip found himself at Azotus, and as he was passing through the region, he proclaimed the good news to all the towns until he came to Caesarea. (Acts 8:26–40)

The story of the Ethiopian eunuch has polyvalent significances.[26] Getting into the contours of this story allows for a better reading of the overall argument of this book.[27] It explains why more attention should be paid to this narrative.

Here are the key details of the chapter and the particular episode. Philip has accomplished the mission of bringing the gospel to the Samaritans (Acts 8:5–13). While describing Philip, Luke gives us clues that he is certainly speaking of a child of God. Philip is full of the Spirit (6:5). He works miracles (8:6). He is even carried away in a manner similar to Elijah and possibly Jesus (8:39).

A child of God is replicating himself. Luke also tells us that Peter and John come from Jerusalem to spread the reach of the Spirit among the Samaritans after the Samaritans were baptized (Acts 8:14–17).[28] With this accomplished, God leads Philip to go down from Jerusalem toward Gaza (8:26).[29] There, he encounters a single person, an Ethiopian who is riding in a chariot while reading the prophet Isaiah (8:26–34).[30] This Ethiopian is a eunuch and a treasurer who oversees the entire treasury of the Candace, the queen of the Ethiopians (8:27).[31] Luke interjects, narrating the text of Isaiah that the Ethiopian read (8:32–34).[32] From this reading, Philip explains the text and preaches the gospel to the eunuch (8:35). The eunuch readily receives the message gladly and is baptized, with Philip descending in the waters with him (8:36–39). After the Ethiopian's baptism, Philip is snatched away to Azotus and then preaches until he comes to Caesarea, while the Ethiopian eunuch returns home rejoicing (8:39–40).[33]

One of the main concerns regarding this story is the ethnic status of the Ethiopian and how Luke's audience would have perceived him.[34] There is a tendency in scholarship to suppress or ignore the ethnography of the Ethiopian.[35] One could argue that we cannot be sure about the racial status of the Ethiopian.[36] Or, one could argue, that the Ethiopian's origin is inconsequential.[37] Another could argue the ethnic status as an Ethiopian is not Luke's main concern but of some importance.[38] Another view could suggest that Luke's stress on Cornelius and subsequent references to him (Acts 10–15) were because he did not want his audience to think of the Ethiopian as the first gentile convert.[39]

One might propose that Luke *seems* to portray the Ethiopian as a gentile but ultimately leaves ambiguous whether he is a gentile.[40] But then this view also argues that the Ethiopian cannot be a gentile because this would conflict with Cornelius. Luke clearly begins the gentile mission with Cornelius. It could not have begun earlier.[41]

Quite to the contrary, and evidently, Luke did not see the difficulty that modern interpretations perceive in his account. Luke describes the man as an Ethiopian. It is certainly possible that this man is an Ethiopian Jew.[42] Luke describes African Jews and proselytes who had come to Jerusalem for Pentecost (Acts 2:10). This man, too, had come to Jerusalem to worship (8:27). It is more likely, however, that he is gentile[43] and probably a God fearer.[44] In this case, the evidence suggests against deeming this man a Jewish person.[45] When there might be a lack of clarity, Luke specifies if a person is Jewish. With Elymas, who was in the court of a gentile ruler, for example, Luke tells us that he was a Jewish person (13:6–8). The same can be said for Apollos, who, as an Alexandrian, lived in the Diaspora (18:24). As stated, the Ethiopian eunuch is a gentile, possibly a God fearer, or at least someone sympathetic to Judaism, since he could not become a full proselyte because of his eunuch status (Deut 23:1).[46] His attempt to worship in Jerusalem may have been met with failure[47] or at least only permission to worship in the outer court.[48]

Concerning his social status, he had a complex identity, to be sure. It can be argued that he has "status inconsistency." In terms of financial status, the textual descriptions suggest that we should think of this man as a wealthy servant.[49] He was riding in a chariot and commanded it to stop, suggesting that he had servants. Luke says that he oversaw the "entire" treasury of the Candace. And as discussed earlier, the treasury he stewarded was of a nation considered quite wealthy. He was also reading a scroll in his chariot, which suggests that he was literate. But this does not mean that he was completely socially accepted. Both his ethnography and eunuch status mean that he may not have been viewed favorably by many in the community.

The Ethiopian's narrative in Acts is unique in that it does not involve an apostle. One view proposes, then, that Cornelius's conversion was the "official" beginning of the effort for the gentiles.[50] The Ethiopian eunuch's story does not speak of *many* gentiles coming to repentance in direct terms (see Acts 17:34). But this narrative is essential to how Luke frames the mission because it features a gentile eunuch coming to faith, which in Isaianic terms was a sign of God's restoration of Israel (Isa 56:1–8).[51] The eunuch's salvation suggested not only that God was accepting gentiles, eunuchs, and the like, cleansing them from their sins, but that Israel was being restored (Isa 56:8). Despite the lack of an apostle, the narrative suggests that Israel not only was being a light but received that light itself (Acts 13:47).[52]

African Peoples and Biblical Missiology

Luke's auditors would have recognized one other prominent feature of the narrative: we are discussing an Ethiopian. That an Ethiopian, a black-skinned African, has come to faith suggests that Israel has been renewed and the nations are being invited to repentance (Isa 11:1–11; 19:25). We must remember, the restoration of Israel was umbilically tied to the reclamation of the world. And in the corpus of Israel's Scripture, there was a unique place given to the children of Cush, Africans, in the narrative of salvation in the life of Israel.[53]

When Isaiah spoke of the return of Israel from exile, he argued that God made a claim upon not only Israel but also Assyria and Egypt (Isa 19:25). It is important to note that the Egypt being discussed at this moment was under Cushite (Ethiopian) occupation.[54] Indeed, in the previous chapter of

Isaiah (Isa 18)—which is a description of Cushites, Black Africans—we have what one view calls the closest example of a Cushite "ethnography."[55] At any rate, Isaiah proclaimed that from the nation of Cush, "gifts will be brought to the Lord of hosts from a people tall and smooth, from a people feared near and far, a nation mighty and conquering, whose land the rivers divide, to Mount Zion, the place of the name of the Lord of hosts" (Isa 18:7; see also Ps 68:31; Zeph 3:10). This oracle of Ethiopia is not often connected to the next one by New Testament scholars. A very similar prophecy is given about Egypt:

> On that day there will be an altar to the Lord in the center of the land of Egypt, and a pillar to the Lord at its border. It will be a sign and a witness to the Lord of hosts in the land of Egypt; when they cry to the Lord because of oppressors, he will send them a savior, and will defend and deliver them. The Lord will make himself known to the Egyptians; and the Egyptians will know the Lord on that day, and will worship with sacrifice and burnt offering, and they will make vows to the Lord and perform them. The Lord will strike Egypt, striking and healing; they will return to the Lord, and he will listen to their supplications and heal them. On that day there will be a highway from Egypt to Assyria, and the Assyrian will come into Egypt, and the Egyptian into Assyria, and the Egyptians will worship with the Assyrians. On that day Israel will be the third with Egypt and Assyria, a blessing in the midst of the earth, whom the Lord of hosts has blessed, saying, "Blessed be Egypt my people, and Assyria the work of my hands, and Israel my heritage." (Isa 19:19–25)

It must be noted that when speaking of Ethiopia in Isaiah 18 and Egypt in Isaiah 19, this is speaking of the Nubian empire. Isaiah 20 confirms this. Isaiah is told to engage in a prophetic symbolic action, walking naked for three years. This portended that Egypt and Ethiopia would be placed in bondage by the Assyrians. Isaiah announces, "So shall the king of Assyria lead away the Egyptians as captives and the Ethiopians as exiles, both the young and the old, naked and barefoot, with buttocks uncovered, to the shame of Egypt"

(Isa 20:4). Again, the clue that we are speaking of a single empire, or at least that these nations are being grouped together, is that the "shame" is not separated between the nations but given to "Egypt."[56]

The children of Noah's son Ham[57] (Ethiopians, Egyptians, Libyans, Sabeans; Gen 10:6–8) are often grouped together in the Bible broadly.[58] In other words, Isaiah is not marginal in his description of African peoples. They are often discussed in concert in Israel's Scripture. In many cases, this is probably for historical reasons because the texts may have been discussing the Nubian empire or the alliances these African peoples made. Another reason may have been because they shared the same customs and looked similar; in a world of brown-skinned people, they were the darkest brown.

That Luke's audience would have also perceived the commonality of these peoples is more certain when we see the Second Temple and Greco-Roman evidence.[59] Again, Ethiopians, Egyptians, and Libyans are often not only seen as allied nations but described in similar terms. This is not only for geopolitical reasons but, as the evidence would suggest, for cultural and phenotypical reasons. When African peoples are discussed in Luke/Acts (Acts 2:10), it is probable that Luke does so to indicate the expected victory the gospel will have in reaching every human being.[60] Luke uses black-skinned people, against pejorative associations with their phenotype and culture, to express that the gospel will reach every nation. Among many other groups, Luke uses black-skinned people to display God's restoration of divine childship to the world, dignifying their blackness as a God-given trait. And second, Luke upholds black-skinned people as a symbol of God's intention to rescue the entire world, all of Adam's gentile children.[61]

SEEING BLACK IN THE ANCIENT WORLD: GRECO-ROMAN VIEWS

Again, establishing the context in which Luke wrote is necessary. Exploring the Greco-Roman evidence is important, as many of these views would have been ubiquitous in Luke's time. This evidence shows that Luke is discussing blackness in a pronounced way. The significance of the color black itself is where this investigation must start. Ancients of all stripes considered the color black to be a portent of death and evil.[62] This perception was irrespective of particular ethnographic origin.[63] The association of the color black with a skin color did not always yield a deleterious opinion. Calling someone Black did not *always* mean that one considered someone problematic aesthetically and culturally.[64] For people who perceived themselves as non-black-skinned, it did, however, cause them to consider black-skinned people as *other*, but not always in a negative sense.[65]

Greeks and Romans thought Ethiopians and other African peoples were Black.[66] A summary of the primary words used for Black people explains this: "The most common Greek words applied to the Ethiopian's color were *melas* (black) and its compounds . . . *melanochroos* ('black-skinned'). . . . In Latin the adjective most frequently used for this purpose was *niger*."[67] The non-Black ancients focused on what seemed the most obvious trait of difference for the Ethiopians, their skin color.[68] Literally, the word Ethiopian in Greek is the contraction of *aitho* (burn) and *ops* (face, appearance), which suggests Ethiopians were deemed "burnt peoples." But other African peoples, like Egyptians, could be equally considered Black. Thus, the term *Ethiopian* in some of its earliest usage in Homer was fluid, marginally tied to geopolitical and cultural association. Homer considered there to be at least two different sets of Ethiopians—those in India and those in Ethiopia (*Od.* 1.21–25), a people where the sun rose and set.[69]

Essentially, to say "black" in some cases (*melas*, or "*niger*") was to say "Ethiopian": "Blackness and the Ethiopian, therefore, were in many respects synonymous. The Ethiopian's blackness became proverbial."[70] By the same token, to say "Ethiopian," and in some cases "Egyptian," was also to say "black."[71]

The phrase *Aegyptius dies*, "an Egyptian day" or "a black day," shows the difficulty that arises with making skin color proverbial. That a person's skin complexion could become thematized can be problematic. But to be sure, the theme was not automatically a negative one. Nonetheless, the ancient reader would perceive a reference to an Ethiopian, or possibly a Libyan or Egyptian, to be a reference to a black-skinned person. This is certainly the case with the Ethiopian eunuch and most likely the case with Simeon

Niger.[72] Aristotle[73] sums up many Greek and Roman views of black-skinned people: "Thus black men like Ethiopians and the like have white teeth as well as white bones, but their nails, like the whole of their skin, are black" (*Hist. an.* 3.9.517a [Peck, LCL]). In essence, Ethiopians and other Africans *are Black*.

Some evidence suggests that the views of the ancients toward Blacks were not as denigrative as they later became in Europe and America.[74] In the ancient world, at least as it pertains to the writers of the biblical texts, what appears to be the case seems to be more "racialism" instead of "racism."[75] "Racialism" is a more neutral view that does not degrade the humanity of another because of differences. Although there was no systematic attempt to reject and devalue Black people among those who considered themselves "white," to be fair, in their evaluations of black-skinned people, what resulted was a form of essentialism. This is not to say, however, that in every case, all observations of the curious appearances of black-skinned people were *meant* to degrade. Some texts sound strange to modern ears but probably reflect a sense of curiosity rather than a desire to demean. Black people, like other ancients (Scythians, etc.), were observed and essentialized in various ways because of their skin color. Among some writers, the apparent displeasure of black skin led people to consider the "crude" appearance of black skin to scare away evil.[76]

The past should not be whitewashed. One of the interpretations considered most authoritative on African peoples in classical literature has held that there were no real problems with Greek and Roman views regarding Black people. The problem with this view is that biases came through quite prominently in this reading of ancient texts. Many attempt to absolve the ancients of color and ethnographic biases in part because race was such an ill-defined conception in antiquity. But this prominent interpretation, bent on exposing the incredulity of racism in the twentieth century, wanted to argue for a complete disconnect with Western society's ancient sources. But this allowed extremely problematic summations. One such summation was of a Christian view: "By Ethiopians, all nations were signified: Christ came into the world to make blacks white."[77] Unwittingly, it may be that this perspective has admitted in this one statement that white racists are, in fact, correct. Black skin is cursed; white skin is blessed. Even if this thinking did not necessarily lead to a categorical and legal denial of personhood for Black Africans in antiquity, the views that elicited such a sentiment are still to be critiqued.[78] A faithful reading cannot avoid the evidence and the obvious implications of the language used against black-skinned people in Roman antiquity.[79] Scholarship that has affirmed Black presence in Greco-Roman literature should be commended.[80] But the biased reading of it, sadly, has served to prop up the very reasons these texts have been ignored.[81]

BLACK-SKINNED PEOPLE
AND THE "ENDS OF THE EARTH"

In Greco-Roman literature, Black-Skinned people are said to have inhabited an extremity of the earth. Homer[82] says that the Ethiopians were in fellowship with the gods.[83] In the *Iliad*, Thetis proclaims, "But you, sitting by your swift seafaring ships, continue your wrath against the Achaeans and refrain entirely from battle; for Zeus went yesterday for a feast to the incomparable Ethiopians at the Ocean, and all the gods followed with him; but on the twelfth day he will come back again to Olympus, and then I will go to the house of Zeus with its threshold of bronze, and will clasp his knees, and I think I will persuade him."[84] The picture is that of a distant people in a distant land. Living at one of the extremities of the earth granted them the ability to commune with the gods. Fellowshipping with the gods rightly accords the designation that these people are "incomparable." The presence of Zeus, especially, gives them greater dignity. They are worthy of the presence of the king of the gods. In Homer's *Odyssey*, the narrator describes Poseidon's interaction with them: "But now Poseidon had gone among the far-off Ethiopians—the Ethiopians who dwell divided in two, the farthermost of men, somewhere Hyperion sets and somewhere he rises—there to receive a hecatomb of bulls and rams, and there he was taking his joy, sitting at the feast; but the other gods were gathered together in the halls of Olympian Zeus."[85] In this passage, Homer discusses Poseidon's foray to visit the "far-off Ethiopians." We must note that Homer does not describe the Ethiopians as Black, even though we are aware they are by the very title. Second, his use of the term *Ethiopian* is not regional or cultural. He is speaking of black-skinned people at two ends of the earth, Africa and India.[86] Principally, for Homer, these people are distant people. Indeed, they are the "farthest among men." They are *other*, but in a positive sense. They are worthy of fellowship with the gods.

Herodotus[87] notes that Ethiopians are at the "ends of the earth" in Libya, where there are gold and other precious resources in abundance (*Hist.* 3.114–15; see also Heliodorus, *Aeth.* 9.23). Strabo[88] also says that Ethiopians were the most distant at one of the ends of the earth (*Georg.* 1.2.27–28; 2.2.2).[89] In Aeschylus's play *Prometheus vinctus*,[90] Prometheus discusses an Ethiopian at the extremity of the world (*Prom.* 809–15). Most likely, in these cases, the writers are speaking of ancient Nubians. In the case of Herodotus, specific geopolitical distinctions are not stringent, since he groups together Libyans and Ethiopians. Greek and Roman ancients considered Ethiopians and other black-skinned people to live at the "ends of the earth."

THE BLACK SKIN OF ETHIOPIANS

The most noticeable and discussed characteristic of Ethiopians by other nations was their blackness[91] (Herodotus, *Hist.* 2.29–32; 3.17–24; 4.183, 197; Seneca, *Nat.* 4A.2.18; Heliodorus, *Aeth.* 1.2; 4.8; 8.16).[92] Not only Ethiopians were known for their black skin and other phenotypical features. Egyptians, Colchians, and Libyans were also recognized for being black-skinned. Herodotus[93] notes the different peoples who were considered black-skinned:

> For it is plain to see that the Colchians are Egyptians; and this that I say I myself noted before I heard it from others. When I began to think on this matter, I inquired of both peoples; and the Colchians remembered the Egyptians better than the Egyptians remembered the Colchians; the Egyptians said that they held the Colchians to be part of Sesostris' army. I myself guessed it, partly because they are dark-skinned and

woolly-haired;[94] though that indeed counts for nothing, since other peoples are, too; but my better proof was that the Colchians and Egyptians and Ethiopians are the only nations that have from the first practised circumcision. (*Hist.* 2.104 [Godley, LCL])[95]

Herodotus places Egyptians, Colchians, and Ethiopians under the same phenotypic banner.[96] Colchians were not Africans but were still considered Black by Herodotus. These groups may be culturally and regionally diverse, but they are all categorized as Black people. This shows the fluidity of the terminology.

Diodorus Siculus[97] discusses Ethiopians in laudatory terms (*Hist.* 3.2.1–4).[98] Ethiopians were the first among people and pious. He falls in line with the tradition of considering the Ethiopians as "noble barbarians."[99] Though noble, some Ethiopians and other black-skinned people were very much barbarians:

But there are also a great many other tribes of the Ethiopians, some of them dwelling in the land lying on both banks of the Nile and on the islands in the river, others inhabiting the neighbouring country of Arabia, and still others residing in the interior of Libya. The majority of them, and especially those who dwell along the river, are black in colour and have flat noses and woolly hair. As for their spirit they are entirely savage and display the nature of a wild beast, not so much, however, in their temper as in their ways of living; for they are squalid all over their bodies, they keep their nails very long like the wild beasts, and are as far removed as possible from human kindness to one another; and speaking as they do with a shrill voice and cultivating none of the practices of civilized life as these are found among the rest of [hu]mankind, they present a striking contrast when considered in the light of our own customs. (*Hist.* 3.8 [Oldfather, LCL])

Ethiopians and other African peoples, says Diodorus, are black-skinned, kinky-haired, and in some cases, wild and beastly. This is not to say that Diodorus necessarily associates the blackness of the skin or the hair texture of these people to be indicators of this wildness. The literary and historical implication of Diodorus's description, we can say, helps us see the otherizing aspect of Greco-Roman views of black-skinned Africans. This otherization may simply be the consequence of noting what he considered oddities or curiosities. But the Ethiopian is no less *other*. Ethiopians' and Indians' black skin made them so different, claimed Herodotus, that their nails and semen were also theorized as Black (*Hist.* 3.101).[100]

The blackness of Ethiopians, in particular, was the most black among the skin colors.[101] Pseudo-Aristotle held that these black-skinned Africans were the darkest of all: "Why are the teeth of the Ethiopians white, and whiter than those of other people, but their nails are not? Are their nails (not white) because their skin is dark, and darker than that of other people, and the nails grow from the skin? But why are their teeth white? Is it because whatever the sun extracts moisture from, without dyeing it, becomes white, such as wax? Now it dyes the skin, whereas it does not dye the teeth, but the moisture is evaporated from them owing to the warmth" (*Prob.* 10.66 [Mayhew, LCL]).[102] Ethiopians have the whitest teeth but the blackest skin. The contrast between the two colors may speak to the extreme nature of their location. It was quite common in Greek and Roman thought to consider the spread of physical traits to be resultant of the environment. In particular, following Homeric thought, and with others, the consensus view was that Black Africans and Ethiopians in particular had dark skin and curly hair because of the extreme heat of Africa.[103] The extreme differences in features were explained by the differences in region and climate, which also explained the phenotypic differences from Scythians.[104]

The passage of Black phenotypic traits was a point of inquiry for the children of African and Greek people.[105] This view suggests that it was possible that Black phenotypic traits could not be hidden or overcome by white phenotype. There is an interesting but tenuous connection between this view of descent and the later "one drop rule."[106] But we must be careful to not think that later racist ideologies have a strong foundation in this kind of ancient thinking on phenotypical theorization.

BLACKNESS AND PHYSIOGNOMY

Another part of the calculus of skin color, environment, and other physical traits was the notion that they had a bearing on character. The consideration that physicality spoke to internal and invisible human characteristics and nature is called physiognomy. Many ancients considered physiognomic rationalization to be an essential way to evaluate people. Physicality bespoke who one was. In essence, how one looks on the outside tells us what is on the inside, morally.[107] As is the case now, many ancients thought this way.

Aristotle assessed that the Greeks were the best of all people. Their physical environment allowed them to share in the best of character traits. This was not so for other Europeans:

> Let us now speak of what ought to be the [Hellenic] citizens' natural character, now this one might almost discern by looking at the famous cities of Greece and by observing how the whole inhabited world is divided up among the nations. The nations inhabiting the cold places and those of Europe are full of spirit but somewhat deficient in intelligence and skill, so that they continue comparatively free, but lacking in political organization and capacity to rule their neighbours. The peoples of Asia on the other hand are intelligent and skilful in temperament, but lack spirit, so that they are in continuous subjection and slavery. But the Greek race participates in both characters, just as it occupies the middle position geographically, for it is both spirited and intelligent; hence it continues to be free and to have very good political institutions, and to be capable of ruling all mankind if it attains constitutional unity. The same diversity also exists among the Greek races compared with one another: some have a one-sided nature, others are happily blended in regard to both these capacities. (*Pol.* 7.6.1–2 1327b [Rackham, LCL])

For Aristotle, the physical environment affected also physical traits. It is safe to assume, also, that he linked physical traits with character traits and intelligence. For him, Greeks occupied a space in the world that allowed for them to demonstrate the best of humanity. Some Greeks showed better character traits than others, Aristotle says. But on the whole, their "middle position" granted them a unique position in the world to be an exemplary nation.

Pseudo-Aristotle's physiognomic system continues the theme of the "middle" being the best. He explicitly pairs physicality with differences of internal nature:

> Those who are too black are cowardly; this applies to Egyptians and Ethiopians. But the excessively fair [too white] are also cowardly; witness women. But the complexion that tends to courage is in between these two. . . . Those whose eyes are excessively black are cowardly; for it was shown above that an excessively black colour signifies cowardice. But those who are not excessively black but who incline to a tawny colour are stout-hearted. Those whose eyes are grey or whitish are cowardly; for a whitish colour has been shown to be a sign of cowardice. But those whose eyes are not grey but bright are stout-hearted; witness the lion and the eagle. Those whose eyes are wine-dark are gluttonous; witness the goats. Those who have flaming eyes are shameless; witness the dogs. Those who have pale and blotchy eyes are cowardly; this refers to the affection, because men who are terrified turn pale with a complexion which changes. But those who have gleaming eyes are sensual; witness cocks and ravens. (*Physiogn.* 812a–b [Hett, LCL])[108]

Black-skinned people, Egyptians and Ethiopians, are cowardly because of the blackness of their skin. People who are too white are also cowardly, but he does not give an ethnographic group for this assessment. He describes women as representative of this particular trait.[109] Pseudo-Aristotle comes back to his assessment of blackness. Those whose eyes are black are cowardly because the color black signifies cowardice. If one is considered Black, then because of the nature of the color itself, that suggests that the person is inherently cowardly. The color scheme in the world has appropriated traits for humans. The black color, for him, bespeaks the antinomy of courage, which was visible in those whose color was in between, in the middle. Greek men, in particular, would embody this trait.

Some readings of this material dismiss widespread color prejudice in antiquity and argue that prejudice was marginal at best. One such view says the majority of ancients thought there is dignity in black-skinned people[110] and that Pseudo-Aristotle is in the minority.[111] One of the flaws in this argument is that it fails to see the fraught nature of a standardized color or ethnicity. By discussing people with differences as inherently *other*, writers opened the way for combining character traits with ethnography and geography, as did Aristotle.

These negative valuations of black complexion can move from the level of observation to mockery. Juvenal states, "It should be the man who walks upright who mocks the man who limps, the white man who mocks the black (literally, 'Ethiopian')."[112] Juvenal thinks that a person who is white should be able to mock a Black person because white is better than Black, apparently.[113] In the Greek school lessons, students were taught this concerning Ethiopians:

Seeing a fly on his table, he said:

"Even Diogenes keeps parasites."
Seeing a woman being educated, he said:
"Wow! A sword is being sharpened."
Seeing a woman giving advice to a woman, he said:
"An asp is being supplied venom from a viper."
Seeing an Ethiopian eating white bread, [he said]:
"Look! Night is swallowing day."
Seeing and Ethiopian defecating, he said:
"Look! A kettle with a hole in it."[114]

It is supposed in these instances that blackness is subnormal or against accepted standards of beauty. Beyond the physiognomic criticism of blackness and its attendant phenotypic traits beheld in black-skinned peoples, these aesthetic valuations assume something is inherently wrong with Black appearance. It is not simply because it matches a color that it is considered evil. The Black traits themselves do not meet Greco-Roman standards of beauty and are, thereby, worthy of criticism. The same goes for many northern Europeans, to be sure, but this recognition does not diminish the sting of the criticism for black-skinned people.[115]

Iconography of black-skinned people accentuates the deleterious implications of the textual descriptions. Although Agatharchides claimed that the white person only had fear of black-skinned people as a child, this raises the question of why this fear existed at all.[116] This notion of fear is matched by observations of images found in Pompeii.[117] Though strictly defined racism is not in play, somatic differences of black-skinned people were considered so grotesque that they had an apotropaic effect. Black people were so ugly that they scared evil away![118]

Ethiopians, Egyptians, and black-skinned people were also otherized because of their appearance and, more, their "barbaric" culture. For some Greeks and Romans, the two went hand in hand. This truth is clearly seen in the Greek novels.[119] Tatius's *Leucippe and Clitophon* (ca. second to third century CE) narrates Leucippe's interaction with Egyptians along the seas. The description is telling. These Egyptians are Black and barbaric:[120]

> As we were sailing past one city, we suddenly heard a great outcry. Our sailor said, "Rangers." . . . All large and black (not deep black like Indians but as black as, say, a half-Ethiopian might be) bareheaded, heavyset but quick on their feet. They all shouted in a foreign language. . . . I began to cry . . . "O gods and spirits, if you do exist, hear our prayers, what great crime did we commit, to be overwhelmed by this avalanche of adversities? Now you have put us in the hands of Egyptian bandits to deprive us even of a sympathetic hearing." A Greek bandit would respond to our speech, and his hard heart might melt at our prayers. Speech often succeeds on its mission of mercy. . . . But now in what language will we frame our requests? . . . I can only communicate my cause by expressive gestures, display my desires in sign language. (*Leuc. Clit.* 3.9–10)

Like Homer, Herodotus, and others, Tatius sees a connection between the Ethiopians of the South (Nubians) and the East (Indians). Interestingly,

Tatius uses Indians as the measure of blackness and describes the Egyptian as a "half-Ethiopian" (see Ps. Aristotle, *Prob.* 10.66). In this portrayal, we must note the connection between their color description and their foreignness. After emphasizing how Black these bandits were, the writer tells us that there would be no way the main character could understand the bandits. His only resort would be to communicate with them via "gestures." Blackness in Greco-Roman eyes was a sure indicator of foreignness. Indeed, these black-skinned Egyptians were barbarians, *other*.[121]

Another instance in another Greek novel, Heliodorus's *An Ethiopian Story*,[122] sounds quite similar to Tatius's narrative: "The bandits moved round and stood in front of her. They seemed to be on the point of taking some action when the maiden looked up again and saw their dark skin and unkempt faces" (1.3).[123] The opening scene of the novel portrays another one of the essential characters—Theagenes, the husband of Chariklea—as "gleaming white" (1.2). The color contrast is unmistakable between this noble Greek and these ignoble Egyptian bandits. This contrast is also coupled with an inability to understand Greek when Chariklea cried to the Egyptians, but "they could understand not a word" (1.3). Again, blackness directly corresponds with being a barbarian.[124]

In the context of the novel itself, this beginning scene demonstrates a certain denigration of black-skinned people that will take place throughout the novel.[125] A complex tale, the story centers on Chariklea, who is a white-skinned Ethiopian, unheard of in the ancient world. She obtains her whiteness through impression.[126] Her mother and father are the queen and king of Meroe, the Nubian kingdom. They are described in noble as well as barbarian terms. This representation of Ethiopians is to be expected. They are recognized for their noble characteristics but also lightly reprimanded for their backward, non-Greek ways. It is clear in the narrative that their royalty does not allow them to escape being considered *other*, foreign to the Greek world. This theme is integral to the function of the narrative; blackness means foreignness, even barbarianism (1.2, 19).

Chariklea embodies this relegation and confinement of blackness to a world wholly other to the Greek world. Her white skin grants her the privilege to live as a Greek but also rule as an Ethiopian (2.36; 10.40–41). She was born with shining white skin, as her mother, Persinna, told her, "But you, child I bore, had a skin of gleaming white, something quite foreign to Ethiopians" (4.8).[127] Persinna's comment to her daughter captures the point: Ethiopians are not white people. But still, in the end of the story, the controlling narrative oracle is fulfilled: a "crown of white on brows of black" (2.36) means that Chariklea and her husband become the rulers of Ethiopia. In the end, a white Ethiopian with her white, Greek husband bring a new era to the Ethiopians.

Heliodorus's portrayal of black-skinned people, again, is not at all completely negative. His narrative does not neatly find a strong parallel with later racist ideologies. But it was certainly essentialist. It pays close attention to blackness and signifies blackness with foreignness, otherness. As such, Heliodorus—though having written a highly imaginative tale, certainly with a white-skinned Ethiopian—aligns with the otherizing views that are prominent in Greco-Roman perspectives on black-skinned people.[128]

Among Greeks and Romans, black-skinned people took strong notation of physical differences. This was done not always to vilify but to chronicle. In some cases, the goal was to designate black-skinned people as *other*. They were fundamentally different from white-skinned people. They had physical features that were also unappealing to some white-skinned people. This otherized status could elicit a kind of praise, as in Homer and Herodotus. It could also generate disdain, as in the case of Juvenal.

SEEING BLACK IN THE ANCIENT WORLD: JEWISH VIEWS

The concept of blackness as an unusual trait among African peoples is not as prominent in Jewish scripture and Second Temple sources. Philo of Alexandria certainly pays attention to the blackness of Ethiopians and the children of Ham, but this feature of African peoples is not as predominant in other Jewish literature in the New Testament period (*QG* 2.81–82). Rabbinic sources certainly pick up and emphasize the blackness of African peoples who are documented in Scripture.[129] Rabbinic literature, especially in the medieval period, reflects the development of racist ideologies that led toward the dreadful "curse of Ham" theology. The level of vituperation present in later rabbinic literature is not at all present in biblical and early Second Temple discourse.[130]

The African Children of Ham
and the Biblical Record

Ethiopians were considered to live at the end of the earth in the biblical record (Esth 1:1; 8:9; Ezek 29:10; Zeph 3:10).[131] Also, terms used for Ethiopians vary. They are called *Kush*[132] in the original Hebrew, but the Greek is often translated as Ethiopia. When Cush, the child of Ham, is mentioned in Genesis 10:6, the Greek translators transliterated it as *Cous*.[133] This is rare, however, as the vast majority of times, *Kush*[134] is translated in its various forms as Ethiopia.[135]

In the Jewish story of the origination of the world, Ham, the son of Noah, is said to be the father of African peoples and Canaan (Gen 10:6–8). Among his sons in Africa are the Ethiopians, Egyptians, Libyans, and Sabeans. In their various ways, all of these children of Ham play a key role in salvation history.[136]

Ethiopia and Egypt are essential to the salvation of Israel. In Isaiah 11, 18–20, many of the references to Egypt and Ethiopia are probably references to the Twenty-Fifth Dynasty, when Nubia ruled Egypt. Taharqa, one of the most famous Nubian rulers of this dynasty, aids Israel against the Assyrians.[137] Ebed-Melech, the Ethiopian eunuch, rescues Jeremiah from certain death (Jer 38:7–8; 39:16).[138] There are negative characterizations, oracles of doom, as well (e.g., Isa 43:3; Zeph 2:12). But overall, Jews would have recognized the strength of the connection they had with African peoples.[139]

There are only two references in the biblical tradition from which we can infer that Jews thought that blackness was the prominent feature in African peoples. The first is Jeremiah 13:23, which does not state that Ethiopians are Black, but it assumes that Jews recognize that Cushites have black skin.[140] Song of Songs 1:5–6, the other passage, makes no reference to the character as an Ethiopian.[141] It has been assumed by patristic writers that this is so.[142]

There is no major emphasis on the blackness of the African's skin. When there is a reference to it, it is without negative assessment.[143]

Black-Skinned Africans
in Second Temple Literature

In Second Temple literature, discussions of African peoples are consistent with biblical literature.[144] Other notable historical events not documented in the biblical texts are also mentioned in pseudepigraphal literature.[145] Judith 1:10 suggests a continued belief that Ethiopians occupied the extremity of the world.

The Sibylline Oracles are rife with references to Ethiopia grouped with other African nations, as noted earlier.[146] In Sibylline Oracles 5:179–99,[147] the writer discusses the destruction against Egypt.[148] An Ethiopian is said to raze Syene in southern Egypt (5:194).[149] In 5:195, the writer says, "Dark-skinned Indians will occupy Teuchira by force."[150] It is noted that book 5 represents an Egyptian Jewish provenance.[151] If this is the possible context, one wonders why this text would describe Indians as black-skinned. Again, we should be reminded that in Hellenistic depiction, Indians, Ethiopians, and other black-skinned people are often mentioned in the same breath when discussing phenotypical similarities.

One of the most important of the traditions that grabs the attention of Jewish writers is the marriage of Moses to an Ethiopian woman (Num 12:1–2).[152] None of these traditions discusses the physical traits of Ethiopians and other African peoples. Jubilees, in particular, follows the grouping tradition of Genesis 10:6, assuming that the children of Ham are African peoples.[153] In Jubilees 7:7–13, the tradition is maintained that Noah cursed Canaan and not Ham.[154] Because of Noah's curse, Ham and his sons (Cush, Mizraim, Put, and Canaan) leave Noah (Jubilees 7:13) and eventually go to where traditions held Nubia was located (Jubilees 8:22, 24; see also Gen 2:13). Japheth also leaves, but Shem remains with Noah (Jubilees 7:14–19). That Noah did not curse Ham is stated in emphatic terms in 4Q252 2:7, which says, "But he did not curse Ham, but only his son, for God had blessed the sons of Noah."[155]

Jubilees 9:29–30 claims that the portion of land that Japheth inherited is cold and Ham's inheritance is hot.[156] Shem's land is "not hot or cold" (Jubilees 9:30). This tradition may reflect the wider-believed view that Ethiopians were closer to the sun, while northern Europeans (e.g., Scythians) were farther from it.[157] Shem (read Jews) thought of themselves in the middle, just as the Greeks did. The environmental description may imply color distinctions; it may be implied only slightly.[158]

There are prophecies of doom against Ham, which may reflect oracles of destruction against Ethiopians and other African peoples (e.g., Isa 20:3–5). Testament of Simeon 6:4 foresees doom for the "land of Ham" with the rise of Israel (6:5) in the eschaton. In 1QM 2:13–14, the congregation will fight against the "sons of Ham and Japheth" to obtain the victory of Israel.

The discussion on color appears in the Apocalypse of Moses. Apocalypse of Moses 35:4 reports that Eve saw Ethiopians. In this passage, the following explanation is given by Seth: "'These are the sun and the moon, and they themselves fall down and pray for my father Adam.' And Eve said to him, 'And where is their light, and why have they become dark?' Seth said to her, 'They are not able to shine before the light of all, and this is why the light is hid from them'" (Apocalypse of Moses 36:1–3). Here the writer perceives that to speak of an Ethiopian is to speak of a black-skinned person. In this respect, however, the purpose is not to denigrate them. They are described by the feature that stood out, their blackness. But they are the sun and the moon, who remove their glory to honor God. This example suggests that the Ethiopian's skin color could be used in a symbolic way to refer to a spiritual concept.[159]

Josephus and Philo both group Ethiopia together with other African nations, particularly Egypt and Libya.[160] Most interesting for our study is Philo's discussions of Ethiopia and the children of Ham. In his commentary *Questions and Answers on Genesis*, Philo establishes that he considers Cush,[161] his child Nimrod, and their blackness to signify wickedness:

Why is Ham's eldest son "Cush?" The theologian has expressed a most natural principle in calling Cush the eldest offspring of evil, (since he is) the sparse nature of earth. For earth that is fertile, well-stocked, well-watered, rich in herbage and in grain, and well-forested is distributed and divided into the products of fruit. But sparse and dusty earth is dry, unfruitful, barren and sterile, and is carried off and lifted up by the wind, and why did Cush beget Nimrod who began to be "a giant hunter" before the Lord, wherefore they said, "like Nimrod a giant hunter before God?" It is proper that one having a sparse nature, which a spiritual bond does not bring together and hold firmly, and not being the father of constancy either of soul or nature or character, but like a giant valuing and honouring earthly things more than heavenly, should show forth the truth of the story about the giants and Titans. For in truth he who is zealous for earthly and corruptible things always fights against and makes war on heavenly things and praiseworthy and wonderful natures, and builds walls and towers on earth against heaven. But those things which are here are against those things which are there. For this reason it is not ineptly said, "a giant before God," which clearly is opposition to the Deity. For the impious man is none other than the enemy and foe who stands against God. Wherefore it is proverbial that everyone who is a great sinner should be compared with him as the chief head and fount, as when they say, "like Nimrod." Thus the name is a clear indication of the thing (signified), for it is to be translated as "Ethiopian," and his skill is that of the hunter. Both of these are to be condemned and reprehended, the Ethiopian because pure evil has no participation in light, but follows night and darkness, while hunting is as far removed as possible from the rational nature. But he who is among beasts seeks to equal the bestial habits of animals through evil passions. (*QG* 2.81–82 [Marcus, LCL])

For Philo, the Cushite's black skin is a symbol of wickedness. Here Nimrod becomes the essential locus for his understanding of the nature of the Ethiopian. Nimrod (Gen 10:8–9; 1 Chr 1:10) as a Cushite is malevolent, a hunter, and bestial (see Diodorus, *Hist.* 3.8). Nimrod, and thereby the Ethiopian, is what his color says about him, a representative of darkness and, thereby, evil.

Philo's discussion of Cush, however, must be balanced with his discussion of the Ethiopian woman who married Moses (Num 12:1–12):

For the external sense, being really shameless and impudent, though considered as nothing by God the father, in comparison of him who was faithful in all his house, to whom God himself united the Ethiopian woman, that is to say, unchangeable and well-satisfied opinion, dared to speak against Moses and to accuse him, for the very actions for which he deserved to be praised; for this is his greatest praise, that he received the Ethiopian woman, the unchangeable nature, tried in the fire and found honest; for as in the eye, the part which sees is black, so also the part of the soul which sees is what is meant by the Ethiopian woman. (*Leg.* 2.67 [Colson and Whitaker, LCL])

In a discussion about the shamelessness and impudence (*Leg.* 1.65–66), Philo allegorizes the marriage of Moses to the Ethiopian woman.[162] Here Philo argues that Moses is to be commended for marrying a woman who represents what cannot be changed, something that is burnt and black. Philo indicates that the Ethiopian woman's blackness signified that Moses's soul was wedded to honesty.

But Philo's interpretation of the Ethiopian's blackness cannot be completely disconnected from a negative valuation. Even though he speaks positively of the Ethiopian woman's blackness, he concludes that Ethiopia, itself, symbolizes "cowardice" and "humiliation":[163]

"And the name of the second river is Gihon. This is that which encircles all the land of Ethiopia." Under the symbol of this river courage[164] is intended. For the name of Gihon being interpreted means chest, or an animal which attacks with its horns; each of which interpretations is emblematical of courage.[165] For courage has its abode about the chest, where also is the seat of the heart, and where man is prepared to defend himself. For courage is the knowledge of what is to be withstood, and of what is not to be withstood, and of what is indifferent. And it encircles and surrounds Ethiopia, making demonstrations of war against it; and the name of Ethiopia, being interpreted, means humiliation.[166] And cowardice[167] is a humiliating thing; but courage is adverse to humiliation and to cowardice.[168] (*Leg.* 1.68)[169]

Philo interprets the depiction of the garden of Eden in Genesis 2:13 and its many rivers. In Genesis, the river Gihon surrounds the land of Cush (Ethiopia). Philo reads this river as a force of might against the "cowardice" and "humiliation" that is Ethiopia. Interestingly, there is no reference to color. It is assumed that Ethiopia, itself, means blackness in the same sense as Pseudo-Aristotle characterized it. We can certainly conclude, based on these texts, that Philo considered blackness to be the defining trait of Ethiopian peoples.

But what did the blackness of Ethiopians mean? Whether he claims that the Ethiopian's blackness is a symbol of wickedness (*QG* 2.82) or symbolic of honesty (*Leg.* 2.62), Philo argued that their blackness defined their character. Consequently, he could also believe, based on his acceptance of a Hellenistic physiognomic worldview, that such blackness could mean that Ethiopians, and possibly other black-skinned people, are cowardly and humiliated. Their appearance meant that they were a humiliated people.

No explanation is given as to why either Pseudo-Aristotle or Philo understood Black physiognomy in this manner.[170] It could be that the black skin of Egyptians and Ethiopians was extreme. They were "too black." They did not fit the Hellenistic or Roman norm of acceptable appearance. Their blackness suggested that they were cowardly in their character. To be cowardly in this sense could indicate blackness is like femininity.[171] The juxtaposition of blackness with being a hunter may counter this position.[172] We cannot be sure as to why Pseudo-Aristotle claimed blackness in Ethiopians and Egyptians meant cowardice. In the same way, it is unclear as to why Philo added "humiliation" to this conception of blackness. It seems that to have black skin meant that there was something wrong, something unacceptable in the Ethiopian, Egyptian, or Libyan black-skinned person. And in this way, following Pseudo-Aristotle and other Greco-Roman thinkers, Philo also upheld the view that black-skinned people were properly otherized. He is out of step overall with many of the Jewish views of his period. Most did not problematize black-skinned people for being black-skinned.[173] The majority of Jewish views prior to the rabbis were value neutral on the question of black skin.[174] Philo stands as an outlier.[175]

When God's Black Children Come Home

With this evidence, it is easier to understand why Luke places emphasis on African peoples' blackness in his narrative. Luke features Jews, proselytes, and black-skinned people from African nations. All of the following reasons are interlinked. First, when Jews and proselytes in African nations hear the gospel, this signifies the return from exile and the exaltation of Israel (e.g., Isa 19:25; Ps 68:30–32). Second, the preaching of the gospel to the Ethiopian and the prophetic status of Simeon Niger demonstrate the first point and provide another example, respectively, of Luke's stress on the gospel's power to uplift the socially excluded and downtrodden (Luke 4:18–19; see also Isa 61:1–5). Last, which is the most common interpretation of the Ethiopian, Luke shows us that the gospel will reach the ends of the earth because through the Ethiopian, it has already symbolically reached an end of the earth (Acts 1:8; see also Isa 49:6). In other words, that all the nations will see the light of salvation is revealed in and through the salvation of black-skinned people. These themes emerge through the inclusion of the Ethiopian eunuch and Simeon Niger.

Through black-skinned Africans, Luke reveals the restoration of the rest of Adam's children to their divine childship status. Just as Jesus was doing this in his own ministry through the woman bent over by disease (Luke 13:11–17) or Zacchaeus (Luke 19:1–10), the reclamation of the black-skinned children of God disrupts denigrative perceptions of black-skinned people.[176] The best way to read the discussion of the Ethiopian eunuch and other mentions of black-skinned people in the narrative is against a backdrop that considers them at best negligible and at worst objectionable.[177] Luke intends to accentuate their presence in the same way he did the poor, women, and even uncircumcised centurions (Luke 7:1–10; 23:47; Acts 10:1–8). Each group in their own way was resented and rejected by another group. Black-skinned people, in particular, elevate Luke's agenda in a special way because they were *others* among *others*. Their reception and participation in the gospel mission showed in no uncertain terms that the mission of the gospel to restore the divine childship of the world would be successful.

There are three major claims to be made based on the evidence. First, the proper way to understand Lukan anthropology is that all humans are God's children who have lost their status as God's children (Acts 17:26–31). All of Adam and all of his descendants had lost their status. Israel, even, had lost its favored status. Thus Jews needed their divine childship status restored, and therefore, all human beings need the same restoration. Second, salvation through Jesus concerns the restoration of God's children to their proper status (Luke 15:11–32). Third, Jesus, the Son of God, restores Adam (Israel and the nations; Acts 1:8). The restoration of Israel has begun full force in Jerusalem, Judea, and Samaria. And as biblical prophecy dictates, the restoration of Israel is inextricably linked with the salvation of the world.

Now, this reading suggests that the rest of the world is symbolized and proleptically saved through the restoration of the black-skinned children of God.[178] There are protests that any proleptic expectation of the eunuch weakens its narrative and theological functions.[179] Luke is able, however, to use individuals and groups symbolically. Indeed, a prominent theme is the return from exile at Pentecost (Acts 2:1–13; see also Isa 43:6). Luke is fully aware that Jews are still spread out and the four winds had not carried them all back to the homeland.[180] Moreover, all of the gentiles had not been saved when Cornelius and his party came to faith in Caesarea (Acts 10). People in Acts serve to make the reader look forward to a brighter future when the promises Jesus made in the Gospel are to come to pass in their fullness (Luke 6:35; 20:36), when the children of God are revealed.

The Ethiopian eunuch confirms the theme we first see in Acts 2:10. Simeon Niger furthers the theme. By bringing attention to black-skinned people, Luke is explaining that perceptions of *the other* are being undone through the work of restoration. The gospel brings the children back home. An integral way to elucidate this theme is to offer a story that makes this case in the most obvious terms. Discussing the salvation of an Ethiopian (Isa 11:11; 19:25) who is a eunuch (Isa 56:1–8) and a treasurer (Ps 68:31; Zeph 3:9–10) representing the Candace, the queen of the Ethiopians (1 Kgs 10:1–13; Luke 11:31), accomplishes a lot for Luke.[181] It is the perfect story that demonstrates the global capacity and the sociocultural subversiveness of the gospel. Luke's inclusion of Simeon Niger reaffies this subversiveness and says to his readership that God is no respecter of persons but uses all, despite and in opposition to color and cultural biases.[182]

THE ETHIOPIAN EUNUCH

The story of the Ethiopian functions to establish that God is reclaiming a child of his. This story, which parallels the resurrection account of Jesus (Luke 24:13–35), shows the work of the divine childship Spirit.[183] In the narrative, Philip, having been part of the scattering of the Jerusalem church, extends the mission of the church to Samaria (Acts 8:1–24). The strengthening of the legitimacy of that mission had been confirmed by the descent of the apostles from Jerusalem (8:14). After leaving Samaria, an angel speaks to Philip to go to the location where the Ethiopian is (8:26). The Spirit speaks to Philip to join the Ethiopian in his chariot (8:29). After Philip is done, the Spirit transports him to Azotus, where he commences preaching again all the way to Caesarea (8:40).[184] The Spirit had ordained this Ethiopian unto life (see 11:18; 13:48). Luke's emphasis on God's direct communication with Philip suggests that what we have learned about the Spirit still applies. God is reclaiming God's children by the Son through the Spirit. Even though there is little outward evidence of a filling of the Spirit in the Ethiopian beyond his joy, it is certain that he has shared in the baptism that Jesus had promised.[185] He shared in the Abrahamic covenant blessings declared by Peter (2:38–39).

The absence of apostolic influence does not diminish the potency of the Spirit's work. Paul's conversion takes place without an apostle present, and Luke tells us plainly that Ananias is meant to be the conduit through whom he receives the Spirit (Acts 9:17). The nonapostolic status of Philip, as in the case of Ananias, in no way detracts from the pivotal nature of the narrative. God has moved, and the presence of the Spirit suggests that a child of God has been restored.

In such a Spirit-filled narrative, it makes sense that some manuscript traditions include that the Ethiopian was filled with the Spirit.[186] If not original, it is not necessary, since he walked away with joy. The Ethiopian's joy would signal an encounter with the Spirit.[187]

Why does God give so much attention to this individual Ethiopian? There are three moments in Acts when God (through an angel, Jesus, or the Spirit) directly communicates for the evangelization of an individual (Acts 8:26–40; 9:13–15; 10:9–17).[188] Each of these conversions is essential for the conversions of the gentiles. Through these conversions, Luke builds his theological case for the inclusion of the gentiles into the people of God. The conversion that begins this sequence is that of the Ethiopian. His conversion functions as a turning point for the conversion of the nations as seen in the conversion of Paul and Cornelius.

THE ETHIOPIAN AND THE PLAN OF SALVATION

Second, this story conveys Luke's focus on the gospel's impact on Africa and, thereby, fulfills the prophecy for the restoration of Israel and the world. Luke carries the tradition of the judging "queen of the South" (Luke 11:31; see also Matt 12:42).[189] In the Gospel, Luke says "from the ends of the earth" to talk about the African queen's inquest of Solomon's wisdom.[190] She would be the judge to condemn the people of Israel for their lack of faith in Jesus. Her appearance in the Gospel says that "Luke also abolishes racial-ethnic barriers when he makes an African the symbol of appropriate belief. Indeed, this will not be the last time in Luke's Gospel that an African is at the forefront."[191] In Acts 8:27, to continue this theme, an Ethiopian who is understood to be from the South (Homer; Zeph 3:10) and a representative of the queen of Ethiopia comes to Jerusalem to worship. Josephus considers the queen of Sheba (1 Kgs 10) to be the queen of Egypt and Ethiopia (*Ant.* 8.159, 165). It is possible that in the mind of Luke and his readers, the current queen of Meroe, through her representative, was offering worship as well. The Ethiopian eunuch came to Jerusalem to worship the God of Israel, fulfilling prophecy both as an Ethiopian and as a eunuch (Isa 56:1–8).

As an Ethiopian, he represented the gospel's reach to the extremity of the world.[192] This is proleptic.[193] Luke is capable of proleptically announcing major theological milestones throughout his narrative.[194] All conversions, therefore, point forward to a greater reality. Contrary to some views, this proleptic move does not devalue the narrative of the Ethiopian. The return from exile at Pentecost in no way violated the greater Jewish mission throughout the Diaspora (Acts 2:1–13). Indeed, the conversion of Cornelius did not negate the effect that Paul's presence would have in Rome (Acts 10). Luke is capable of exploring multiple symbolic fulfillments; indeed, that is what the entire book of Acts is. This is why Acts ends with the promise of the greater gentile mission (28:28). Luke had no intention of concluding that all of the work that needed to be done to win the gentiles had been accomplished with Paul in prison in Rome.

Furthermore, by coming to Jerusalem, the Ethiopian was brought to the center of the universe, the place where God's house was.[195] And more, he came to worship, which made him a prime candidate to receive the oracles of God, similar to Cornelius (Acts 10:1–4; see also Luke 7:3–4). An end of the world had been reached through this black-skinned man's restoration to divine childship status. From this point forward, Luke seems to intimate, the whole world will hear without hindrance (Acts 8:36; 10:47; 11:17; 28:31).[196]

The Ethiopian embodies and epitomizes the fact that God has eliminated his distance from the world. Luke is not the only New Testament writer to use the term *makran*, "far away."[197] Nevertheless, Luke may have been hinting at the Ethiopian in Acts 2:39. In Peter's sermon, he says that the promise of God is to those in Jerusalem and "for all who are far away . . . whom the Lord our God calls to him" (2:39). The narrative suggests two meanings: the reconciliation of all Jews, in the land and in the Diaspora, and the salvation of the gentiles.[198] The Ethiopian exemplifies this for the gentiles. He is the most distant in geography, culture, and appearance. His conversion would mark the reach of the gospel to the nations.

He, then, personifies the argument about the return of God's children home (Luke 15:11–32; Acts 17:26–30). Luke's theme of divine childship restoration involves not only the return of Israel (Luke 15) but the return and repentance of God's offspring (Acts 17). Both texts bespeak status restoration for God's children through repentance. In the case of the Ethiopian, this concept is intensified. He was perceived, in his blackness and his eunuch status, to be marginal, "far away," outside of the society. He was considered distant by Jews, Greeks, and Romans. Through him, and his "humiliation," Luke is showing that God is intent on reconciling the world.

The Ethiopian and the Restoration
of the Image of God

While saying all of these things, third, Luke also emphasizes this man's blackness. The Ethiopian can be viewed with an intersectional paradigm. Some Greco-Roman views on blackness held that it was an otherizing trait, and others thought of Blacks as *others* in a benign way. Luke uplifts the Ethiopian to overturn all otherizing views.[199] The Ethiopian illustrates Luke's emphasis on inclusion and "universalism."[200] Indeed, the very appearance of black skin evoked a barbarian to Greco-Roman eyes. The essentialist views vaunted in Greco-Roman society promoted the notion that blackness should be stigmatized (Ps. Aristotle, Philo, Juvenal). But Luke was against such views.

One might object that to argue such a case reads something into the text that is not there. But it can be cogently argued that Luke intended to upset physiognomic conventions when he announced that the gospel had been preached to the Ethiopian.[201] One can interpret that Luke was attacking ethnographic, anatomical, and zoological conventions, but Luke, in this view, hopes primarily to subvert the anatomical and zoological arguments.[202] This view is based on Luke's continued reference to the Ethiopian as a eunuch (Acts 8:27, 34, 36, 38, 39). The Isaiah 53:7–8 reference is meant to accentuate that the eunuch has been included in the family of God. But this interpretation notwithstanding, it appears that Luke intends to place the focus on the Ethiopian's blackness rather than his being a eunuch.

Not to split the atom, as it were, but it is clear that Luke sees in this Ethiopian multiple meanings—several barriers are being broken through his conversion. Yes, the Ethiopian is referenced as a eunuch more than anything. But the first reference emphasizes not only that he is an Ethiopian but that he served the Candace of the Ethiopians. The second instance of "Ethiopian" not only serves to define who the Candace is, but it also serves as a point of emphasis. When he is "returning home" (Acts 8:28), the reader remembers that he is going back to Ethiopia. When we are told that he "went on his way" (8:39), the way is the way home, back to Ethiopia. The last thing the reader sees is that a eunuch was going to ancient Nubia excited about his inclusion in the family of God. Therefore, his geographic origin—and his skin color, thereby—is likely the most prominent feature of the text.

Isaiah 53:7–8 provides the integral theological backdrop for understanding this story.[203] Here, again, emphasis falls on his being an Ethiopian.[204] To be sure, Luke is resisting Pseudo-Aristotle's physiognomy. But a text much closer to, and probably relying on, Pseudo-Aristotle is Philo. The argument that blackness means cowardice is dominant in both writers. But it may be that Luke shapes his narrative to directly rebuke Philo. Some other scholars have noted Philo's discussion of Ethiopia in *Legum allegoriae* 1.68.[205] But few have explored the implications of this connection between Luke and Philo.

Luke's emphasis is on the Ethiopian's origin and skin color, in resistance to a belief held by Philo of Alexandria and many others in the Mediterranean world. Greeks and Romans were concerned with otherizing blackness. And yet when God wanted to launch the gentile mission, the first person, the first *other*, was a black-skinned person—indeed, the blackest of the black (Ps. Aristotle, *Prob.* 10.66). Luke frames his discussion of the Ethiopian without any otherizing features. Luke goes out of his way to dignify this Ethiopian not only in terms of his social status but even in his religious orientation (Acts 8:27–28). Luke wants his readership to see in this conversion story that God was concerned with the salvation of black-skinned people, and their salvation signified the reclamation of divine childship status for the rest of the nations.

God continues to bring the world back together in this section (Acts 8–10; see also Gen 10:1) with representatives from Ham (the Ethiopian), Shem (Paul), and Japheth (Cornelius).[206] It would actually appear that this framework is in use prior to the Ethiopian's narrative. Acts 1:8 shows us the new Adam's salvific itinerary, which is to be taken up by the eschatological children of God. Shem represented beginning in Jerusalem and extending to the Samaritans (Acts 1–8). The representative of Ham's conversion (Acts 8:26–40) opens the way for Japheth (Acts 10). Instead of describing the declaration of war against Ham and Japheth, as in 1QM 2:13–14, Luke explicates their salvation.

God's blackest, and thereby most foreign, children are symbolically and representatively having their status restored. Luke arranges the material to specifically identify the Ethiopian with Jesus himself. In the citation of Isaiah 53:8, Jesus is the one who is humiliated: "In his humiliation,[207] his judgment was removed, who will explain his generation, because his life was taken away from the earth."[208] Jesus was in "humiliation," ready to be sheared like a sheep and slaughtered (Acts 8:32–33). In the physiognomic system, augmented by Philo's own reading of Ethiopic nature, black skin was a sign of humiliation in and of itself. The whole land of Ethiopia, Philo claimed, represented "cowardice" and "humiliation." But in Luke's view, Jesus represented anything but these things. In his suffering, he endured humiliation; his muted disposition was probably perceived as cowardice (Luke 23:9). But Jesus's death was necessary, since it brought to fulfillment all of what the prophets had spoken so that the Son might enter his glory (Luke 24:26–27, 44–47; Acts 3:18; 26:23).

Jesus's rejection in his crucifixion not only mirrors the Ethiopian's rejection because of his appearance but is also the basis for the Ethiopian's divine childship reconciliation. Juvenal said that Ethiopians should be mocked (*Sat.* 2.23), and Jesus was mocked and scorned (Luke 23:11, 35–36, 39). The death of Jesus and his resurrection opened the way for the Spirit to be sent (Luke 24:49; Acts 1:8), restoring all of God's children back to their status. It was the Spirit who orchestrated the Ethiopian's conversion (Acts 8:29).

Jesus's suffering allowed him to be identified with all humans (Luke 22:19–20; see also Acts 14:22). Luke, playing with the language he would know from physiognomic ideology, cites this part of the text most likely to suggest that Jesus has disturbed the views of Greeks and Romans who would consider the Ethiopian's anthropology inherently objectionable. He was the blackest and most distant of all. And yet in his reconciliation, he portended the reconciliation of all of Adam's gentile children. God brings the blackest children back home (Luke 15:24, 32).

And furthermore, if blackness means humiliation (Ps. Aristotle, Philo) and Jesus was humiliated, then Jesus has identified as Black. He is identifying with this man in what others could call his humiliation. To be sure, Jesus identified with rejected people. Ham was inveighed as a drunkard and gluttonous and called a friend of tax collectors and sinful people because of his associations (Luke 7:34).[209] Jesus's identification made Jesus like those whom he rescued. In this passage, Jesus has identified with the Black *other*, taking on humiliation like him in order to rescue him from his lost status.[210]

The Ethiopian's question and Philip's response (Acts 8:34–35) commend this interpretation. The Ethiopian asks if Isaiah was speaking of himself or someone else. This question most likely works on several levels. When Jesus raised the boy in Nain, the crowd proclaimed that God had visited them (Luke 7:16). At face value, the reader is not sure if Jesus is speaking of God, the sender of Jesus, or Jesus himself. Both readings are probably intended. In the same way, Luke probably winks at his auditors when the Ethiopian asks this question. So was Isaiah speaking of himself, Jesus, or the Ethiopian? Of course, the text is about Jesus (Acts 8:35). Philip begins from that very point to explain Jesus to the Ethiopian. But the narrative effect is to suggest that Jesus has identified with this man in his physicality.

His baptism, contrary to patristic writers, was not to wash him white (Acts 8:36–39).[211] This is the only time in Acts when the baptizer is baptized along with the baptized (8:39). Philip's baptism assures us that the baptism was not meant to suggest agreement with the Ethiopian's color degradation. His blackness could not "prevent" him from being baptized (8:36), just like Cornelius and his party's lack of circumcision could not stop them (10:47). God had willed his conversion, and Jesus had identified with him and all the nations through his rescue.

SIMEON NIGER, BLACKNESS, SALVATION, AND GOD'S DIVINE IMAGE RESTORATION

The explosive spread of the Spirit, witnessed in the salvation of the Ethiopian, also generated a second Jerusalem in Antioch. From here, God would ordain Paul and Barnabas as heralds of the divine childship mission: "Now in the church at Antioch there were prophets and teachers: Barnabas, Simeon who was called Niger, Lucius of Cyrene, Manaen a member of the court of Herod the ruler, and Saul. While they were worshiping the Lord and fasting, the Holy Spirit said, 'Set apart for me Barnabas and Saul for the work to which I have called them.' Then after fasting and praying they laid their hands on them and sent them off" (Acts 13:1–3).

In the second Jerusalem, was another Black person. Evidence suggests that through Simeon Niger, Luke lifts another black-skinned person to a prominent position.[212] In Acts 13:1–3, prophets and teachers gather in Antioch, the second base of Christian ministry (Acts 11:26). Gathered there are Paul, Simeon Niger, Lucius the Cyrenian, Manaen, and Barnabas (13:1). This is an extremely important gathering because from here, Paul begins his missionary journeys, which make up the primary narrative of the remainder of Acts of the Apostles.

Simeon has the name that is most peculiar of those mentioned in this chapter.[213] There are good reasons to assume that "Niger" is a nickname,[214] a name to describe Simeon as a black-skinned African.[215] First, Luke gives him a name that could easily have described him. This happens with Justus Barsabbas, called the "son of consolation" (Acts 4:36; my translation). Second, the pattern of grouping African nations was widely used in Greco-Roman and Jewish literature. Luke would have inherited this tradition. One should expect this given his collocation of Egypt and Cyrene (Acts 2:10). Third, Luke most likely would have been aware that the name *Niger* itself bespoke a black-skinned African, possibly an Aethiops but most likely a North African Black person.[216] It is likely that Luke wants his readers to recognize that there was a black-skinned African present when Paul was commissioned for his apostleship with Barnabas.

This recognition of blackness continues Luke's retrieval of biblical traditions that connect the presence of black-skinned Africans to Israel's reconciliation, the gospel's triumph (Isa 19:25). Luke shows that a black-skinned African was essential for the launch of the gentile mission (Acts 8:26–40). It only makes sense, in this pivotal scene, for a black-skinned African to be associated with the reassertion of that mission through the apostle to the gentiles, Paul (Acts 13:2–3).

In so doing, Luke also continues to dignify black-skinned people. He shows that the aspersions one might cast against them for their black skin are inherently problematic (Juvenal, Ps. Aristotle, Philo). Or, we might go further: the so-called observational arguments are being questioned (Herodotus, Aristotle, Diodorus). These are not distant peoples, foreign peoples, at least to the God of Israel.

One of the prophets/teachers who laid hands upon Paul and who is of immense importance for the second half of Acts was a black-skinned African. Some of Luke's readers, if they were so inclined, could not easily dismiss or casually insult Black African members of the church.[217] Despite their differences, God had included them as part of God's divine rescue because of their appearance. That is, their appearance was given by God and did not warrant rebuke. Black-skinned people were part of the multicolored Adam, who represented all of the nations of the world. Their inclusion into the people of God was necessary for Adam to be complete (see Luke 15:1–11).

Additionally, Luke's concentration on the blackness of their skin implicitly rebuts common Hellenistic and Roman tropes that confined black-skinned people. Heliodorus's very common conception was that Black people were necessarily *other*, they were out of place in the Greco-Roman world, and they most naturally fit in African places.[218] Luke, however, undermines this view. Yes, the Ethiopian was returning to Meroe, but his conversion took place in the wilderness outside of Jerusalem. In the same way, a black-skinned African, Simeon, was present in Antioch and part of the ministry occurring there. Luke shows us that black-skinned people cannot be considered an *other* among the people of God. They belong among the restored children just like all other people, fully participating in the life and spread of the message of the Son of God.

The Ethiopian, Simeon Niger, and the Rescue of God's Children

Taking seriously the possibility that the ancient mindset was color conscious, in addition to focusing on geography and culture, Luke appears to be focusing on the importance of blackness. The Ethiopian provides a "graphic illustration and symbol of the diverse persons who will constitute the church."[219] Adding Simeon to this "illustration" provides a beautiful black picture in

Acts. Luke knew that when he discussed an Ethiopian and a person called *Niger*, his auditors would envision both as black-skinned people.

Bringing the weight of the Greco-Roman and Jewish evidence together suggests not only that to speak of some African peoples was to say black-skinned. It also suggests that for some, black-skinned people were inherently problematic. To be black-skinned meant that one was foreign and, among some, inherently ugly. Within this framework, to be black-skinned could also indicate that one was a portent of a curse, doom, or death. Being Black was so evil that it could scare away demons!

Luke does not discuss black-skinned people in this way. The Ethiopian and Simeon are depicted as essential in the spread of God's blessings. The Ethiopian's salvation symbolizes the restoration of the rest of Adam's gentile children. Simeon is present and a contributor to Paul and Barnabas's mission to enact the salvation of the world. Luke's narrative approach is intentional. He works his sources to expose his community to the church's diverse origins. In his view, the repentance of the children, their approach home, involved the most distant and foreign people. Black-skinned people allowed him to say this in a very pronounced way that illustrated in the most explicit terms that God was bringing his children back home. Through black-skinned people, Luke discloses the fulfillment of biblical prophecy and the controverting of Greco-Roman negative views that denigrated the application of the image of God to all. The purpose of the divine childship mission was to reclaim the children of God, to reassert that humans were made in God's image and likeness. Therefore, Luke accomplishes his aim: the outcast is accepted; the foreigner is welcomed; the children of God—Jews and gentiles—have returned home through the symbolic display of black-skinned people. Black lives mattered to Jesus.

* * *

Ethiopians and other Africans, Black and distant peoples, exemplify the pursuit of the nations of Luke/Acts. As I have argued, the lost son should be understood in juxtaposition with the lost nations. Luke clarifies that the status of Israel as a lost child applied to all of the children of Adam. All were lost and in need of salvation and restoration to divine childship. Therefore, the mission of the church was to restore the divided and spread-out children of Adam to their original place in the house of God, with their status as children restored.

Luke envisions this mission taking place through Israel, embodied first through the Son of God, Jesus. Jesus's coming to Israel, his proclamation of the kingdom of God, his call to repentance, and his death and resurrection brought about the restoration of Israel itself. This restoration allows the restored Israel to become a restorative agent for the rest of the world. Again, this is why Luke discusses Jesus as a child of Adam (Luke 3:38) and describes the mission of the gospel to all the offspring of God; those who descended from Adam come back to God through the man whom God raised from the dead (Acts 17:26–31). The children of God were lost in Adam, but they are found in Jesus. The mission of divine childship allows the ages of existence to meet through Adam and Jesus, allowing paradise to be available to all once again (Luke 23:43).

To express this worldwide mission to rescue Adam's children, the children of God, Luke describes the restoration of all the people through the coming of the Spirit and the spread of the message of Jesus (Acts 1:4–8; 2). Israel's proleptic return from exile and reconfiguration under the messiahship of Jesus provided the key signal that the whole world was being invited to Jerusalem to worship in God's holy mountain (Isa 2:1–4; 11:1–11).

To further express the call of the non-Jewish nations to repentance, Luke discusses the call of African Jews and black-skinned people (Acts 2:10; 8:26–40; 13:1). The appearance of African Jews and other Black people fulfilled prophecy, the restoration of Israel and the turning of the whole world to the true God (Isa 11:11; 19:25; Zeph 3:10; Ps 68:29–32). This fulfillment occurs through focusing on black-skinned people in Acts.

Among the lost people, in Greco-Roman and Hellenistic Jewish opinion, black-skinned people personified the *other*. It would make sense, then, that Luke would use them as the symbol of God's reclamation of the rest of Adam's children. The physiognomic conclusions drawn about them may have separated them from society. But God, through these flawed, biased views, demonstrated that God is making all people near, making them among the first gentiles to hear the news of God's coming kingdom.

The Ethiopian eunuch, portraited with asymmetric status, epitomizes this mission. Luke characterizes him as a wealthy elite who would have been marginalized because of his black skin, and foreignness thereby, and eunuch status. But Luke intimates that the kingdom of God subverts such aesthetic and social marginalization. Luke describes him in a manner that only exalts and approbates him. Furthermore, Luke connects him to Jesus through his use of Isaiah 53:7–8, identifying Jesus with his blackness.

With Simeon Niger, there is not as much textual description, but he is no less important. The Ethiopian, in the minds of Luke's auditors, would have painted the picture of a black-skinned person. The descriptive term for Simeon would have done the same. In his case, Luke clarifies his identity as a black-skinned prophet/teacher. He is present and connected to Paul and Barnabas's expansive apostleship. In him, Luke finds an essential way to express that the church is diverse in its leadership. By discussing someone who would be considered an *other* by virtue of his skin color, Luke is proclaiming that all colors, thereby all nations, are welcome at the Lord's table and called to serve.

Luke's portrait exhibits that racial thinking in the ancient world was connected to color beliefs. People believed that color was attached to ethnography and culture. Luke, however, uses this cultural, aesthetic focus only to describe the gifting of the church to be a universal community. By accentuating descriptions of people who would have been considered marginal, symbolizing the very edge of the world, Luke shows that their uplifting means the restoration of the gentile children of Adam through the increase of Abraham's family. God's restoration of divine childship status, the image of God, is done through the welcoming of all the nations that are God's children, Adam's descendants. This only occurs through mission of divine childship taken up by the church that obeys its Messiah, Jesus.

CONCLUSION

Black Lives Mattered and They Matter

A look at the evidence should caution against charges of racism with respect to essentialist views in the Greco-Roman world.[1] But it is also true that an incipient concept of race does not negate the reality of racial insensitivity.[2] Ancients believed in categorizing people in groups on the basis of their ethnographic and phenotypic similarities (e.g., Herodotus, *Hist.* 2.104; Ps. Aristotle, *Prob.* 10.66; *Physiogn.* 812a). Herodotus, for example, grouped Egyptians, Ethiopians, and Colchians (*Hist.* 2.104). Homer and the Sibylline Oracles could speak of Ethiopians and Indians in one breath (*Od.* 1.21–25; Sibylline Oracles 5:195). Care must be taken when describing ancient perspectives on race, ethnicity, and phenotypic diversity not to impose modern assumptions upon the ancients. But there is a form of racial description that is easily relatable to modern versions.

Therefore, an appropriate way to discuss many African peoples is as black-skinned. The common term used for them was *black-skinned*. Other phenotypical traits typically accompanied this one. But we know that skin color was the most commonly described trait and the most definitive for the group.

Race, noting that was not exactly the same as it is now, can be an essential term to utilize.[3] And racism, in this sense, expresses the essentialist views that manifest judgments on the basis of color and phenotype.[4] There was no systematic oppression generated against black-skinned people because of their appearance. But some Black slaves were treated differently because of their appearance. It is impossible to know what was occurring on the ground. But if black-skinned people were hacked up because their skin was a bad omen, it is likely that other acts of prejudice occurred (Appian, *Bell. civ.* 4.17.134). There is also mockery and derision because of black skin color. Jim Crow did not appear among the ancients, but the foundation was laid for him in the thoughts and beliefs of these ancients.

When considering the dispersion of the gospel to the nations, then, we can say that Luke offers a christocentric critique of negative racial beliefs. In particular, Luke's theological approach combats racist beliefs rooted in aesthetic color biases. Again, Luke's theology is argues for preferential treatment for the downtrodden. It is no wonder that he would also shape his history to prominently include people who would be considered out of place in the Greco-Roman world because of their skin color.

By arranging his material to begin with the blackest and most phenotypically criticized of all of Adam's children, Luke is making a statement about color distinctions. The mission of divine childship restoration confounds arbitrary color essentialism. Luke's theology is founded on a *Jewish person* whom he proclaims is "Lord of all" (Acts 10:36) in Caesar's empire. At the same time, Luke will report that one of this Lord's most ardent and successful heralds was arrested, tried, and placed under Roman confinement.[5] Luke's aim was to give focus to those who modeled the impossible possibility of the gospel of Jesus (Luke 1:37). Concentrating on black-skinned people accomplished this feat. Luke removes the stigma of color essentialism by showing God's choice of one of the most essentialized among the nations.

BLACK LIFE AND THE VALUE OF COLOR DISTINCTIONS

Thereby, when considering Adam, Luke can say two things at the same time about racial beliefs. First, God ordained the color distinctions. Even though Luke did not mention skin color for all of the various populations he references, this does not mean that Luke is unaware of the views surrounding color and phenotype. Indeed, the fact that he discusses the Ethiopian while speaking of "humiliation" and Simeon with the word *black* suggests he is well aware. But Luke tells the story of these black-skinned people with dignity. No shame is to be found in referring to their color. As such, Luke is implying that their distinctive color was God ordained and necessary. The coming together of the nations as restored children of God of all colors and backgrounds honors their distinctiveness as God-given. For Luke, this was important: "Ethnic difference ultimately was not an obstacle but an opportunity, a resource in theological reflection on the expansion of the followers of Jesus in the diverse lands ringing the Mediterranean."[6]

Second, this distinctiveness, though of divine origin, cannot thwart the unity God accomplishes through Jesus. There is no explicit command for the church to be "one" in Luke/Acts as there is in John (e.g., 17:11, 21–22). It is implied that God delights in the unity of the church (Acts 2–3, 10–11, 15). But Paul, in his Areopagus speech, discusses the unitary origin of all people "from one man" and the Diaspora of all of Adam's children under God's watchful ordination. God determined the diversity of humanity according to God's will. But this diversity was from a unity (Acts 17:26). This is why the requirement for restoration is the same for all. Repentance is necessary for both Jew and gentile (2:38; 17:30). The necessity of repentance, turning back, is explained in James's declaration that God is reclaiming the remainder of Adam, those who had lost fealty to the God who made them (15:17). Therefore, all nations are demanded to return to the one God by "the man" whom God raised from the dead (17:31; my translation). Each nation in its distinctiveness will return to make up the one people of God through the one who will judge all people in righteousness.

Speaking in racial terms, each nation is part of Adam. The colors, the distinctions in phenotype, cannot be stratified. Caste systems cannot be made on the basis of physical differences. God gave these equally, and they are aesthetically pleasing to God and cannot be used to give an advantage to one group over the other.

In their diversity, through the Son of God, God is calling all of God's children, the dispersed nations, to repent and return home. Under the reign of Jesus the Messiah, these diverse peoples can be one. They are meant to be one with their diversity. There are no environmental explanations in Luke/Acts for the diversity in the Adamic family. Their diversity is pleasing to God

131

when the nations choose to return to the true God, eschewing and destroying their divisive idols in the process (Acts 17:29; 19:18–20).

Seeing the Beauty of Black Life

But when left to idolatrous manipulation, this diversity has been the cause of terrible tragedies. Racism, as understood by moderns, may have not been a problem for the ancients, but it is certainly a problem today. This is ever-more present in Christian scholarship. Scholars were trained in an era when ethnographic physiognomy was not only acceptable but promoted. Western intellectualism's project openly demeaned black-skinned people in the past and present. The elements from their ancient culture that were considered the best were culled by many white scholars and whitened. One interpretation could easily claim that the ancient Near Eastern people relevant for Old Testament study were composed of "Caucasians" and "whites."[7] Indeed, most people were Caucasoid, with the exclusion of Cushites, but this view concludes those Cushites were not "negro[es]."[8] Ethiopians were not really Ethiopians—or, at least, the Ethiopians of the past had no relationship with the Black people of the present. In the "Africa" entry in a famous biblical dictionary of 1930, the following opinion is expressed concerning Black people and the Bible: "It will thus be seen that the Negro districts were practically unknown to the ancient Hebrews, though men and women of Negro race must have come within their ken. It seems doubtful, therefore, whether there be, in the Bible, any reference to that race, either collectively or individually, the word Cushite standing, not for Negro, but for Ethiopian. This term is applied to Moses' (first) wife . . . and it will probably be admitted that the great Hebrew lawgiver was not likely to have espoused a Negro woman."[9] Sadly, the opinion expressed in the updated version (1979–88) of this entry is not better:

> It is evident that all of the peoples who can be identified as "African" [in the Bible] are Caucasoid. There are no nations mentioned that can be identified anthropologically as Negroid. The Nubians, and for that

matter the Ethiopians, while black-skinned, do not fit the anthropological description of the Negroes. (It might be mentioned at the same time that the Table of Nations does not include any peoples that can be identified in any way with the Mongolian race.) We can only conclude that the Bible limits its references to the peoples of the Eastern Mediterranean and adjacent areas; and so far as Africa is concerned, this means North Africa and the Nile Valley to Nubia.[10]

This same approach is even more readily seen among Egyptians.[11] We have to be careful not to make every person in Scripture Black.[12] But at the same time, we have to realize that many critics have already set a standard that everyone, including Jesus of Nazareth, was white.[13] This kind of mentality makes seeing the color diversity emphasis in Scripture quite difficult. Until we deal with the propensity toward whiteness in scholarship, we will never be able to see the biblical texts in their multicolored original format.[14]

Going back to these texts while eschewing the tendency to relegate everything black to the pile of "humiliation" is the proper course of action. The way of Jesus mandates that the people of God place great focus on what God dignifies. Even speaking globally, multitudes of people have been convinced that God is white and that to have any color darker than what is considered white is a problem. The gospel of Jesus should alert the careful reader that when such views become standard, become exalted, God has a problem. Jesus explained that what human beings exalted, God found abominable (Luke 16:15). Therefore, a reconsideration of perspectives that have led not only toward physical violence and discrimination but also toward hermeneutical violence done to the Scripture is necessary. God intended the world to be diverse in color. Even what was considered white was a color in the eyes of God. But still, when God desired to show how he was intending to save the white person, God used, first, a Black person's testimony.

Coming to this conclusion demonstrates the beauty of blackness. This is not to say that there is no beauty in other colors. But one is compelled to argue for the beauty of blackness in light of modern views but also of ancient ones. These perspectives that have built upon one another generation after generation have yielded an array of confused racist perspectives that seem to have humanity in an inextricable tangle of folly. Racism persists, it seems, without any real solution as people divide over things that they did not choose for themselves. And yet the gospel of Jesus, not only as presented in Luke/Acts, but all throughout Christian Scripture, demands recognizing the beauty in all that God has given humanity. Because God gave it, because skin color and other phenotypical distinctions are indications of humanness, it is evidence that Black people are made in the image of God. They, too, are God's descendants. But through Jesus, they too, like all of God's descendants, can be favored, can be discerned as covenantally blessed. When Paul says there is not Jew or Greek (Gal 3:28), he does not do so to say that there are no distinctions. It is a matter of fact that God made all of his creatures with differences. Not even two snowflakes are alike. Rather, Paul means that the tendency toward hierarchical oppressive comparisons is done away. God has exhibited in his Son that all are brought together. All are given grace. All can be redeemed from the diseases that have led to the foul treatment that God's children continue to utilize toward each other. But to realize this truth, God's children must see each other as God has made them and choose to accept that each belongs in the house of God together.

*   *   *

C. Herbert Woolston, in the nineteenth century, wrote the lyrics to a song that children still sing in many churches: "Jesus loves the little children, all the children of the world." It is in the completion of this verse where there has been a problem: "Red and yellow, black and white, all are precious in his sight." The problem relates to the equity of Jesus. Are "all" precious in the sight of Jesus, truly? A quick look at American history will say that no, they are not. Some are considered more precious than others, especially in the minds and hearts of many people who have claimed allegiance to Jesus as their savior. Among these colors, it became apparent that Black lives did not matter.

The great sin of slavery in America begs us never to forget the evils committed based on this belief. In the Constitution of the United States,

Africans were understood as part human and part property. The three-fifths clause stipulated that Black people were almost nonpersons in the eyes of the state. Black lives, in effect, did not matter as far as the majority of this country was concerned.

The Christian church came to bear witness to the truth of this degradation. Theologians and ministers of the Christian church testified that Black people were cursed by God. Slavery was an attempt to save them from their savagery. Without the help of white people, they would be left to their own barbarism. Their enslavement was an act of God, rescuing them from themselves and their curse.

This theological justification demanded that more be done. After the Civil War, after Reconstruction, laws were made that propped up the legal and theological predisposition that Black lives did not matter. Indeed, it has been legitimate to live out the words of Juvenal in America. The white person has been more than justified in her mind to mock the Black person, to dehumanize, to demonize, to denigrate. Mountains of evidence can be marshaled to demonstrate this truth. One need not only look at codified laws and established traditions. The images of our culture have more than affirmed the worthless nature of Black life. Racism has fluidly moved throughout this country touching each and every aspect of American life. What was true in the preaching of the pulpit was also true in the courtroom; it was also true in books, even children's books, reaching to the extent of toilet usage. The "truth" that prevailed in America for the past several hundred years is that Black lives do not matter.

The sad reality is that this state of affairs is no mere nadir in the annals of human events. The evidence suggests that there has been a long path to get to this point. With ease, not only could a Black life be hanged from a tree as "strange fruit," but that life could be snuffed out with a knee on his neck for almost nine minutes. The same principality has been ruling that has deceived the minds of many to believe that the lives of some colors are simply better than the others. God made distinctions not just in appearance but in fundamental worth in this world. The follower of the Jesus of the New Testament cannot be blind to this reality. For she who follows Jesus believes in the gospel and, therefore, condemns all of the purveyors of chaos. All of the elemental spirits that drive a wedge between God and God's creation can be clearly seen by those alive to the power of Christ. Indeed, the follower should realize that through Jesus, his purpose is to destroy such powers. The task of the Christ follower is to dethrone demons, to unseat them through the Messiah.

The Christ follower will be oblivious to this vocation if he carries the label but eschews the practice seen through the prism of God's own activity. The mission of God unveiled in the coming of the Messiah has spoken quite clearly, despite numerous attempts to reject God's missional voice. All people have been made in the image of God. The writer Luke, through his historical presentation, expresses this point with lucidity. All people come from Adam; they are therefore made in the image and likeness of God. Divine childship, then, is inherent within God's human creation. All people made in God's image and likeness are, therefore, descendants of God.

To be a descendant of God is not sufficient for a relationship with God, however. That is, good parents want their children to enjoy fellowship with them. Such is also the case with the God who created the cosmos. After human failure, the God revealed in Christian Scripture chose Israel to be the conduit through which all of God's children were brought back to God. And because of Israel's own failure, their God became a Jew to become the means by which Israel could be what it was always supposed to be.

The inherent dignity given to God's descendants, notwithstanding, compels the actions of God who had become a Jew in Jesus. Since God had invested God's self into human beings, God desired to have humans back. God was taken with the work of God's hands because God loves what God made.

This love was made manifest to Israel; this is without dispute. What was obfuscated is that when God wanted to reveal this love to the rest of the world, when God wanted to demonstrate God's desire to save and express God's desire for all of the nations, God sought a Black person. Indeed, Luke wanted to clarify this emphasis on the importance of blackness by talking about Africans at Pentecost and at Antioch. In other words, Black lives mattered to Jesus.

But they did not matter only because they reflected the immense diversity that God intended for God's people. They mattered because they mattered. The Spirit drove Philip to the Ethiopian. And Luke's description of Isaiah persuades the reader to think differently of not only this man but all Black people. Their blackness did not mean humiliation. Their black skin was a gift. So much so that Jesus himself identified with this Black man through his own humiliation. This action is expected of a figure whose task was to identify with all the descendants of Adam, for in him, creation was beginning anew. So in this way, in racial terms, Jesus identified with Cornelius as an uncircumcised white-skinned person as well. This reading in no way restricts the love of Christ to confer divine childship, to restore God's relationship with humans.

But particular focus must be given to Black people. In this time, this message is necessary. The ills that have been discussed above, rooted in ancient ideas about Black people and blackness, find their redress in the person of God's own Son. Proper Christian teaching is obligated to reject, in all of its forms, any view that attempts to exclude God's Black children. Their skin, their bodies, all of who they are, are just as much from God as everyone else. Luke shaped his narrative to give this message. Luke wanted his audience to recognize that God started his mission to the nations with a Black person. God even included a Black person as part of Paul's mission to the nations.

And their inclusion signaled that God would not tolerate mistreatment of them or any other person on the basis of how God made them. Through Jesus, their divine childship had been restored. And their example suggested that God would reach all of the world, bringing all of the colors of the world back to him.

This inclusion did not just matter then; it certainly matters now. More than ever, all people need to recognize that God chose a Black person on purpose. This was a choice; this was an act of God's favor. In our culture, which has done all it can to make Black people and other people of color feel like they do not matter, God proclaims they matter. Again, certainly all people matter to Jesus. But it must be said, when we look at the biblical text, when we view the contours of Scripture, it is loudly spoken that Black lives matter to Jesus.

NOTES

CHAPTER 1: BLACK LIVES MATTER, JESUS, AND HISTORY

1 On the whole, the reader will note that the case being made in this work is wholly unknown because scholars have seen no relevance to the notion of skin color in the biblical text, let alone black skin.

2 The justifications of the "curse of Ham" theology are evidence of this. White Christians, picking up on poorly interpreted traditions from years prior, some reflected in rabbinic traditions, held to the notion that Black people were inherently inferior according to Genesis 9 because they were the descendants of Noah's son Ham. As such, God had relegated them to live out their lives as sub-human slaves. One need not look far for this kind of aberrant interpretation of Scripture. Former president of the Southern Baptist Convention W. A. Criswell is noted for his sermon "The Scarlet Thread through the Bible," in which he declares the children of Ham, with reference to Africans, are a "servant people." See W. A. Criswell, "The Scarlet Thread through the Bible (Part 1)," wacriswell .com, December 31, 1961, https://tinyurl.com/2w7y6f34.

3 Eric Metaxas issued a comment on Twitter claiming that Jesus was "white." See "Uh, Eric Metaxas Said That Jesus Was White?," *Relevant*, July 28, 2020, https://tinyurl.com/69t8s48h. He would later try to explain that racial categories are unimportant, Jesus was Jewish, Jews are white. But this in no way alters Jesus's significance. See Megan Briggs, "Eric Metaxas on His 'Ill-Considered' Jesus Was White Tweet," churchleaders.com, July 29, 2020, https://tinyurl.com/2us66vmh. But this comment of retraction was in response to backlash against a likely belief in Jesus's whiteness. The many representations of Jesus we see around the world would certainly back up the sentiment that Jesus was considered to look like a white European. This is the most common depiction of Jesus but has no basis in history.

4 On the pernicious nature of "color blindness" and scriptural interpretation, see Kristopher Norris, "Race and Resurrection: Contesting Colorblind White Supremacy with Biblical Resources," *Theology Today* 77, no. 1 (2020): 33–46.

5 See chapter 5 for a discussion of notions of the ideal body among Jews.

6 See Mikeal C. Parsons, *Body and Character in Luke and Acts: The Subversion of Physiognomy in Early Christianity* (Waco, TX: Baylor University Press, 2011).

7 For example, Aristotle, *Gen. an.* 5.3.782b; Ps. Aristotle, *Prob.* 14.4.909a; and Polybius 4.20–21.

8 See discussion below in chapter 4 regarding character and its relationship to physicality.

9 Parsons, *Body and Character*, 126–41.

10 Esau McCaulley, *Reading While Black: African American Biblical Interpretation as an Exercise in Hope* (Downers Grove, IL: IVP, 2020), 96–97.

11 See David T. Adamo, *Africa and the Africans in the Old Testament* (San Francisco: International Scholars, 1998); and David T. Adamo, *Africa and Africans in the New Testament* (Lanham, MD: University Press of America, 2006).

12 I use the term *childship* instead of *sonship*, which is the more common term. To be more inclusive, I use the neutral term *child* to refer to our status as male and female children of God.

13 We must remember that the church in Acts is majority Jewish. It was only after the conversion of the Ethiopian in Acts 8 that non-Jews were sought out.

14 Ps. Aristotle, *Prob.* 10.66.

15 Appian, *Bell. civ.* 4.17.134.

16 Martin Luther King Jr., *Where Do We Go from Here: Chaos or Community?* (Boston: Beacon, 1968).

17 It bears mentioning that in the ancient world, there is no such thing as race as moderns view it. Nor is there such a thing as ethnicity, for that matter. See Eric Barreto, "Ethnic Negotiations: The Function of Race and Ethnicity in Acts 16" (PhD diss., Emory University, 2010). I only use the word *race* for heuristic purposes to say that when one group of ancients speaks against another group, they had in mind, in many cases, more than just geographic origin and language. We will see that physiognomy is in view in much of the caustic speech used by ancient thinkers. They are thinking of origin, skin color, culture, and so on. These are all, in many ways, involved in racialized thinking today. The language itself is not precise for what the ancients believed, but it at least allows us to engage them, though we will need to nuance it. For another framework for how the ancients perceived racial thinking, see the concept of "racialism" used by Rodney S. Sadler, "Can a Cushite Change His Skin? Cushites, 'Racial Othering,' and the Hebrew Bible," *Interpretation* 10, no. 6 (2006): 386–403.

18 If this were so, then there would not be different rules for Jews and gentiles. Yes, they are supposed to sit at the same table. But Jews are allowed to embrace and practice circumcision, while Paul proclaims a curse for gentiles who do the same (Gal 3:10).

CHAPTER 2: DIVINE CHILDSHIP AND ITS
RELEVANCE TO BLACK LIVES IN LUKE/ACTS

1 Here I follow Parsons and Pervo, who believe Luke and Acts were not a two-volume set, but I hold to the view that Luke provides similar narratological and theological paradigms in both works. For the prevailing view that Luke intended Luke and Acts to be Luke-Acts, see Henry J. Cadbury, *The Making of Luke-Acts*, 2nd ed. (Peabody, MA: Hendrickson, 1958). For the view I am taking, see Mikeal C. Parsons and Richard I. Pervo, *Rethinking the Unity of Luke and Acts* (Minneapolis: Fortress, 1993). Following their argument, I speak of Luke/Acts instead of Luke-Acts.

2 Each reference provides the citation of the comments first on Luke 6:35 and then on 20:36. Joel B. Green, *The Gospel of Luke* (Grand Rapids, MI: Eerdmans, 1997), 274–75, 720–21; François Bovon, *Luke 1: A Commentary on Luke 1:1–9:50*, trans. Christine M. Thomas (Minneapolis: Fortress, 2002), 231; François Bovon, *Luke 3: A Commentary on the Gospel of Luke 19:28–24:53* (Minneapolis: Fortress, 2012), 70–71; F. Godet, *A Commentary on the Gospel of St. Luke*, trans. E. W. Shalders and M. D. Cusin (New York: I. K. Funk, 1881), 208, 437; P. M.-J. Lagrange, *Évangile selon Saint Luc* (Paris: J. Gabalda et Cie, 1948), 197, 515–16; A. Plummer, *A Critical and Exegetical Commentary on the Gospel according to Saint Luke*, 5th ed., ICC (London: T&T Clark, 1898), 189, 469–70; Craig A. Evans, *Luke* (Peabody, MA: Hendrickson, 1990). Evans does not comment on divine childship language in 6:35 but does comment on 20:36 (see Evans, 349). I. H. Marshall, *The Gospel of Luke: A Commentary on the Greek Text*, 1st ed., NICGT (Grand Rapids, MI: Eerdmans, 1978), 263–65, 741; John Nolland, *Luke 1–9:5*, WBC 35A (Dallas: Word Books, 1989), 299–300, 965–66; Darrell Bock, *Luke: 1–9:50* (Grand Rapids, MI: Baker Academic, 1994), 1:602–3; Darrell Bock, *Luke: 9:51–24:53* (Grand Rapids, MI: Baker Academic, 1996), 2:1624; William Arndt, *The Gospel of St. Luke* (St. Louis, MO: Concordia, 1956), 195, 411; John T. Carroll, *Luke: A Commentary* (Louisville, KY: Westminster John Knox, 2012), 153–54, 407; Craig F. Evans, *Saint Luke* (London: SCM, 2008), 336, 717–18; Norval Geldenhuys, *Commentary on the Gospel of Luke* (London: Marshall, Morgan &

Scott, 1952), 213, 513; Josef Ernst, *Das Evangelium nach Lukas* (Regensburg, Germany: Friedrich Pustet, 1993), 228, 545–46; Joseph A. Fitzmyer, *The Gospel according to Luke (I–IX): Introduction, Translation, and Notes*, AB 28 (Garden City, NY: Doubleday, 1981), 640; Joseph A. Fitzmyer, *The Gospel according to Luke (X–XXIV): Introduction, Translation, and Notes*, AB 28 (Garden City, NY: Doubleday, 1985), 1306; Stephanie B. Crowder, "The Gospel of Luke," in *True to Our Native Land: An African American New Testament Commentary*, ed. Brian K. Blount (Minneapolis: Fortress, 2007), 166; James R. Edwards, *The Gospel according to Luke* (Grand Rapids, MI: Eerdmans, 2015), 183, 470–71; Mikeal C. Parsons, *Luke*, Paideia Commentaries on the New Testament (Grand Rapids, MI: Baker Academic, 2015), 111, 296–97; Luke Timothy Johnson, *The Gospel of Luke* (Collegeville, MN: Liturgical, 1991), 109, 112, 313–14; David Tiede, *Luke* (Minneapolis: Augsburg, 1988), 144, 348–49; Eduard Schweizer, *The Good News according to Luke*, trans. David Green (Atlanta, GA: John Knox, 1984), 80–81, 307; William Manson, *The Gospel of Luke* (London: Harper and Brothers, 1930), 70, 225–26; Robert H. Stein, *Luke*, New American Standard Commentary 24 (Nashville, TN: Broadman & Holman, 1992), 209, 503; A. R. C. Leaney, *A Commentary on the Gospel of St. Luke*, 2nd ed. (London: Adam, Charles & Black, 1966), 138, 252–53. Frederick Danker, *A Commentary on the Gospel of Luke: Jesus and the New Age* (Philadelphia: Fortress, 1988), 149, 322–23, is an outlier in that he does give significant weight to divine childship in his commentary. He argues that salvation regards the return of God's children to the "the Parent."

3 This is especially so if we follow a synchronic reading of Genesis 1–10. Though in Genesis, no human is explicitly called God's child—although what looks to be heavenly beings are in Genesis 6:2, 4—within the (ancient Near East) ANE, humans would have been understood as God's children, since they were made in God's image. This may explain why Paul could so easily refer to Jesus as both the image of God and God's Son (2 Cor 4:4; Rom 8:29). What is explicit in Paul seems to be implicit in Luke's narrative portrayal of the story of Jesus and the church. Jesus is known by Luke as the child of God's image, who is referred to as God's Son (Luke 3:38).

4 See, for example, Susan Eastman, "Whose Apocalypse? The Identity of the Sons of God in Romans 8:19," *JBL* 121, no. 2 (2002): 263–77. For an Old Testament treatment, see Werner Schlißke, *Gottessöhne und Gottessohn im alten Testament* (Berlin: Kohlhammer, 1973). Adela Collins offers a general treatment of divine childship language for Christological purposes in reference to Mark from both Greco-Roman and Jewish perspectives in the following: Adela Y. Collins, "Mark and His Readers: The Son of God among Jews," *HTR* 93, no. 4 (1999): 393–408; and Adela Y. Collins, "Mark and His

Readers: The Son of God among Greeks and Romans," *HTR* 93, no. 2 (2000): 85–100.

5   Brendan Byrne, *Sons of God, Seed of Abraham: A Study of the Idea of Sonship of God of All Christians in Paul against the Jewish Background* (Rome: Biblical Institute, 1979). Byrne's categorization is an accurate rendering of how the language works in both the Hebrew Bible (HB) and the New Testament (NT).

6   Byrne, 39–40, suggests that Wisdom of Solomon discusses "son of God" language in a variety of ways seldom seen in Second Temple Literature. It is used in both heavenly and righteous senses.

7   Byrne, 213–21.

8   Crispin H. T. Fletcher-Louis, *Luke-Acts: Angels, Christology, and Soteriology*, WUNT (Tübingen, Germany: Mohr Siebeck, 1997), 78–89.

9   Fletcher-Louis has also written on the subject of the pertinence of the angelomorphic category at Qumran. See Crispin H. T. Fletcher-Louis, "Some Reflections on Angelomorphic Humanity Texts among the Dead Sea Scrolls," *DSD* 7, no. 3 (2000): 292–312; and Crispin H. T. Fletcher-Louis, *All the Glory of Adam: Liturgical Anthropology in the Dead Sea Scrolls* (Leiden: Brill, 2002).

10 Joachim Jeremias, "Ἀδάμ," *TDNT* 1:141–43.

11 M. D. Johnson, *The Purpose of Biblical Genealogies: With Special Reference to the Settings of the Genealogies of Jesus*, SNTSMS (Cambridge: Cambridge University Press, 1969), 233–35; Fitzmyer, *Luke (I–IX)*, 498.

12 Craig A. Evans, "Jesus and the Spirit: On the Origin and Ministry of the Second Son of God," in *Luke and Scripture: The Function of Sacred Tradition in Luke-Acts*, ed. Craig A. Evans and James A. Sanders (Minneapolis: Fortress, 1993), 26–45. I do not follow Evans's language. I prefer the notion that Jesus takes on an Adamic vocation. In this chapter, Evans presupposes the central thesis of Jerome Neyrey. Evans, 37. SJ, *The Passion according to Luke: A Redaction Study of Luke's Soteriology* (Eugene, OR: Wipf & Stock, 1985), 165–84. Neyrey answers many of the objections of Marshall Johnson, adapting the background material used by Joachim Jeremias to Luke in a more cogent fashion. But Evans suggests Neyrey's analysis leaves loose ends and is not undergirded with Luke's pneumatology, which Evans sees as the key to understanding the Adam/Christ typology in Luke. Evans, "Jesus and the Spirit," 38. Also, see Charles Talbert, *Reading Luke: A Literary and Theological Commentary on the Third Gospel* (New York: Crossroad, 1982), 46–47, who argues, "The genealogy of Jesus also alludes to Jesus as the second Adam. Like many Greco-Roman genealogies which traced a family back to a hero or a god, Luke's line of descent for Jesus runs through seventy-seven names to Adam and through him to God. . . . Just as Adam was Son of God, that is, a direct creation of God, so is Jesus Son of God, because he too is a direct creation of God (1:35). Read in this way the genealogy evokes

the concept of Jesus as the second Adam." Also, see Charles Talbert, *Reading Luke-Acts in Its Mediterranean Milieu*, NovT Sup (Leiden: Brill, 2003), 99, for similar arguments in defense of this typology.

13 Evans, "Jesus and the Spirit," 42.

14 Evans, 38–40.

15 Evans, 43.

16 Evans, 42–43. Though here he offers a description of Christology, anthropology, and missiology, not stated in these terms, he does not spell out extensively how these particular perspectives work in Luke and Acts.

17 Evans, 42.

18 See Life of Adam and Eve 37:1–3; 44:1–5, where the serpent bites Seth and is rebuked because he is "the image of God." The fact that Jesus gives his disciples "authority" to walk over serpents and scorpions (see Ps 91:13) without *ever* being hurt suggests a restoration of what Seth in this account lost.

19 Evans, "Jesus and the Spirit," 44.

20 Evans, 44, 45.

21 Michael Peppard, *The Son of God in the Roman World: Divine Sonship in Its Social and Political Context* (Oxford: Oxford University Press, 2014), 135. Also, see his earlier article: Michael Peppard, "Adopted and Begotten Sons of God: Paul and John on Divine Sonship," *CBQ* 73, no. 1 (2011): 92–110.

22 Peppard, *Son of God*, 146. For a similar perspective on divine sonship in Luke from a Greco-Roman perspective, see Michael Kochenash, "'Adam, Son of God' (Luke 3:38): Another Jesus-Augustus Parallel in Luke's Gospel," *NTS* 64 (2018): 307–25. He argues that the genealogy of Jesus parallels attempts to describe divine parentage for Augustus.

23 Clarice J. Martin, "A Chamberlain's Journey and the Challenge of Interpretation for Liberation," *Semeia* 47 (1989): 105–35.

24 F. D. Gealy, "Ethiopian Eunuch," *IDB* 1:177–78.

25 Nils Dahl, "Nations in the New Testament," in *New Testament Christianity for Africa and the World: Essays in Honor of Harry Sawyer*, ed. Mark E. Glaswell and Edward Fashole-Luke (London: SPCK, 1974), 62–63. Also, see Ernst Haenchen, *The Acts of the Apostles* (Philadelphia: Westminster, 1971), 314, who is puzzled by the significance of the story. He thinks its tension with Acts 10 completely diminishes its significance. Haenchen grounds his reasoning in the notion that Luke does not tell us if this man is a gentile or not. Thus, he says, "so much for the significance of the eunuch's conversion, in the context of Luke's history of the mission, as a stepping-stone between those of the Samaritans and the Gentiles." In other words, the story has no real worth in the overall narrative. Some scholars resolve this problem by asserting that Luke's chronology is flawed. They argue that this conversion actually comes after Peter

converts Cornelius but that Luke places it before Cornelius to complete the "Acts of Phillip." For this view, see Justo L. González, *Acts: The Gospel of the Spirit* (Maryknoll, NY: Orbis, 2001), 117–18.

26 See Carl R. Holladay, *Acts: A Commentary*, NTL (Louisville, KY: Westminster John Knox, 2016), 188–89; Craig Keener, *Acts: An Exegetical Commentary (3:1–14:28)* (Grand Rapids, MI: Baker Academic, 2013), 2:1538–65; and Mikeal C. Parsons, *Acts*, Paideia Commentaries on the New Testament (Grand Rapids, MI: Baker Academic, 2008), 119.

27 This is not to say that interpreters do not note key implications for his being an Ethiopian. For example, Mikeal C. Parsons, "The Ethiopian Eunuch Unhindered: Embodied Rhetoric in Acts 8," in *"A Temple Not Made with Hands": Essays in Honor of Naymond H. Keathley*, ed. Mikeal C. Parsons and Richard Walsh (Eugene, OR: Pickwick, 2018), 146–60; and Mikeal C. Parsons, *Luke: Storyteller, Interpreter, Evangelist* (Waco, TX: Baylor University Press, 2014), 95–108, explains that the word *eunuch* receives the most emphasis in the passage by usage. Also, see Brittany E. Wilson, "'Neither Male nor Female': The Ethiopian Eunuch in Acts 8.26–40," *NTS* 60, no. 3 (2014): 403–22; Brittany E. Wilson, *Unmanly Men: Refigurations of Masculinity in Luke-Acts* (New York: Oxford University Press, 2015); and H. Moxnes and M. B. Kartzow, "Complex Identities: Ethnicity, Gender and Religion in the Story of the Ethiopian Eunuch (Acts 8:26–40)," *R&T* 17, nos. 3–4 (2010): 184–204; these also place heavy emphasis on the man's being a eunuch. Annette Weissenrieder, "Searching for the Middle Ground from the End of the Earth: The Embodiment of Space in Acts 8:26–40," *Neotestamentica* 48, no. 1 (2014): 115–61, attempts to give strong attention to his being an Ethiopian and a eunuch. Pervo, *Acts*, 221–24, offers an excursus on Ethiopians and Ethiopia. He considers this material to be mythical, mirroring romance novels that portrayed heroes who traveled to Ethiopia to meet the Candace. Similarly, he argues, Philip, by virtue of the Ethiopian's conversion, becomes a hero, a conqueror of Ethiopia. Strangely, he gives no attention to the significance of this man's being a black-skinned person. In his comments on the verses in particular, he only attends to the fact that he is a eunuch.

28 Demetrius K. Williams, "The Acts of the Apostles," in Blount, *True to Our Native Land*, 213–48; Abraham Smith, "'Do You Understand What You Are Reading?' A Literary Critical Reading of the Ethiopian (Kushite) Episode (Acts 8:26–40)," *Journal Interdenominational Theological Center* 22 (1994): 48–70.

29 Clarice J. Martin, "The Function of Acts 8:26–40 within the Narrative Structure of the Book of Acts: The Significance of the Eunuch's Provenance for Acts 1:8c" (PhD diss., Duke University, 1985). In her dissertation, Martin argues that the Ethiopian eunuch has "foreshadowing" functions in the narrative

(222). These two functions are to "inaugurate" (223) the gentile mission and exhibit its universality.

30 Martin, "Chamberlain's Journey," 120, 116. From another angle, Beverly Gaventa, *From Darkness to Light: Aspects of Conversion in the New Testament* (Philadelphia: Fortress, 1986), 98–107, argues that the Ethiopian is an ideal for conversion candidates in Acts (see Beverly Gaventa, *The Acts of the Apostles* [Nashville: Abingdon Press, 2003], 145.), setting the mold for what other converts should look like.

31 Martin, "Function," 226–27.

32 Martin, "Chamberlain's Journey," 117–19. A similar argument is made by Aaron Johnson in "The Blackness of Ethiopians: Classical Ethnography and Eusebius's Commentary on the Psalms," *HTR* 99, no. 2 (2006): 165–86. He argues that Eusebius sees the preaching of the gospel to the Ethiopians as symbolic of the gospel's reach to all of the world.

33 Cain H. Felder, *Race, Racism, and the Biblical Narratives* (Minneapolis: Fortress, 2002), 44–45. There is literary evidence for this inference. One of the major arguments of this dissertation is that Luke included this story precisely to subvert possible Greco-Roman prejudice against black-skinned people. Luke leaves in this story despite the tension it causes with Acts 10 and 15, which suggests that he did so intentionally.

34 Smith, "'Do You Understand?,'" 70.

35 See, for example, Boykin Sanders, "In Search of a Face for Simon of Cyrene," in *The Recovery of Black Presence: An Interdisciplinary Exploration: Essays in Honor of Dr. Charles B. Copher*, ed. Randall C. Bailey and Jacquelyn Grant (Nashville, TN: Abingdon, 1995), 51–63. Sanders proposes that Simon of Cyrene was a Black African. I do not specifically include Simon, but I find it important that Luke includes several African people in his narrative. Many of them may have been Black Africans, which suggests that Luke intends to dignify black-skinned people as part of the foundation of the church. If true, then, among other things, he is attempting to subvert concepts that would marginalize such people.

36 Martin, "Chamberlain's Journey," 111.

37 Gay L. Byron, *Symbolic Blackness and Ethnic Difference in Early Christian Literature* (London: Routledge, 2002), 28, 30, 2, 55–76.

38 Byron, 108–9.

39 Byron, 111–15.

40 Byron, 114–15 (italics in the original).

41 Eric Barreto, *Ethnic Negotiations: The Function of Race and Ethnicity in Acts 16* (Tübingen, Germany: Mohr Siebeck, 2010). My citations come from Barreto's dissertation "Ethnic Negotiations." See pages 17–64 for his view that the terms *race* and *ethnicity* are not anachronistic but applicable to the study of the NT.

He also uses the terms interchangeably. In his understanding, both terms are constructed and, in some ways, mythical.

42 Barreto, "Ethnic Negotiations," 14–15. Though he cites Parsons, *Body and Character*, Barreto's exclusion of Acts 8:26–40 means that he did not engage material ripe for a discussion of physiognomics in the taxonomy of ancient conceptions of ethnicity and race. Color semiotics play essential roles in ancient perceptions of people's ethnicities, as is clear in Pseudo-Aristotle and others. But this analysis plays no key role in Barreto's argumentation.

43 On Luke's universalism, see one of Barreto's recent works: Eric Barreto, "A Gospel on the Move: Practice, Proclamation, and Place in Luke-Acts," *Interpretation* 72, no. 2 (2018): 175–87.

44 Barreto, "Ethnic Negotiations," 245.

45 Parsons, *Body and Character*, 123–41.

46 Barreto, "Ethnic Negotiations," 5–6n6, cites Parsons but has no further engagement with his work. The same can be said for Gay Byron. He has no extensive engagement with her arguments about the polyvalent functions of blackness in polemical mode.

CHAPTER 3: GOD'S CHILDREN IN THE BIBLICAL WORLD

1 For divine childship in the HB, see H. Ringren, "אָב," *TDOT* 1:1–19; H. Haag, "בֵּן," *TDOT* 1:145–58; G. Quell, "Πατήρ: B: 'The Father Concept in the Old Testament,'" *TDNT* 5:959–74; H. Haag, "Sohn Gottes Im Alten Testament," *TQ* 154 (1974): 223–31; Schlißke, *Gottessöhne*; P. M.-J. Lagrange, "La Paternité de Dieu: Dans l'Ancien Testament," *RB* 5, no. 4 (1908): 481–99; H. Neil Richardson, "The Old Testament Background of Jesus as Begotten of God," *BRev* 2, no. 3 (1986); and Gerald Cooke, "The Israelite King as Son of God," *ZAW* 32, no. 2 (1961): 202–25. For general studies of uses of divine childship in the NT, see Gerhard Kittel, "Ἀββᾶ," *TDNT* 1:5–6; and G. Fohrer, "Υἱός," *TDNT* 8:347–53.

2 Recently, an edited volume of works on the meanings of divine childship in Second Temple Judaism and early Christianity called *Son of God: Divine Sonship in Jewish and Christian Antiquity* was produced. Many of these works are quite helpful and will be important throughout this chapter. But there is scant attention paid to Luke/Acts. These works include Reinhard Kratz, "Son of God and Son of Man: 4Q246 in the Light of the Book of Daniel," in *Son of God: Divine Sonship in Jewish and Christian Antiquity*, ed. Garrick V. Allen et al. (University Park, PA: Eisenbrauns, 2019), 9–27; George J. Brooke, "Son

of God, Sons of God, and Election in the Dead Sea Scrolls," in Allen, *Son of God*, 28–40; Garrick V. Allen, "Son of God in the Book of Revelation and Apocalyptic Literature," in Allen, *Son of God*, 53–71; N. T. Wright, "Son of God and Christian Origins," in Allen, *Son of God*, 118–34; Michael Peppard, "Son of God in Gentile Contexts (That Is, Almost Everywhere)," in Allen, *Son of God*, 135–57; and Menahem Kister, "Son(s) of God: Israel and Christ: A Study of Transformation, Adaptation, and Rivalry," in Allen, *Son of God*, 188–224.

3 Danker, *Luke*, 3. Also, see N. T. Wright, "Christian Origins," 124, who argues that early Christians went from "Jewish roots to pagan targets."

4 "בְּנֵי הָאֱלֹהִים." This Hebrew phrase is not the only way divine childship is expressed in Hebrew literature. More will be explored throughout this book.

5 Archie T. Wright, *The Origin of Evil Spirits: The Reception of Genesis 6:1–4 in Early Jewish Literature*, rev. ed. (Minneapolis: Fortress, 2015), 51–95, discusses the history of interpretation of this passage. He notes that some rabbinic Jews objected to interpreting these beings as angels. Some held that "son of God" meant descendant of Seth or a righteous person. Also, see P. S. Alexander, "The Targumim and Early Exegesis of 'Sons of God' in Genesis 6," *JJS* 23, no. 1 (1972): 60–71, for a thorough discussion of how this particular subject was treated in the Targumim.

6 Hosea 2:1 in the Masoretic Text (MT).

7 Here I disagree with Schlißke, *Gottessöhne*, 13–14, who argues there are four rather than three senses in which this language is used. Schlißke includes "Weisheit" (wisdom) as a manifestation of divine childship. I follow Byrne, *Sons of God*, 9.

8 Beyond those I treat in this chapter, there is a metaphorical use of divine childship language in Deuteronomy 1:31; 8:5; Proverbs 3:11; Malachi 1:6; 3:17. Byrne, *Sons of God*, 14.

9 Pharaoh was considered a god and son of a god, the son of Re. See James K. Hoffmeier, "Son of God," *BRev* 13, no. 3 (1997): 44. There are similarities with other traditions in ANE that suggest the gods were the fathers of the nations. See Byrne, *Sons of God*, 13, on this. He notes that Numbers 21:29 may suggest this tradition.

10 "בְּנִי בְכֹרִי יִשְׂרָאֵל."

11 The Hebrew is "בָּנִים אַתֶּם לַיהוָה אֱלֹהֵיכֶם."

12 See Byrne, *Sons of God*, 14.

13 Mark A. O'Brien, OP, *Restoring the Right Relationship: The Bible on Divine Righteousness* (Hindmarsh, South Australia: ATF Theology, 2014), 31, posits that the use of divine childship language confirms that YHWH will be faithful to Israel in the future despite their inevitable failures.

14 O'Brien, *Right Relationship*, 25, suggests the language of Deuteronomy 32:5 is "corrupt."

15 For various views of this verse—Deuteronomy 32:8—see Paul Winter, "Der Begriff, 'Söhne Gottes,' Im Moselied Dtn 32, 1–43," *ZAW* 67, no. 1 (1955): 40–48; Emanuel Tov, *Textual Criticism of the Hebrew Bible* (Minneapolis: Fortress, 1992), 269; Jan Joosten, "A Note on the Text of Deuteronomy xxxii 8," *VT* 57 (2007): 548–55; David E. Stevens, "Does Deuteronomy 32:8 Refer to 'Sons of God' or 'Sons of Israel'?," *BSac* 154, no. 614 (1997): 131–41; and Michael Heiser, "Deuteronomy 32:8 and the Sons of God," *BSac* 158, no. 629 (2001): 52–74.

16 In the Hebrew, it is בָּנָיו וּבְנֹתָיו.

17 The only other instance in the HB where the people of Israel are referred to as God's "sons" and "daughters" is in Isaiah 43:6.

18 To speak of age at this point would be the only time age would be mentioned in the entire discourse. Most likely, when God speaks of them as children, he is speaking of them as his children.

19 O'Brien, *Right Relationship*, 29–30, states that the MT here is also "corrupt" and that there are major differences between the Septuagint (LXX), the Samaritan Pentateuch, and other versions.

20 O'Brien, 30.

21 John D. W. Watts, *Isaiah 1–33*, WBC 24 (Dallas: Thomas Nelson, 2005), 24, argues that the language of "rebellion" is meant to emphasize the emotional tone of a father fighting with his children.

22 John D. W. Watts, *Isaiah 34–66*, WBC 25B (Dallas: Thomas Nelson, 2005), 902, says that this is a refutation of the charge of Isaiah 1:2.

23 Byrne, *Sons of God*, 14, calls this verse an example of the "father-creator" motif. This is repeated in Malachi 2:10.

24 Klaus Balzer, *Deutero-Isaiah: A Commentary on Isaiah 40–55*, trans. Margaret Kohl (Minneapolis: Fortress, 2001), 160.

25 Hans W. Wolff, *A Commentary on the Book of the Prophet Hosea*, trans. Gary Stansell, Hermeneia (Minneapolis: Fortress, 1974), 25, notes the tension in the language. He does not think that this more positive claim—that these will be God's children—is at odds, authorially, with the former claim, "You are not my people" (Hos 1:9). Instead, the disjunction is the result of a later editor who arranged the statements of Hosea for his purposes.

26 Wolff, 197. For Wolff's treatment of the theme of love in this section of Hosea, see 197–99.

27 The Hebrew term is יְרָחֵ֑ם.

28 For a combination of exile and exodus motifs in Jeremiah, see 16:14–15; 23:7–8; 31:32–36.

29 Kister, "Son(s) of God," 196, notes that this verse raises the question about when sonship is conferred upon Israel among the Qumran scrolls. The tension is raised about the status of sonship at Sinai and the lack of it in subsequent periods. The tension is resolved at Qumran by suggesting that the sonship for Israel in the eschatological period is a restoration of divine childship status.

30 This theme will become important in our discussion of the Ethiopian eunuch.

31 It is not clear whether this reference to "sons and daughters" is discussing "sons and daughters" of God or "sons and daughters" of Zion. See Abraham Sung-Ho Oh, *That You Would Rend the Heavens and Come Down! The Eschatological Theology of Third Isaiah* (Cambridge: James Clark, 2014), 46–89, on the universalizing nature of Isaiah 56:1–8 and issues of interpretation. He connects the reference to "sons and daughters" to Isaiah 54, where the children are the children of Zion. Watts, *Isaiah 34–66*, 820, connects this prophecy to the charge in Isaiah 1:2–3 regarding Israel's neglect of God as Father.

32 There are several places where heavenly beings are discussed in divine childship terms in Second Temple literature. See 1 Enoch 6:2; 13:8; 14:3; 39:1; 101:1; 1Qap Gen ar 2:5; 4:16; 5:3–4; 6:11; 1QS 4:22; 11:6; 1QH^a 11:22. They can also be called "sons of the gods" (1QH^a 23:10; 4Q381 frag. 16, 6–7) or "gods" (4QShirShabb^a 1:1). See also Wisdom of Solomon 5:5.

33 There seems to be some indication that the Davidic descendant is known as God's child in 4 Ezra 7:29; 13:32, 37, 52; 14:9. But this is disputed. Byrne, *Sons of God*, 59, argues that the translation should be "servant" rather than "son" in these instances. We cannot be sure, however, that the ancients would have made such a hard distinction between these concepts with use of the term παῖς and its cognates. See Michael E. Stone, *Fourth Ezra: A Commentary on the Book of Fourth Ezra*, Hermeneia (Minneapolis: Fortress, 1990), 207–8, who suggests it should be translated as "servant."

34 Unless otherwise indicated, all references to the pseudepigraphal works in this section are from *OTP* 1–2.

35 See also Sibylline Oracles 3:702–14; 5:200–205, which I do not address in this chapter.

36 See also Judith 9:4, which catalogs the punitive actions of God as Father on behalf of his people.

37 Written ca. first century CE.

38 J. Priest, "Testament of Moses: A New Translation and Introduction," in *OTP*, 1:920.

39 Written ca. early second century.

40 A. F. J. Klijn, "2 (Syriac Apocalypse of) Baruch: A New Translation and Introduction," in *OTP*, 1:616–17. This text, as well as 4 Ezra, would have been composed in part through oral performance according to Matthias Heinze, "'4 Ezra'

and '2 Baruch:' Literary Composition and Oral Performance in First Century Apocalyptic Literature," *JBL* 131, no. 1 (2012): 181–200.

41 Written in late second century BCE to third century CE.

42 George W. E. Nickelsburg Jr., *1 Enoch 2: A Commentary on the Book of 1 Enoch Chapters 37–82*, Hermeneia (Minneapolis: Fortress, 2012), 59–60, notes that there is an ongoing dispute about the dating of this document. The consensus, however, holds that this part of 1 Enoch is later than the Book of the Watchers.

43 Written ca. 100 CE.

44 Composed most likely after the destruction of the temple, ca. 100 CE, this text is essential in demonstrating the conceptions of the elect status of the people of Israel and how God determines their righteousness. See B. Metzger, "4 Ezra," *OTP* 1:520–21; see also Stone, *Fourth Ezra*, 9.

45 Stone, *Fourth Ezra*, 189, provides parallels in Second Temple texts and in the Jewish literature for use of "firstborn" language.

46 For example, 4 Ezra 3:20–27; 4:38–39.

47 This conception—that God's people are both his "first-born" and his "only child"—is similar in Psalm of Solomon 18:4. See 4 Ezra 5:23–27 for notions of how special Israel is and verse 40, which says that God has a "goal of love" for his people.

48 H. Anderson, "3 Maccabees: A New Translation and Introduction," in *OTP*, 2:510, dates this book from 217 BCE to 70 CE, based on the depiction of the Battle of Raphia and its discussion of the Jerusalem temple.

49 J. R. C. Cousland, "Reversal, Recidivism and Reward in 3 Maccabees: Structure and Purpose," *JSJ* 34, no. 1 (2003): 50, argues the motif of reversal, shown in divine protection, is the result of God's "fatherly benefactions" for Israel.

50 There are allusions in this story to Numbers 22:20–38 and 2 Kings 19:35.

51 Also see further confirmation of the point of this account in 3 Maccabees 7:6, where it is stated that God protects the Jews like a father protects his children.

52 See Byrne, *Sons of God*, 38–47, for discussion of Wisdom of Solomon. He notes that Wisdom of Solomon appears to have three main divisions (1–5, 6–9, 10–19) and has divine childship references in all three sections. For a recent treatment, see Jan Joosten, "Son of God in Wisdom 2:16–18: Between the Hebrew Bible and the New Testament," in Allen, *Son of God*, 41–52. He argues that divine childship language is meant to honor Jewish heroes rather than denote their righteousness or royalty. I disagree with his assessment, as I will demonstrate in this section.

53 See Liber antiquitatum biblicarum 32:10–17.

54 In Wisdom of Solomon 12:19, 21, divine childship is discussed in the context of repentance. The discipline of God's children is mentioned in 14:3. The

writer calls God "father" in 16:26. In 18:3–4, God gives substance to his children and punishment for wicked, in verse 13.

55 In this case, the Greek word is παῖδα (son/child/servant), which is more ambiguous than υἱός (son).

56 Although παῖς is an ambiguous Greek word and could mean "child" or "servant" (BDAG), in this context, the best translation is "child," given the other usage of divine childship language in this chapter. See Wright, "Christian Origins," 131, positing that the use of παῖς brings together the concepts of "servant and son" in the NT. Peter W. von Martitz, "Ὑιός, Ὑιοθεσία Α," *TDNT* 8:335, notes that in Homeric Greek, the words υἱός and παῖς were often interchangeable.

57 Here the Greek word is υἱός.

58 See Psalm 22:8.

59 Wisdom of Solomon 5 addresses this turn of events throughout but especially in verses 1–4.

60 Streeter S. Stuart, "The Exodus Tradition in Psalm 105 and the Wisdom of Solomon: Notable Similarities," *EQ* 90, no. 2 (2019): 135, considers the reason the impersonal language of "sons" is used is for transferability. In finding analogs between Wisdom of Solomon and Psalm 105, Stuart argues that generic use of titles in both is meant to allow the current, reflecting generation to claim God's protection as God's righteous as their forebearers. They are "sons" just like those in the wilderness.

61 Adam and Eve also used to eat "angels' food," as reported in Life of Adam and Eve 4:2. Also, see Joseph and Aseneth 16:14.

62 Wisdom of Solomon has another instance where the author uses divine childship language: when Solomon calls God's children his "sons and daughters" (9:7). Byrne, *Sons of God*, 43, argues the divine childship concept is least important in this section (chapters 6–9). The context, however, in which this statement is found speaks to the concept of human authority in the earth, how the king of Israel is related to this cosmic vocation among God's children, how the building of the temple is part of that vocation, and how that temple is patterned after the one "from the beginning" (9:1–8).

63 Written in the first century BCE.

64 Byrne, *Sons of God*, 36, says this is divine childship in the "eschatological reconstitution of Israel."

65 See Jubilees 2:20, which calls Israel God's "firstborn son" chosen from all of the nations to be God's sanctified child.

66 "Liber antiquitatum biblicarum" is the title used in scholarly discourse.

67 See also Atar Livneh, "The 'Beloved Sons' of Jubilees," *Journal of Ancient Judaism* 6, no. 1 (2015): 85–96, who looks at Shem, Isaac, and Jacob as "beloved sons" in this work.

68 See Jubilees 19:28–29, where Abraham prays for his grandchildren that Mastema will not rule over them. The reference to angels and spirits recognizing the sonship of Israel may suggest not only the good angels but also the evil angels.

69 See Psalm of Solomon 17:26–32 for the return from exile and the restoration of the kingdom theme. This restoration comes after David's "son" is said to arise in Israel. The whole of chapter 17 gives attention to God's promise to send the Davidic Messiah. See Nathan Johnson, "Rendering David a Servant in Psalm of Solomon 17.21," *JSP* 26, no. 3 (2017): 235–50, who offers an uncommon interpretation of 17:21. This verse is often translated as having Israel as "servant." Johnson believes David is the "servant" who reigns. On the similarities and differences between the messianic portrayal in Psalms of Solomon and the NT, see Brad Embry, "The Psalms of Solomon and the New Testament: Intertextuality and the Need for a Re-evaluation," *JSP* 13, no. 2 (2002): 99–136.

70 Byrne, *Sons of God*, 32, calls this a "nomistic" reading of divine childship. Kister, "Son(s) of God," 207–8, traces this conception of divine childship to Justin Martyr in his *Dialogue with Trypho*, in which there is also a claim that Israel's sonship had to be renewed.

71 In this book, there is more on the childship theme that cannot be covered in this chapter. There are variants between the Greek and the Hebrew versions, especially on the question of divine childship. Sometimes the Hebrew has uses of the language that the Greek does not and vice versa. See Sirach (Greek) 23:1, 4; 36:17; (Hebrew) 4:19; 44:23; 51:10. For more on this, see Byrne, *Sons of God*, 25–27.

72 Dating for the Dead Sea Scrolls ranges from the mid-third century BCE to the first century. See Eibert Tigchelaar, "The Dead Sea Scrolls," in *Early Judaism: A Comprehensive Overview*, ed. John J. Collins and Daniel C. Harlow (Grand Rapids, MI: Eerdmans, 2010), 207.

73 Note the use of both plural and singular for childship terminology. There is no semantic difference.

74 Unless otherwise noted, all English translations of Dead Sea Scroll (DSS) texts come from Florentino García-Martínez and Eibert Tigchelaar, eds., *The Dead Sea Scrolls Study Edition* (Grand Rapids, MI: Eerdmans, 2000).

75 Greg Sterling et al., "Philo," in Collins and Harlow, *Early Judaism*, 253, say Philo is said to have lived between 20 BCE and 50 CE. Steve Mason, James S. McLaren, and John M. G. Barclay, "Josephus," in Collins and Harlow, *Early Judaism*, 290–91, say Josephus lived between 37 CE and 100 CE. Both are essential witnesses for the varied possible ways Jews of the first century understood Jewish literature and culture within the Greco-Roman world. Philo, in particular, shows us the flavor of Alexandrian Judaism that was heavily influenced by allegorical readings of texts. For how these perspectives fit within

the wider scope of diasporic Judaism, see John M. G. Barclay, "Paul among Diaspora Jews: Anomaly or Apostate?," *JSNT* 60 (1995): 89–120.

76 In *Ant.* 1.73, Josephus angelizes the Genesis 6:2, 4, tradition.

77 See *Opif.* 74; and *Gig.* 60.

78 The Hebrew term is אָדָם. Although many Jewish traditions primarily refer to Adam, it is important to note that Genesis 1–3 describe Adam and Eve as essential to the flourishing of the human race.

79 Adam also seems to be in view in Job 15:7–8. Lester Grabbe, "'Better Watch Your Back, Adam': Another Adam and Eve Tradition in Second Temple Judaism," in *New Perspectives on 2 Enoch: No Longer Slavonic Only*, ed. Andrei Orlov and Gabriele Boccaccini (Leiden: Brill, 2012), 273–82, interprets Ezekiel 28, the warning against the king of Tyre, as a metadescription of Adam to critique the king of Tyre. In my view, the text seems to function better as a description of Satan.

80 Genesis 1:26–28; 2:7, 15–3:24; 5:1–5. There are all sorts of discussions surrounding the historical order and the sources of the various texts pertaining to Adam. It is generally agreed by critical scholars, for example, that Genesis 1, said to be the P source, is actually later than Genesis 2. Jon D. Levenson, *Creation and the Persistence of Evil: The Jewish Drama of Divine Omnipotence* (San Francisco: Harper & Row, 1988), 5–6. The task of this inquiry is to determine the various significances that Adam would have had for Luke's audience. We are not as concerned with a diachronic evaluation of development. Thus as I attempted in the previous chapter, I will attend more to themes than chronology within the various literary groupings.

81 *BDB*.

82 The Hebrew term is אָדָם.

83 Levenson, *Creation*, 3.

84 There are also questions about what YHWH means when he says, "Let us make [humanity] in our image" (Gen 1:26). Gordon J. Wenham, *Genesis 1–15*, WBC 1 (Dallas: Word Books, 1987), 28, relates that in the history of interpretation, Jewish readers like Philo and the rabbis have held to the notion of the heavenly court composed of God and the angels as an option. Recently, he notes, many scholars hold to the view that this language speaks of "self-deliberation." God is encouraging God's self to create humanity. Christian interpreters have taken this particular conception to include the Father, Son, and Holy Spirit.

85 The Hebrew is "בְּצֶלֶם אֱלֹהִים."

86 Nahum M. Sarna, *Genesis: The Traditional Hebrew Text with New JPS Translation* (Philadelphia: Jewish Publication Society, 1989), 12.

87 John H. Walton, *The Lost World of Adam and Eve: Genesis 2–3 and the Human Origins Debate* (Downers Grove, IL: IVP Academic, 2015), 89.

88 Walton, *Lost World*, 89.

89 Wenham, *Genesis*, 28; Levenson, *Creation*, 114–15.

90 Levenson, *Creation*, 114–15.

91 Claus Westermann, *Genesis 1–11: A Commentary*, trans. John J. Scullion (Minneapolis: Augsburg Fortress, 1984), 153, opposes this view, opting instead for the perspective that image language had to do with a special relationship with God. Wenham convincingly rebuts this argument, drawing on the ANE background and similar use of "image and likeness" language in Genesis 5. Wenham, *Genesis 1–15*, 95.

92 Levenson, *Creation*, 113–14; William P. Brown, *The Seven Pillars of Creation: The Bible, Science, and the Ecology of Wonder* (Oxford: Oxford University Press, 2010), 42–43.

93 Walton, *Lost World*, 42, 41. The imitation of God (*imitatio Dei*) is an essential part of the original conception of the *imago Dei*. Levenson argues that human participation in the Sabbath is another way humans represent the presence of God on earth, imitating his enthronement on the Sabbath. Levenson, *Creation*, 119.

94 Richard J. Middleton, *The Liberating Image: The Imago Dei in Genesis 1* (Grand Rapids, MI: Brazos, 2005), 88.

95 J. Daniel Kirk, *A Man Attested by God: The Human Jesus of the Synoptic Gospels* (Grand Rapids, MI: Eerdmans, 2016), 223.

96 Another valence of significance in this same vein for the image is God's care for God's image. Nahum M. Sarna suggests that in addition to being God's authority on earth, humans also have inherent worth because they are made in God's image: "In other words, the resemblance of man to God bespeaks the infinite worth of a human being and affirms the inviolability of the human person. The killing of any other creature, even wantonly, is not murder. Only a human being may be murdered." Sarna, *Genesis*, 12. Here Sarna refers to Genesis 9:5–6, where after the flood, God forbids the murder, not the killing, of animals on the grounds that people are made in the image of God. Humans are the only creatures made in God's image; their creation is the apex of God's creative action in the world. God allows other creatures to be killed for food, but humans are to protect each other, since they represent God. See Wenham, *Genesis*, 31–32.

97 There is a question of the cursedness of humanity in Genesis 9. Noah is clearly an Adamic figure. Noah is commanded to expand and multiply (Gen 9:1, 7). He and his children also have authority over the animals (Gen 9:2), and God swore never to curse the ground again (Gen 8:21). Without question, the Genesis writer frames Noah as an Adamic figure. For more discussion of Noah traditions, see Fletcher-Louis, *All the Glory*, 33–41.

98 See also Liber antiquitatum biblicarum 13:8–9 for this theme.

99 See Sirach 24:28–29, which says, "The first man did not know wisdom fully, nor will the last one fathom her. For her thoughts are more abundant than the sea, and her counsel deeper than the great abyss." This statement is a direct contradiction of Wisdom of Solomon 10:1–2. John R. Levison, *Portraits of Adam in Early Judaism: From 2 Sirach to 2 Baruch*, JSPSupp (Sheffield: Sheffield Academic Press, 1988), 44–45, contends that the *Tendenz* of the author in this passage is to exalt wisdom at the expense of Adam. But still, this claim may be an allusion to Adam.

100 4 Ezra 3:4–10; 4:30; 6:53–59; 7:11–13; 7:118; Jubilees 3:25; Liber antiquitatum biblicarum 37:3; 2 Baruch 4:3; 17:2; 18:2; 23:4–5; 48:46 (sin is increasing with those born from Adam); 54:15, 19 (Adam's sin affects all, but each person is held responsible for him or herself); 56:5; 2 Enoch 30:10–14; 31:1–8.

101 See Levenson, *Creation*, 96.

102 1QHᵃ 4:14–15; 1QS 4:22–23; CD 3:19; 4Q171 3:1–2. For more on Adam traditions in Qumran, see Nicholas Meyer, *Adam's Dust and Adam's Glory in the Hodayot and the Letters of Paul: Rethinking Anthropogony and Theology* (Boston: Brill, 2016).

103 This view was represented in texts outside of Qumran. See Testament of Levi 18:10–12. Christian texts like Revelation 22:2 perfectly illustrate the belief that within the Second Temple landscape, Jews believed that the end would be like the beginning.

104 Written around 200 BCE to 100 CE. See also Richard Bauckham, "Is 'High Human Christology' Sufficient? A Critical Response to J. R. Daniel Kirk's *A Man Attested by God*," *BBR* 27, no. 4 (2017): 511. M. D. Johnson, "Life of Adam and Eve: A New Translation and Introduction," in *OTP*, 2:252, argues the text is Jewish in origin, showing no real signs of Christian interpolation.

105 In Life of Adam and Eve 2:2, Eve refers to Adam as "lord." This is meant to be not because he is only Eve's overseer but because Adam is assigned to be lord over creation. As exalted figures, Adam and Eve were allowed to eat the food of angels but had to eat animals' food after their sin (4:1–3). Adam was the "image of God" in a sense that would have resonated well with the pagan context (12–15). They represented the presence of the Deity. Satan's deception of Adam and Eve is rationalized by Satan because he was forced to worship Adam. Michael demanded that Satan worship him, but he refused and was banished from paradise.

Also, in Life of Adam and Eve, Adam and Eve were on par with the angels in the beginning but lost their status because of sin. Later, their descendants will lament because of the evil that was brought upon them through their parents

(44:4). During Adam's death, the sun and the moon are darkened (46:1), signs of an apocalyptic occurrence.

Adam and Eve's failure in the garden, however, did not change the fact that glory still remained in them. Cain was illuminated (21:3), and Seth would still be able to wield the authority that Adam lost. Seth is still called the "image of God" by Eve when an animal bites him (37:1–3). Seth rebukes the animal (he says, "The Lord rebuke you"), calling it a "chaotic destroyer" and referring to himself as the "image of God" (39:1–3). The animal is allowed to attack him because of Adam and Eve's disobedience to God (38:1–3). The creature only responds to Seth, however, because he is the "image of God."

The antagonist of the narrative is Satan. After their expulsion from the garden, Adam asks Satan about his anger toward them because he thinks they have stolen his glory (11:1–3). Satan's answer (12–16) is that he felt slighted because he was made to worship God through Adam and Eve, the image of God.

But humanity's failure is not the end. Seth is able to partake of the "oil of life" (36:1–2). But Michael warns that Seth cannot take it until the last days, in the time of the resurrection (42:1). In that time, Adam "shall sit on the throne of him who overthrew him" (47:3).

Apocalypse of Moses 2:1 also refers to Adam as "lord." But human authority is lost because of the first humans' disobedience (10–13; 24:4). Seth was bitten by a creature who explains to Eve, when she was exasperated at the sight of a creature biting Seth, that her disobedience caused this violence. Seth is able to rebuke it, and it obeys because he is God's image. This document, however, does make clear that Eve is also made in the image of God (29:10), but she seems to not have the same authority as Seth.

The failure of Adam and Eve is explained as their attempt to take "glory" from the forbidden tree (18:1–6). The "glory" was not enough, however; in this version of the story, the serpent, being used by Satan (16:1), sprinkled covetousness on the fruit of the tree (19:1–3). Covetousness is explicated as the "origin of every sin" (19:3).

But like Life of Adam and Eve, there is a future for humanity beyond the great failure in the garden. Seth is able to obtain the divine oil, which he will be allowed to partake of in the resurrection (13:2–6). At that time, humans will be freed from sin because the evil heart will be removed (13:5). In this time, the serpent will be crushed (26:4), and humans will again have access to the tree of life (28:4).

106 Originally, the Greek here is "Ethiopians" (Αἰθίοψ).
107 For "father" language for Zeus in Greek, see Homer, *Il.* 2.371; 4.68; 5.426; 8.49; 11.182; 8.69; 10.154; Homer, *Od.* 1.28; 4.340; 5.7; 7.311; 12.63; 13.51; Hesiod, *Theog.* 457; Hesiod, *Op.* 169; Pindar, *Nem.* 5.33; Pindar, *Ol.*

1.57; 2.28; and Pliny, *Ep.* 1.7.1. For Latin texts, see Vergil, *Aen.* 1.60, 691; 3.251; Vergil, *Georg.* 1.121, 283, 328; Catullus, *Carm.* 64.21; and Ovid, *Metam.* 1.154. For a general discussion of "son of God" language in the NT, its origins, and its analogs, see von Martitz, "Υἱός, Υἱοθεσία," 334–40. It is on this work that Martin Hengel, *The Son of God: The Origin of Christology and the History of Jewish-Hellenistic Religion* (Philadelphia: Fortress, 1976), 24, bases his judgment against the relevance of Greek and Roman conceptions of sonship for discussion of the NT. He insists that the numerous passages where Zeus, for example, is known as father have no relationship with Jewish and Christian usage. He also argues against the relevance of the emperor for the discussion. Collins, "Greeks and Romans," 85–87, counters Hengel, noting that his earlier work documented Hellenism's unmistakable connection with Judaism in the first century. Thus there must have been, in the least, a way both Jewish and Greco-Roman hearers of the first Gospel would have connected their conception of divine childship with that which comes from Greco-Roman religiosity.

108 Homer, *Il.* 3.374–75.

109 Both Collins, "Greeks and Romans," 86, and Peppard, *Son of God*, 30, note the rarity of this language outside of Jewish and Christian use, save for the Roman emperor. N. T. Wright, *The Resurrection of the Son of God* (Minneapolis: Fortress, 2003), 724, argues that "son of God" language would immediately bring up the emperor as a close referent in the first-century context. See discussion below concerning the emperor.

110 Cited from W. E. L. Broad, *Alexander or Jesus? The Origin of the Title "Son of God"* (Eugene, OR: Pickwick, 2015), 9–10.

111 For deity reproduction in Greek religion, see Homer, *Il.* 3.374–75; 14.194–95; Homer, *Od.* 8.334; Hesiod, *Theog.* 1003.

112 Walter Burkert, *Greek Religion*, trans. John Raffan (Cambridge, MA: Harvard University Press, 1985), 203.

113 Emily Kearns, *Ancient Greek Religion: A Sourcebook* (West Sussex: Wiley-Blackwell, 2010), 50. Kearns notes that goddesses also sleep with mortal men. One famous instance is when Kalypso seduces and sleeps with Odysseus. Kearns, 50, 57 (Homer, *Od.* 5.118–32, 134–36).

114 Von Martitz, "Υἱός, Υἱοθεσία," 336.

115 Such is the case in terms of Heracles, who is reputed to have special powers, overcoming this- and otherworldly creatures like the Hydra. Hesiod, *Theog.* 309–35 (see Euripides, *Herc. fur.* 359). The hero Perseus is said to have killed the Gorgon Medusa (Pindar, *Pyth.* 12).

116 Cited from Kearns, *Greek Religion*, 18.

117 Burkert, *Greek Religion*, 203–7, argues that this cult was part of "chthonic," earthbound, god-worship among Greeks. He says that an essential difference

between the worship of the gods and the heroes was that the cult was "always confined to a specific locality: he acts in the vicinity of his grave for his family, group or city. The bond with the hero is dissolved by distance" (206).

118 Kearns, *Greek Religion*, 18.

119 Arrian, *Anab.* 3.3; Plutarch, *Alex.* 2.1; 5; Von Martitz, "Υἱός, Υἱοθεσία," 336.

120 Ory Amitay, *From Alexander to Jesus* (Berkeley: University of California Press, 2010), 9.

121 Peppard, *Son of God*, 70, argues that his divine childship indicated divine election to rule.

122 Adela Y. Collins and John J. Collins, *King and Messiah as Son of God: Divine, Human, and Angelic Messianic Figures in Biblical and Related Literature* (Grand Rapids, MI: Wm. B. Eerdmans, 2008), 50–53; Von Martitz, "Υἱός, Υἱοθεσία," 336–37.

123 Arrian, *Anab.* 3.3; Broad, *Alexander*, 32–34.

124 Collins and Collins, *King and Messiah*, 49–50, 50–51, 53.

125 Mary Beard, John North, and Simon Price, *Religions of Rome* (Cambridge: Cambridge University Press, 1998), 1:31.

126 Peppard, "Gentile Contexts," 136; Wright, *Resurrection*, 724.

127 If nothing else, it was well reported that Augustus came from divine parentage.

128 Cited from Peppard, 140. The source is *OGIS* 2.583, trans. Peppard.

129 Peppard, "Gentile Contexts," 136–37.

130 Peppard, *Son of God*, 43.

131 Ovid, *Metam.* 15.760; Suetonius, *Div. Aug.* 94.4; Cassius Dio, *Roman History* 45.1.2–3. Tacitus, *Ann.* 4.2.9, reports that Julius Caesar and Augustus both discussed their connections to Aeneas, probably in an effort to promote their supposed divine ancestry. For more on Caesar's claim, see Cassius Dio, *Roman History* 41.34.1. Tacitus, *Ann.* 15.74, says that there was a discussion to build a temple to Nero with public funding. Some took it to mean that Nero was about to die, since, in Tacitus's view, the Caesar was to be worshipped after death.

132 Peppard, *Son of God*, 48. Also, see Kochenash, "Jesus-Augustus," 307–25.

133 Peppard, *Son of God*, 66.

134 This question, in many cases focusing on Deuteronomy 32, is taken up by the rabbis (*b. B. Bat.* 10a; *b. Kid 36a*; *Sipre* on Deut 32:19). The best way to understand this line of reasoning is that status as God's children can be lost. Even if one is a member of Israel, the nation that is God's child, disobedience to the law causes one to lose the status as a child of God.

135 Against Brooke, "Election," 39, who suggests the "begetting" language at Qumran is metaphorical. It is meant to signify "election." The birthing language does, in the case of Deuteronomy 32, for example, demonstrate the notion that

the people of Israel have been chosen by God as his special people. But as I will demonstrate in the next chapter, the birthing language is linked to the notion that Israel is in right relationship with the real creator, the one who birthed Adam and, thereby, all human creatures. The divine childship language is not just metaphor.

136 Terence L. Donaldson, *Judaism and the Gentiles: Jewish Patterns of Universalism (to 135 CE)* (Waco, TX: Baylor University Press, 2007), 499–501.

137 For example, Genesis 12:3; Isaiah 2:2–4; 11:10–12; 49:6; 55:5; 60:3; Jeremiah 3:17; Micah 4:2; Zechariah 14:16.

Chapter 4: Jesus and the Salvation of God's Children

1 See Kochenash, "Jesus-Augustus," 307–25, who argues that Luke has written this genealogy under the influence of the tradition of Augustus and other Roman rulers to define a divine lineage for themselves. This is not what Luke is doing, in my view. Luke explores the notion of Adam as God's child in a different way and extends the divine childship umbrella to all humans in Paul's Areopagus speech in Acts 17:24–31. Luke is attempting to demonstrate that all humans are made in the image of God.

2 My translation of the Greek text is "Καὶ αὐτὸς ἦν Ἰησοῦς ἀρχόμενος ὡσεὶ ἐτῶν τριάκοντα, ὢν υἱός, ὡς ἐνομίζετο, Ἰωσὴφ τοῦ Ἡλί." See Green, *Luke*, 189, who interprets this passage to suggest that Jesus is "the apparent son of Joseph." Luke's audience (e.g., 1:32, 35; 2:49) knows better: Jesus is God's Son.

3 In the Greek, this is "τοῦ Ἀδὰμ τοῦ θεοῦ."

4 Martin M. Culy, Mikeal C. Parsons, and Joshua J. Stigall, *Luke: A Handbook on the Greek Text*, BHGHT (Waco, TX: Baylor University Press, 2010), 120.

5 I will discuss below why I think Luke's Jesus demonstrates a divine childship that takes and transcends other previous notions we have explored. Jesus, in my view, is a divine Son. He is not just a heavenly Son as the angels are described in Jewish literature. Jesus is the Son of God, YHWH. Though he does not argue for Jesus's divine position as Son, Rodney T. Hood, "The Genealogies of Jesus," in *Early Christian Origins: Studies in Honor of Harold R. Willoughby*, ed. Allen Wikgren (Chicago: Quadrangle, 1961), 1–15, argues that the genealogy is not simply to announce Jesus's universal connection to humankind. It establishes that Jesus is "and had been all along" the Son of God (14).

6 Adam is likely alluded to in Mark's temptation narrative. I have already discussed this interpretation given by Joachim Jeremias in his *TDNT* article on Adam: "Ἀδάμ," *TDNT* 1:141–43. See also Dale C. Allison Jr., "Behind the

Temptations of Jesus: Q4:1–13 and Mark 1:12–13," in *Authenticating the Activities of Jesus*, ed. Bruce D. Chilton and Craig A. Evans (Leiden: Brill, 1999), 195–213; and Brandon Crowe, *The Last Adam: A Theology of the Obedient Life of Jesus in the Gospels* (Grand Rapids, MI: Baker Academic, 2017), 26–28.

7 See Joel W. Parkman, "Adam Christological Motifs in the Synoptic Traditions" (PhD diss., Baylor University, 1994). Parkman argues that two of the most prominent titles of Jesus—"son of man" (133–61; based on Dan 7:13–14) and "son of God" (162–89; based on Gen 5:1–3)—both speak to Jesus's Adamic representation. Parkman argues that early Christology, broadly understood in the NT, relied heavily on the Adam motif, which was founded on the theme often seen in traditions of Jesus concerning the Endzeit matching the Urzeit. Crowe, *Last Adam*, 37–53, argues that the four Gospels portray Jesus as the "son of man" to establish an Adamic typology. His argument, based in part on Daniel 7:13–14, 18, is that the "son of man" figure in canonical use builds on "royal imagery" and resounds with Genesis 1–2 and Psalm 8, which also speaks of humans in royal terms (39–40). Crowe states that Jesus, as "son of man," demonstrates the "royal dominion of humanity" (43). He goes further to exhibit this fulfillment through Jesus's work, suffering, and coming glory (43–53).

8 The Mark narrative provides an Adam allusion at best. If we can accept the Adam-Christ connection there, it should be even more acceptable in Luke, especially if Luke's audience knows Mark already. Parsons, *Luke*, 71.

9 Crowe, *Last Adam*, 34–35, argues the phrase βίβλος γενέσεως only appears in Matthew 1:1; Genesis 2:4; 5:1. It is more than likely that Matthew's genealogy is intent on casting Jesus as an Adamic figure.

10 See Miryam T. Brand, *Evil Within and Without: The Source of Sin and Its Nature as Portrayed in Second Temple Literature*, JAJSup (Göttingen, Germany: Vandenhoeck & Ruprecht, 2013), who notes that Adam is certainly not to blame within Second Temple literature for all of human ills. Also, see John J. Collins, "The Origin of Evil in Apocalyptic Literature and the Dead Sea Scrolls," in *Congress Volume Paris 1992*, ed. J. A. Emerton, VTSup 61 (Leiden: Brill, 1995), 25–38; Philip R. Davies, "The Origin of Evil in Ancient Judaism," *ABR* 50 (2002): 43–54; and Loren T. Stuckenbruck, "The Book of Jubilees and the Origin of Evil," in *Enoch and the Mosaic Torah: The Evidence of Jubilees*, ed. Gabriele Boccaccini et al. (Grand Rapids, MI: Wm. B. Eerdmans, 2009), 294–308. For discussions in rabbinic Judaism, see Johann Cook, "The Origin of the Tradition of the of the יצר הטוב and יצר הרע," *JSJ* 38 (2007): 80–91.

11 Fitzmyer, *Luke (I–IX)*, 498. See Carroll, *Luke*, 99; Sharon Ringe, *Luke* (Louisville, KY: Westminster John Knox, 1995), 57.

12 See also Crowder, "Luke," 163.

13 Also, see Kirk, *Man Attested*, 44–77, 218–37, for discussion of an Adam-based framework for an "idealized humanity" within which Jesus's Christology makes the most sense. Kirk believes that Jesus's Christology is properly understood as an eschatological Adam. Like Adam, he would have been thought of as Son of God, king, and priest. It is not necessary, in his view, to think that Luke, or Matthew or Mark, portrayed Jesus as a divine figure in his narrative. I respond to Kirk more fully below. But to be sure, it is important to note that to say that Jesus is an Adamic figure for Paul did not impede him from also claiming that Jesus is a "life-giving Spirit" (1 Cor 15:45). If this is so, it is possible for the gospel writers to characterize Jesus using human figures and mean, at the same time, that he was God in the flesh.

14 See Joel Marcus, "Son of Man as Son of Adam," *RB* 110, no. 1 (2003): 38–61; and Joel Marcus, "Son of Man as Son of Adam: Part II: Exegesis (Continued)," *RB* 110, no. 3 (2003): 370–86, who proposes that "Son of Man" means "Son of Adam." He interprets the Synoptic references to the "Son of Man" traditions to connote that Jesus is Adam's son who is meant to restore the fortunes of Adam in the eschaton.

15 Evans, "Jesus and the Spirit," 36.

16 This argument relies on Philo's discussion of Adam, which requires a bit of analysis. See Evans, "Jesus and the Spirit," 40–42. Philo's treatment of Adam is varied and complex. For more on this, see Levison, *Portraits*, 63–88; and Marcus, "Son of Man as Son of Adam," 50–51. Philo describes Adam as God's child through his unique creation through wind, being made an immortal (*Virt.* 1.203–4). Adam's immortality was lost through his sin (*Virt.* 1.205). Adam, however, was God's "firstborn" (*Conf.* 63), and the children of God, like Adam, are meant to be understood in light of the "image of God," who can also be called God's "firstborn son" (*Conf.* 145–47). According to Philo, true children of God can be called Adamic.

A further portrayal of Adam in Philo asserts that there were two Adams (*QG* 1.4). Philo says there was a corporeal Adam and a spiritual Adam. Evans perceives that this view of Adam was picked up by Paul in 1 Corinthians 15, the Adam from the earth and the one from heaven (1 Cor 15:45–47). Evans, "Jesus and the Spirit," 41, is helpful for this point. It could be that Luke holds to this same two-Adam conception. Both exist because of God's Spirit, and both are ideal humans, but Adam failed and Jesus, as Adam's son and redeemer, fixes Adam's failure. See Evans, "Jesus and the Spirit," 41–42, 44. See also Talbert, *Reading Luke-Acts*, 99: "Whereas those who came before were disobedient, Jesus as second Adam and as the true culmination of Israel's heritage is obedient. He has reversed Adam's fall and Israel's sin."

The connection between Philo's interpretation and Luke's treatment of Adam is not obvious. Luke is not attempting Philo's sophisticated allegorical reading. Philo's argument, however, expresses that Jews in the first century are thinking of more than one Adam, even though Philo does not seem to be thinking of it eschatologically or apocalyptically as Paul would. But Acts 17:26–31 confirms that Luke is thinking of Jesus as a kind of Adam, the beginning of a new order.

17 Talbert, *Reading Luke*, 46–47.

18 Petr Pokorný, *Theologie der Lukanischen Schriften* (Göttingen, Germany: Vandenhoeck & Ruprecht, 1998), 115.

19 Pokorný, 113. He argues, "neuen Menschen und den wahren Adam nach dem Bilde Gottes." See Jacques Dupont, OSB, *The Salvation of the Gentiles: Studies in the Acts of the Apostles*, trans. John Keating, SJ (New York: Paulist, 1979), 32, who says that Luke's narrative includes two Adams.

20 Parsons and Pervo, *Luke and Acts*, 105.

21 Here Parsons and Pervo follow Hans Conzelmann, *The Theology of St. Luke*, trans. Geoffrey Burswell (New York: Harper & Row, 1961), 227n2, the English translation of Hans Conzelmann, *Der Mitte der Zeit: Studien zur Theologie des Lukas* (Tübingen, Germany: Mohr Siebeck, 1954).

22 Parsons and Pervo, *Luke and Acts*, 104.

23 Parsons and Pervo, 104.

24 This saying in Luke 3:7, with use of the term *vipers* to indicate sinfulness, also appears in Matthew 3:7, but Matthew reports John saying this "when he saw many Pharisees and Sadducees" coming to the Jordan. Luke expands it to the "multitude" (my translation).

25 Parsons and Pervo, *Luke and Acts*, 103, contend—following Schuyler Brown, *Apostasy and Perseverance in the Theology of Luke* (Rome: Pontifical Biblical Institute, 1969), 121—that Luke has erased the notion of the cosmic power of sin and its effect on anthropology. Acts 26:18 undermines this notion. Evidence against this notion is also found not only in Jesus's fight with Satan in Luke 4:1–13 but also in the parable of the sower, where Satan inhibits the hearing of the word (Luke 8:12). Additionally, Satan has chosen to attack Jesus through Judas (22:3) and attack his disciples (22:31–32) through their apostasy, their sinful unbelief. The Sanhedrin is certainly under the power of Satan when they arrest Jesus (22:53). Jesus must give the disciples power, through the Spirit, to overcome this cosmic evil (10:17–20; Acts 1:8). Thus we must conclude, against Parsons and Pervo, that the effects of cosmic evil are inherently anthropological just as much as its counter is.

26 Bovon, *Luke 3*, 70.

27 In this passage, it must be noted that Luke places emphasis on the "times." This most probably is a reference to the "ages" in Luke 20:34–35 (see Luke 12:54–56; 17:22; 18:30; Acts 1:7; 3:19, 21).

28 See Evans, "Jesus and the Spirit," 43, for this insight. See Testament of Dan 5:9–13, which offers a similar messianic prediction to cause the return to Eden. But there is no mention of Adam. Unlike Testament of Levi, the redeemed are not called God's children (v. 12).

29 This text (Testament of Levi 18:10–12) is also important for confirmation of the disciples as children of God. Testament of Levi says that as God's children receive the "spirit of holiness" (v. 11), "Beliar" will be bound by the Messiah (v. 12), and the children will be given powers over evil spirits (v. 12), which is highlighted in Luke 10:17–20. Luke's narrative suggests that Jesus and his people restore Adam to his former glory and restore the fortunes of the people of God as God's children. See Evans, "Jesus and the Spirit," 42–43.

30 Evans, 43. This episode on the cross is solely in Luke.

31 Danker, *Luke*, 96–97. He claims that Jesus can consider his own sonship with God through Adam on "legal grounds."

32 Green, *Luke*, 190.

33 Peppard, *Son of God*, 134.

34 The Greek is "ἄπιστος καὶ διεστραμμένη."

35 See Peter's speech in Acts 2:40, interestingly, also alludes to this text, "σώθητε ἀπὸ τῆς γενεᾶς τῆς σκολιᾶς ταύτης."

36 Danker, *Luke*, 96–97.

37 For a recent attempt to map Luke's Christology, see Nina Henrichs-Tarasenkova, *Luke's Christology of Divine Identity*, LNTS (London: Bloomsbury T&T Clark, 2016). She finds evidence for Richard Bauckham's theory that Luke would have considered Jesus to share God's unique identity. See also Kirk, *Man Attested*.

38 Again, Malcolm Wren, "Sonship in Luke: The Advantage of a Literary Approach," *Scottish Journal of Theology* 37, no. 3 (1984): 310, argues that Jesus's status was key for his own Christology. This is against James D. G. Dunn, *Christology in the Making: A New Testament Inquiry into the Origins of the Doctrine of the Incarnation*, 2nd ed. (Grand Rapids, MI: Wm. B. Eerdmans, 1996), 50, who argues that Jesus's sonship plays no major role in Luke's Christology. As I will demonstrate, the evidence points in quite the contrary direction.

39 In Acts, Luke reports that Jesus is referred to as παῖς (3:13, 26; 4:27, 30). This language could signify divine childship. Wright, "Son of God," 131. Wright believes that Jesus is both a "son" and a "servant" of YHWH.

40 Conzelmann, *Theology*, famously argues against this claim (24, 48–49). He thinks the birth narrative has no bearing on Luke's theology (172). Pace Conzelmann, on the essentiality of the birth narrative for Lukan theology, see Paul S.

Minear, "Luke's Use of the Birth Stories," in *Studies in Luke-Acts*, ed. Leander Keck and J. Louis Martyn (Philadelphia: Fortress, 1980), 130.

41 Matthew's infancy narrative (Matt 1–2) indirectly implies Jesus is God's Son, since he is virgin born (1:20). But there is no explicit reference, as there is in Luke, to Jesus being God's Son. Luke says it twice in the birth narrative.

42 Most often in Luke, humans do not refer to Jesus as "Son of God." Motivated by, most likely, demonic forces, there are instances where Jesus is called "Son of God" by humans (Luke 4:41; 22:70; see also 8:28). Paul is the only human, again, motivated by the Spirit to declare that Jesus is "Son of God." All of the other instances are from God or the devil.

43 Mark L. Strauss, *The Davidic Messiah in Luke-Acts: The Promise and Its Fulfillment in Lukan Christology*, JSNTSup 110 (Sheffield: Sheffield Academic Press, 1995), explores and emphasizes Lukan Christology as an outworking of "Luke's 'proclamation from prophecy and pattern' motif" (15). In this way, Jesus fulfills the promises God made to David. Conzelmann, *Theology*, 75 (also 188–89), resists a Davidic sense, however, to the triumphal entry and other messianic moments, arguing that Luke displays a "non-political Christology." Danker, *Luke*, 362, contends that Luke's Christology is "independent of Davidic messianism." Luke's Christology, on the contrary, takes, adapts, and transcends the notion of Jesus's Davidic sonship. Jesus's comments, for example, in Luke 20:41–44 about how the Messiah could be David's son was not meant to deny his fulfillment of the promises in the Psalms. Rather, it was meant to suggest that those promises are expanded through Jesus. See Luke Timothy Johnson, *Contested Issues in Christian Origins and the New Testament: Collected Essays* (Leiden: Brill, 2013), 157–61, advocating a "prophetic" image that, he believes, incorporates Davidic messianism.

44 Raymond E. Brown, *The Birth of the Messiah: A Commentary on the Infancy Narratives in Matthew and Luke* (Garden City, NY: Image, 1979), 290–92.

45 Simon Gathercole, *The Preexistent Son: Recovering the Christologies of Matthew, Mark, and Luke* (Grand Rapids, MI: Wm. B. Eerdmans, 2006), 282. Also, see Marshall, *Luke*, 71.

46 Robert Tannehill, "The Story of Israel within the Lukan Narrative," in *Jesus and the Heritage of Israel: Luke's Narrative Claim upon Israel's Legacy*, ed. David P. Moessner (Harrisburg, PA: Trinity, 2000), 325–39, states that promise and fulfillment are crucial elements in the infancy narrative.

47 Gathercole, *Preexistent*, 281–282. Joel B. Green, *The Theology of the Gospel of Luke* (Cambridge: Cambridge University Press, 1995), 55, says Luke has moved "beyond a functional understanding of Jesus' sonship"; Jesus is God's Son when he is conceived, not because of the Davidic throne.

48 Brown, *Birth*, 290.

49 Pokorný, *Lukanischen*, 112; Ernst, *Lukas*, 61–62, both assert that a Hellenistic Jewish background explains Luke's inclusion of a virgin birth story. It is most likely that Luke is trying to demonstrate, like Matthew, that Jesus is born of a virgin to fulfill Isaiah 7:14. But it would not be missed on Luke that Jesus's virgin birth would have appealed to Hellenistic sensibilities.

50 Jesus's entrance into the world without a human father, born by way of God's wind, already alluded to Adam. In this sense, Jesus is more than mere human—mere humans are corrupt and sinful. Jesus is the precorruption, ideal human, like Adam was.

51 Crowe, *Last Adam*, 98, notes that Deuteronomy 14:1–2 and Exodus 13:2 require holiness of God's children. Jesus's holiness is manifested in a greater way because he is born holy. His execution of the covenant is not the primary operative mechanism for his sacral nature.

52 Bock, *Luke*, 1:124; Parsons, *Luke*, 39.

53 See Kirk, *Man Attested*, 399, who interprets this passage as illustrating a human Jesus. He is exceptional but still human in the portrayal.

54 C. Kavin Rowe, *Early Narrative Christology*, ZNW (New York: Walter de Gruyter, 2006), 35–49. Rowe observes that Luke uses "Lord" language seamlessly without giving exclusionary distinctions between God the Father as Lord and Jesus the Son as Lord. Jesus is the Son and Lord from birth. Rowe goes on to show the consistency of this view with Acts. C. Kavin Rowe, "Acts 2.36 and the Continuity of Lukan Christology," *NTS* 53 (2007): 37–56. Against this view, see C. F. D. Moule, "The Christology of Acts," in Keck and Martyn, *Studies in Luke-Acts*, 159–85, proposing that Luke has two different Christologies between the Gospel and Acts. In Moule's view, Luke reads back into the Gospel what he thinks about Jesus in Acts, though who Jesus is in Acts is not who he is prior to his resurrection in Luke.

55 Henrichs-Tarasenkova, *Divine Identity*, 189.

56 I. H. Marshall, "The Christology of Luke's Gospel and Acts," in *Contours of Christology in the New Testament*, ed. Richard N. Longenecker (Grand Rapids, MI: Wm. B. Eerdmans, 2005), 122–47, 123. Furthermore, Jesus's birth through a human mother does not preclude that he could be divine; Paul could say something similar (Gal 4:4) and still consider Jesus to be God.

57 Bock, *Luke*, 1:124, determines that in statements like these, we can assume a divine identity for Jesus.

58 Fitzmyer, *Luke (I–IX)*, 485, comments that the tradition in these verses is the only place where Psalm 2:7 is mentioned in reference to Jesus prior to his resurrection.

59 Danker, *Luke*, 96, suggests Jesus heard the decree and not John.

60 Bovon, *Luke 1*, 129, comments that the Spirit's presence at the baptism suggests that Jesus needed to be equipped further. This view seems to have confirmation in

what Luke says in 4:14: Jesus had the fullness of the Spirit in going to Galilee. But Luke tells us that there can be multiple fillings and empowerments with the apostles in Acts (e.g., 9:17; 13:9). Also, we know Luke tells us that John received the Spirit from his mother's womb (Luke 1:15). I am more persuaded by the notion that the Spirit is publicly confirming Jesus. This is why Luke and the other gospel writers discuss a "bodily" form for the Spirit. This form suggests that people saw it.

61 It is ambiguous in Mark 1:10, but Matthew 3:16 tells us that Jesus saw the dove. Danker, *Luke*, 96, interprets the voice to speak to Jesus. See Bovon, *Luke 1*, 129, for discussion of textual issues in this verse.

62 God's possessive language with respect to Jesus is matched by Jesus's possessive language with respect to God (Luke 2:49; 10:22; 22:29; 24:49).

63 Bovon, *Luke 1*, 129, says the event is not an "adoption" but a "revelation"; Jesus was understood to be God's Son. The Spirit's role is to confirm this. Conzelmann, *Theology*, 194, dismissing the importance of the birth narrative, claims the baptism is the introduction of Jesus's sonship.

64 Here I capitalize the name to suggest Jesus's uniqueness as God's Son who defines all other children of God.

65 Green, *Luke*, 196, suggests that obedience and sonship go hand in hand. Jesus's obedience to God affords him the power to overcome the power of Satan. Lukan Christology suggests, however, that Jesus's obedience as a Son is not necessary for his sonship; he is already a Son. His actions are consonant with who he is. He followed the Scripture faithfully because of who he was, not to attain divine childship status.

66 Parsons, *Luke*, 72.

67 On the truthfulness of Satan's challenge against Jesus, see Tucker S. Ferda, "God of the Nations: Daniel, Satan, and the Temptation of Jesus in Luke," *ZNW* 110, no. 1 (2019): 1–20.

68 Fitzmyer, *Luke (I–IX)*, 515, limits the referent of Satan's question to the baptism. This suggestion unnecessarily truncates the totality of Luke's intention to establish Jesus as God's unique Son.

69 Ernst, *Lukas*, 126–27, gives no attention to how divine childship might function in the passage. On the contrary, Danker, *Luke*, 103–4, states the arrangement of the material may have been influenced by the issue of divine childship: "Perhaps the fact that the second temptation did not and could not begin with the words 'if you are the Son of God' was an additional factor in assigning the third position to this temptation. The basic question is: In view of the outcome of events, will Jesus appear to be the Son of God?"

70 Parsons, *Luke*, 71.

71 Consequently, Danker, *Luke*, 104, urges that this would communicate that the "auditors" of Luke's Gospel would, too, have to overcome temptation, not

taking the path of suffering. As such, they must embrace a Jesus of suffering, recognizing his path was the correct Christological one.

72 One of the interesting features of Luke's temptation narrative is Satan's presumptive statement that he could make Jesus the king of the world because this right had been bequeathed to him (Luke 4:6). Matthew does not contain this statement (Matt 4:9). Luke never elaborates on this concept. We never know how Satan received this authority. We just know he has it. Life of Adam and Eve 47:3 and Apocalypse of Moses 39:2 discuss Adam's reclamation of authority from Satan. Adam is promised to regain the authority that Satan had stolen from him by inheriting Satan's throne. In Luke, the fact that Jesus hands authority to his disciples (Luke 9:1; 10:17–20) suggests that he has wrested this authority from Satan. We can only say this by implication. Another possibility is that Jesus always had authority and Satan was lying. In this way, Jesus comes as one who has Adam's authority through his identity as God's Son and Lord of creation.

73 Gathercole, *Preexistent*, 282, does not notice that the Sanhedrin's question may hint at Luke placing this attribution on their lips as well or other instances listed above.

74 Kirk, *Man Attested*, 229–32. Kirk proposes that the function of the transfiguration is to portray Jesus as the representation of Israel and not a preexistent being (232). He bases his judgment on several texts from the Enoch literature that show that an ideal human can appear in heavenly form. One of the major issues with the use of this literature in comparison with Luke's Gospel is intentionality. Luke is writing a history, not a visionary narrative. His narrative includes visions, but his intention is to wed people to faithfulness to Jesus. None of the Enoch literature was attempting to found hero cults for ancient Israelite figures. For more on the conception of divinized humanity, see Crispin H. T. Fletcher-Louis, "The Worship of Divine Humanity as God's Image and the Worship of Jesus," in *Christological Monotheism: Papers from the St. Andrews Conference on the Historical Origins of the Worship of Jesus*, ed. Carey C. Newman, James R. Davila, and Gladys S. Lewis (Leiden: Brill, 1999), 112–28; and Fletcher-Louis, "Angelomorphic Humanity Texts," 292–312.

75 Bock, *Luke*, 2:1011. See John 3:35; 7:29; 10:14–15, for example.

76 This use of the first-person possessive has four instances in Luke (2:49; 10:22; 22:29; 24:49). Interestingly, three of the instances in which it occurs also facilitate a transference from Jesus to his disciples. In the first instance (10:21–24), Jesus transfers relational knowledge of the Father. In the second instance (22:29), Jesus transfers a kingdom. In the last instance (24:49), Jesus discusses the transfer of the Spirit. This phrasing certainly reminds the reader

of Johannine literature (e.g., John 2:16; 5:43; 6:32; 6:40; 8:49; 10:25, 29, 37; 14:2, 7, 20, 23; 15:1, 8, 9, 23–24).

77 Rudolf Bultmann, *The History of the Synoptic Tradition*, trans. John Marsh (Oxford: Basil Blackwell, 1968), 159–60, notes that these verses (particularly vv. 21–22) may have not been a unity in their original setting. See Bovon, *Luke 1*, 40; and Ernst, *Lukas*, 258 (who calls vv. 21–22 "Stichwortzusammenhang"). Some scholars argued an original Hellenistic setting following Bultmann in this judgment. Fitzmyer, *Luke (I–IX)*, 866; Marshall, *Luke*, 432.

78 According to Evans, "Jesus and the Spirit," 30, Jesus's status as one filled with the Spirit enables him to overcome Satan.

79 Rowe, *Narrative Christology*, 137–38.

80 Bauckham, "Human Christology," 517.

81 Fitzmyer, *Luke (I–IX)*, 869, 874, thinks "all things" is a reference to the knowledge of the Son about the Father. This knowledge is certainly included but not a limit in my view.

82 Green, *Luke*, 421. See also Danker, *Luke*, 219.

83 Parsons, *Luke*, 314, suggests the kingdom is "shared," not transferred. Again, the disciples' share in authority is not independent of Jesus. Their reign as judges is based on him.

84 On how Luke narrates the fulfillment of the promise for a kingdom to his disciples in Acts, see David H. Wenkel, "When the Apostles Became Kings: Ruling and Judging the Twelve Tribes of Israel in the Book of Acts," *BTB* 42, no. 3 (2012): 119–28.

85 See Matthew 8:11, which only has "east and west."

86 Evans, "Jesus and the Spirit," 43.

87 Johnson, *Luke*, 378–79, argues that "paradise" is Eden. With respect to the temporal marker, Johnson notes that "today" is mentioned also in Luke 2:11; 4:21; 5:26; 13:22–33; 19:9; 22:34, 61, showing "a special moment of revelation or salvation" (378). He also notes in Isaiah 51:5 which confirms that Luke has Adam in mind when discussing the work of Jesus (379). Johnson cites a striking passage from *b. Ber. 12b*: "How do we know that heaven had forgiven him (i.e., Saul)? Because it says, 'and Samuel said . . . Tomorrow shalt thou and they sons be with me' and R. Johanan said, 'with me' means in my compartment in paradise.'" Cited from Johnson, *Luke*, 379. This text suggests that the rabbis construed the future of Israel to involve the reoccupation of Eden. For this view, Johnson also cites Psalm of Solomon 14:2; 1 Enoch 60:8; 61:12; Lev. Rabb. 26:7.

88 See 2 Corinthians 12:4; Revelation 2:7. In the LXX, see, for example, Genesis 2:8–10, 15–16; 3:1–3, 8, 10, 23, 24. According to the Genesis account, this

place was closed to human entrance because of sin. But this is not mentioned in Luke's Gospel.

89 Parsons, *Acts*, 27, suggests that Luke in this passage is repeating Mark more than his own report of the saying of Jesus in Luke 3:16.

90 See Bauckham, "Human Christology," 517.

91 Romans 8:29.

92 Evans, "Jesus and the Spirit," 42–43.

93 N. T. Wright, *The New Testament and the People of God* (Minneapolis: Fortress, 1992), 268.

94 The question of the rationale for the gentile mission in Lukan studies is hotly debated. One of the prevailing views, advocated by Haenchen, *Acts*, 100, is that the gentile mission was solely the consequence of Israel's disobedience to Messiah Jesus. Jacob Jervell, *Luke and the People of God: A New Look at Luke-Acts* (Minneapolis: Augsburg, 1972), 43, suggests the mission begins only after the division of Israel into "repentant" and "unrepentant" Israel. The obedience of the Jews to Jesus opened the way for the gentiles to be included as an "associate people" (147). The restoration of Israel through the Jewish Christians opens the way for the gentiles. Talbert, *Luke-Acts*, 165, argues that the inclusion of the gentiles was part of God's "divine plan, . . . the means by which God ultimately fulfills the promises God has made to Israel" (162–63). Gentile salvation is prophecy fulfillment (169). See Tannehill, "Story of Israel," 327, on the question of the resistance of Israel and the salvation of the gentiles.

95 Could divine childship be lost? The rabbis took up this question: Kister, "Son(s) of God," 193–94. Some concluded that sonship could be lost and restored. Others concluded that it could never be lost. A key text for their evaluation of this question was Deuteronomy 32.

96 Again, Pervo and Parsons, *Luke and Acts*, 103–4, see an unbroken Heilsgeschichte. But this explanation would not account for why Luke perceives the generation to be "crooked" (Acts 2:40; my translation). Somehow, this generation has been corrupted, but we are not told how.

97 Tannehill, "Story of Israel," 327, calls the story of Israel in Luke's portrayal tragic. The unbelief that met the Messiah continues on to the end of Acts, where Paul encounters the same unbelief (Acts 28:25–28).

98 Luke offers us a regnal note naming Caesar Augustus as world ruler and Herod the Great as the ruler of Israel (Luke 1:5; 2:1).

99 Green, *Luke*, 90, suggests obedience is a demonstration of the "representation of God."

100 Green, 275.

101 See Luke 23:34. Green, *Luke*, 817n19, argues that this verse was original.

102 Crowe, *Last Adam*, 98–102, says that Luke depicts Jesus's entire life as a life of suffering. The disciple is called to mimic Jesus in not only what he does on the cross but his suffering prior to this event.

103 Danker, *Luke*, 149, 179. Danker expresses throughout his commentary that this was one of the main arguments of Luke/Acts, for Jesus to reconnect humanity with "the Parent."

104 This scene echoes the instance when the seventy elders receive the spirit that is upon Moses (Num 11:24–25). A major difference, demonstrating the supremacy of Jesus, is that Moses does not distribute the spirit as Jesus does. Jesus does what God did in Numbers 11.

105 Johnson, *Luke*, 169, cites the various HB texts to speak of this record. Fitzmyer, *Luke (X–XXIV)*, 860, describes the record as the "heavenly registry." My understanding of the passage suggests that something more may be going on than just the notion of a record.

106 Green, *Luke*, 421, proposes that one of the revelations of Jesus to the disciples is that they can, too, call God "father."

107 This faithfulness appears to open the way for God's blessing to the rest of the world. Evans, "Jesus and the Spirit," 42–43, argues that the sending of the seventy could be symbolic of God's desire to reach the whole world, the seventy nations of the earth (Gen 10).

108 Danker, *Luke*, 149.

109 Here the Greek is "οἱ υἱοὶ τοῦ αἰῶνος τούτου."

110 See Luke 3:8; 15:18, 21.

111 Danker, *Luke*, 323, contends that Luke assumes two senses of divine childship, of heavenly beings and of Israelites.

112 Against Turid Karlsen Seim, *The Double Message: Patterns of Gender in Luke-Acts* (Nashville, TN: Abingdon, 1994), 77–81.

113 Bovon, *Luke 3*, 71, sees the connection that this verse has to Luke 6:35 but does not make the leap to discussing the larger theme of divine childship at work in the Gospel and Acts.

114 Speaking of these verses, Bovon, *Luke 3*, 70, states, "Personally, I am of the opinion that the theology of these statements is not far removed from that of the apostle Paul. He is convinced that death entered the world because of Adam and that sin is universal (Rom 5:12–21). In his view, in Jesus Christ sin and death are defeated at the same time. Those who believe in the gospel of Jesus Christ become new creatures. They rediscover the glory that Adam lost in the fall (Rom 3:23)." In Bovon's view, by calling those to be resurrected "God's children," Luke is describing a "juridical decision," an "adoption" (70).

115 Bovon, *Luke 1*, 70, argues that Luke's view of the resurrection, and his eschato-logical schema, is quite similar to Paul's. Adam brought death into the world, and Jesus, as a new Adam figure, reverses the curse of Adam. This is not the scheme we are given in explicit terms in Luke. The evidence suggests, however, that Jesus is viewed as an Adam figure. It could be that Luke assumed that the reader was aware of Adam's failure as the cause of human sin and that Jesus's coming overcame Adam's failure. See Johnson, *Luke*, 315–16.

116 Moreover, they are now able to live in equality with the hosts of heaven. This promise may parallel Daniel 12:3, which describes the resurrection of the just as their ability to shine like the hosts of heaven.

117 The history of interpretation of this parable is long and varied. I cannot engage the breadth of studies on this parable in particular. With this said, how-ever, see Joachim Jeremias, *The Parables of Jesus*, rev. ed. (London: SCM, 1963); J. D. M. Derrett, "Law in the New Testament: The Parable of the Prodigal Son," *NTS* 14 (1967): 56–74; J. D. M. Derrett, "The Parable of the Prodigal Son: Patristic Allegories and Jewish Midrashim," *Stud. Patrist.* 10 (1970): 219–24; Roger D. Aus, "Luke 15:11–32 and R. Eliezer Ben Hyrcanus's Rise to Fame," *JBL* 104, no. 3 (1985): 443–69; Roger D. Aus, "Die Rückkehr des Verlorenen Sohnes: Motive aus der Jüdischen Josefüberlieferung in Lukas 15, 11–32," in *Weihnachtsgeschichte, Barmherziger Samariter, Verlorener Sohn: Studien zu Ihrem Jüdischen Hintergrund* (Berlin: Institut Kirchen und Judentum, 1988), 126–73; Ingo Broer, "Das Gleichnis vom Verlorenen Sohn und die Theologie des Lukas," *NTS* 20, no. 4 (1974): 453–62; Trevor Burke, "The Parable of the Prodigal Father: An Interpretative Key to the Third Gospel (Luke 15:11–32)," *TynB* 64, no. 2 (2013): 217–38; Joel Huffstetler, *Boundless Love: The Parable of the Prod-igal Son and Reconciliation* (Lanham, MD: University Press of America, 2008); Greg Forbes, *The God of Old: The Role of the Lukan Parables in the Purpose of Luke's Gospel* (Sheffield: Sheffield Academic Press, 2000); Greg Forbes, "Repen-tance and Conflict in the Parable of the Lost Son (Luke 15:11–32)," *JETS* 42, no. 2 (1999): 211–29; Rohun Park, "Revisiting the Parable of the Prodigal Son for Decolonization: Luke's Reconfiguration of Oikos in 15:11–32," *BibInt* 17 (2009): 507–20; Kenneth Bailey, *Jacob and the Prodigal: How Jesus Retold Israel's Story* (Downers Grove, IL: InterVarsity, 2003); Kenneth Bailey, *The Cross and the Prodigal: Luke 15 through the Eyes of Middle Eastern Peasants* (Downers Grove, IL: InterVarsity, 2005); and Callie Callon, "Adulescentes and Meretrices: The Correlation between Squandered Patrimony and Prostitutes in the Parable of the Prodigal Son," *CBQ* 75, no. 2 (2013): 259–78. On redactional questions and questions of the source of the parable, see Joachim Jeremias, "Tradition and Redaktion in Lukas 15," *ZNW* 62, no. 3 (1971): 172–89; Jack T. Sanders, "Tra-dition and Redaction in Luke 15:11–32," *NTS* 15, no. 4 (1969): 433–38; and

Marc Rastoin, "Le génie littéraire et théologique de Luc en Lc 15.11–32 éclairé par le parallele avec Mt 21.28–32," *NTS* 60, no. 1 (2014): 1–19.

118 Jeremias, *Parables*, 132. See Bovon, *Luke 1*, 420–21.

119 Derrett, "Law," 68–71.

120 Burke, "Prodigal Father," 229–32.

121 Crowder, "Luke," 175.

122 Fitzmyer, *Luke (I–IX)*, 1085–86, 1090–91.

123 Green, *Luke*, 579. See reference above to Park, "Decolonization," on how this parable disrupts the normal conception of the Greco-Roman household through the father's benevolent behavior.

124 N. T. Wright, *Jesus and the Victory of God* (Minneapolis: Fortress, 1996).

125 Bailey, *Jacob and the Prodigal*, 200 (italics in the original).

126 Bailey, 197.

127 Bailey, 131–35, 199.

128 Amy-Jill Levine, *Short Stories by Jesus: The Enigmatic Parables of a Controversial Rabbi* (New York: HarperOne, 2014), 69.

129 Levine, 57–58, 67–68.

130 Levine, 55–58.

131 Levine, 57.

132 Levine, 69–70.

133 Levine, 69.

134 Christof Landmesser, "Die Rückkehr ins Leben nach dem Gleichnis vom Ver-lorenen Sohn (Lukas 15,11–32)," *Zeitschrift für Theologie und Kirche* 99, no. 3 (2002): 256, notes that it is through the father that the son is restored and not his own self-realization.

135 This distance language is important for how Luke views the plight of Israel and the nations as children of Adam (Acts 17:24–31). Their unfaithfulness to the covenant, like the rest of the nations, has rendered them lost children.

136 Again, Levine, *Short Stories*, 57–58; 67–68, argues against this interpretation.

137 Parsons, *Luke*, 242–43. Jervell, *Luke*, 65–66, says the door is shut at the end of Acts for the rest of unrepentant Israel. I agree with Parsons that the elder brother's self-rejection did not yield in God's total rejection. There is always a possibility in the theological outlay of Luke/Acts for those who have rejected the Messiah to be included in God's people.

138 See Bovon, *Luke 1*, 421, for discussion of the elder brother's unusual inclu-sion into the parable cycle in Luke 15, since none of the other parables have anything like an antagonist, as a sharp polemic against Jesus's opponents. He discusses the redactional issues involved.

139 On the importance and necessity of repentance, see Forbes, "Repentance and Conflict," 225–27. According to David Ravens, *Luke and the Restoration of*

Israel (Sheffield: Sheffield Academic Press, 1995), 169, Jesus is bringing not a new way but an old way that renews through repentance. Repentance atones.

140 There, John says, "ποιήσατε οὖν καρποὺς ἀξίους τῆς μετανοίας καὶ μὴ ἄρξησθε λέγειν ἐν ἑαυτοῖς· πατέρα ἔχομεν τὸν Ἀβραάμ." The parable resounds the question of worthiness and Abrahamic childship and, thereby, divine childship.

141 Landmesser, "Die Rückkehr ins Leben," 257, argues, "Μετάνοια ist die vom Vater, von dem das Leben neu schaffenden Schöpfer, im Akt der Vergebung bewirkte Rückkehr in das Leben," pace Parsons and Pervo, *Luke and Acts*, 104n83, who comment that the prodigal's "self-discovery" led to repentance and restoration. In the parable, when he came to himself, it may have led him to repent, but his condition could have only been restored by his father. Thus his father had to receive his repentance to restore his status. Their argument that the younger son's death did not indicate brokenness does not fit well with Luke's overall point in the narrative in general and these parables in Luke 15 in particular. The sheep, coin, and son do not restore themselves; someone else does. Consequently, we should read the parable in line with Jesus's Spirit-filled power to overcome the other powers enslaving Israel (Luke 4:18–19).

142 To be sure, the son never stopped being a son. He lost his status as a son. In this way, Luke is playing off of motifs from Israel's Scripture and other Second Temple literature. Obedience through repentance is now necessary for the son to be restored.

143 Bailey, *Jacob and the Prodigal*, 85, says that the older son has lost his childship status, acting as a slave. He "obeys the law" like a slave instead of embracing the way of "love" as a son. I think Bailey is correct that the older son has placed himself outside of the house—but like the younger son is still given the ability to return—but I do not think that Luke places "love" and the "law" at odds in the parable. It is clear, in Luke, Jesus is not opposed to the law (Luke 24:44).

144 Fletcher-Louis, *Luke-Acts*, 220, proposes a realized eschatological reading of Luke 15:11–32. He argues that Luke, by use of resurrection language, describes the "ontological transformation of the redeemed in angelomorphic terms." This reading is to be rejected in part because Luke is not using a realized eschatology. Yes, there is an ontological shift that Luke probably intends his readers to understand with regard to their reception of the word of the kingdom, but this happens by the Spirit, anticipating a greater transformation in the future.

145 Marshall, *Luke*, 611.

146 This parable provides the solution to the real issue of the "ungehorsame Sohn Gottes," Pokorný, *Lukanischen*, 115, which is Jesus's own life and ministry as a correction of "vergessen Gottensohnschaft."

147 Parsons, *Luke*, 290.

148 On the Areopagus speech and its importance for Luke/Acts, see C. Kavin Rowe, "The Grammar of Life: The Areopagus Speech and Pagan Tradition," *NTS* 57 (2010): 31–50.

149 See Joshua W. Jipp, "Paul's Areopagus Speech of Acts 17:16–34 as Both Critique and Propaganda," *JBL* 131, no. 3 (2012): 567–88, on how Paul affirms gentile theology in one sense only to undermine it.

150 Craig Keener, *Acts: An Exegetical Commentary: Introduction and 1:1–2:47* (Grand Rapids, MI: Baker Academic, 2012), 1:2645, argues that the audience of Luke's narrative world would not ascertain the "allusion" to Adam, but his readership would. See also C. K. Barrett, *A Critical and Exegetical Commentary on Acts of the Apostles*, ICC (Edinburgh: T&T Clark, 1994), 842; Joseph A. Fitzmyer, *The Acts of the Apostles: A New Translation with Introduction and Commentary*, AB (New York: Doubleday, 1998), 609; Pokorný, *Lukanischen*, 132–36; Danker, *Luke*, 399; Luke Timothy Johnson, *The Acts of the Apostles*, Sacra Pagina (Collegeville, MN: Liturgical, 1992), who remarks that this line of argument is similar to Paul in Romans 5:12; Parsons, *Acts*, 246; Pervo, *Acts*, 435; and Williams, "Acts," 235.

151 See Deuteronomy 32:8. Johnson, *Acts*, 315, catches the allusion to Deuteronomy 32:8 but does not evaluate the possible significance of what it might mean in a conversation where Paul, in the narrative, is discussing human descent from God. In Deuteronomy 32:8, the writer explains that every nation comes from God, but God specifically oversees Israel. Paul has updated the tradition a bit to say that yes, this is true, but now God is calling all nations to account.

152 Here the Greek word is γένος.

153 See Dupont, *Salvation*, 32.

154 Paul does not name either of these individuals specifically, but it becomes clear whom he is discussing by their accompanying descriptions.

155 Rowe, "Areopagus," 43, 44.

156 Fletcher-Louis, "God's Image," 98, suggests that Jesus is the "genus according to which all (Jew and Gentile) were originally created." In his view, this passage proves primacy of Jesus as *the human*.

157 See Stephen G. Wilson, *The Gentiles and the Gentile Mission in Luke-Acts* (Cambridge: Cambridge University Press, 1973), 241.

158 See Ådahl Jonatan, "The Gentiles in Adam: Adam in Amos 9:11–12 and Acts 15:16–18," in *Adam and Eve Story in the Hebrew Bible and Ancient Jewish Writings including the New Testament* (Turku, Finland: Åbo Akademi University, 2016), 313–39, who comments that, despite the differences, Acts 15:17 could be comprehended as a reasonable conveyance of MT Amos 9:12. It is important to note that a tradition related to Adam stands behind the LXX and the NT. The connection of this passage, then, with an Adam tradition only buttresses

Luke's aim to show that in Jesus, all of the children of Adam are being called to repentance and to "seek the Lord" (ὅπως ἂν ἐκζητήσωσιν οἱ κατάλοιποι τῶν ἀνθρώπων τὸν κύριον; Acts 15:17). In Acts 17:27, Luke reports that James says, in a parallel statement, God it made so all people might ζητεῖν τὸν θεόν. For the grammatical and translational concerns with Amos 9:11–12 and Acts, see James D. Nogalski, "The Problematic Suffixes of Amos IX 11," *VT* 43, no. 3 (1993): 411–18; James D. Nogalski, "Three Faces of Hope: Amos 9:11–12 and Acts 15:12–19," *RevExp* 11, no. 2 (2015): 311–15; W. Edward Glenny, "The Septuagint and Apostolic Hermeneutics: Amos 9 in Acts 15," *BBR* 22, no. 1 (2012): 1–26; J. Paul Tanner, "James's Quotation of Amos 9 to Settle the Jerusalem Council Debate in Acts 15," *JETS* 55, no. 1 (2012): 65–85; Richard Bauckham, "James and the Jerusalem Church," in *The Book of Acts in Its Palestinian Setting*, ed. Richard Bauckham, The Book of Acts in Its First Century Setting (Grand Rapids, MI: Wm. B. Eerdmans, 1995), 4:415–80; and Richard Bauckham, "James and the Gentiles (Acts 15:16–18)," in *History, Literature, and Society in the Book of Acts*, ed. Ben Witherington III (Cambridge: Cambridge University Press, 1996), 155–84.

CHAPTER 5: SAVING BLACK LIFE AND SAVING THE WORLD

1 Acts 4:1–2 expresses the process of the resurrection in a way the Gospel never did. The priests and the Sadducees objected to the preaching of the resurrection "through Jesus" (4:2; my translation). As we discussed, Jesus is pivotal because he qualifies Israel for the resurrection of the just. Through the resurrection, the people of Israel, like Jesus, are shown to be God's children.

2 Frank Jabini, "Witness to the End of the World: A Missional Reading of Acts 8:26–40," *South African Theological Seminary* 13 (2012): 51–72, notes that Luke does not tell us about all of the detailed moves the witnesses make in Acts. Galilee has a church (Acts 9:31) but was not part of the missiological agenda (54).

3 Martin, "Function," iii, viii, 123, 222. This view is becoming a consensus view among NT scholars. See Weissenrieder, "Searching," 115–16; Keener, *Acts*, 2:1538–39; Parsons, *Acts*, 119; Gaventa, *Acts*, 140; Smith, "Do You Understand?," 64; and Robert Tannehill, *The Narrative Unity of Luke-Acts: A Literary Interpretation* (Philadelphia: Fortress, 1986), 17–18, 108–9.

4 Conzelmann, *Theology*, 141; Haenchen, *Acts*, 314–15. For Haenchen (314), the Ethiopian's story would contradict Cornelius's and, thus, cannot signify the initiation of the gentile mission. See also Jervell, *Luke*, 44–45, who considers Cornelius as the proper start of the gentile mission. See also Fitzmyer, *Acts*, 410. He affirms the view that "end of the earth" signifies Rome (201). Part of

some scholars' reasoning for excluding the Ethiopian's story is the belief that Luke did not intend for his readers to think of him as a gentile. I will address this issue below. The Ethiopian would have been perceived as a gentile YHWH worshipper.

5   Curt Niccum, "One Ethiopian Is Not the End of the World: The Narrative Function of Acts 8:26–40," in *A Teacher for All Generation: Essays in Honor of James C. VanderKam*, ed. Eric F. Mason et al., vol. 2 of (Leiden: Brill, 2012), 883–900, argues that the Ethiopian eunuch is important in fulfillment of Isaiah 56:1–8 but does not fulfill the missiological itinerary for gentile inclusion. Fulfillment of Isaiah 56:1–8 involved the salvation of eunuchs and the restoration of Israel and the nations. His primary argument is that the consensus view, that the eunuch's story signifies the "end of the earth," is based on external evidence, Greco-Roman evidence. This argument is incorrect (Luke 11:31). But what makes his case even less tenable is that he bases his argument on Isaiah, which is also external to Luke/Acts.

6   See W. C. Van Unnik, "Der Ausdruck (Apostelgeschichte i 8) und sein Alttestamentlicher Hintergrund," in *Sparsa Collecta: The Collected Essays of W. C. Van Unnik*, vol. 1, NovTSup 29 (Leiden: Brill, 1973), 321–27; and Jacques Dupont, "Le salut des gentils et la signification théologique du livre des Actes," *NTS* 6, no. 2 (1960): 132–55. See Niccum, "Ethiopian," above. See also E. Earle Ellis, "'The End of the Earth' (Acts 1:8)," *BBR* 1 (1991): 123–32, who argues that Luke knew Paul wanted to go to Spain, which would have signified the "end of the earth," at least at the Western end.

7   Frank M. Snowden Jr., *Blacks in Antiquity: Ethiopians in the Greco-Roman Experience* (Cambridge, MA: Belknap, 1970), 217.

8   Weissenrieder, "Searching," 122, 137, suggests that "the black eunuch embodies his geographic origin."

9   Among the many texts the Ethiopian is said to fulfill, one chief is Psalm 68:31. See Martin, "Function," 31. In his commentary on the Psalter, the church father Eusebius considered this text important in the Ethiopian's fulfillment of the reach of the gospel to the ends of the earth. See Johnson, "Blackness."

10 On the ridicule the Ethiopian eunuch would have received as an Ethiopian and a eunuch, see Byron, *Symbolic*, 111–12; Wilson, *Unmanly*, 113–15; Moxnes and Kartzow, "Complex Identities"; Parsons, *Body and Character*, 131–40; and Jesse J. Lee, "On Distracting and Disappearing Joy: An Exegetical Comparison of the Ethiopian Eunuch and the Slave-Girl Rhoda in Acts," *HBT* 40 (2018): 67. See Sean D. Burke, *Queering the Ethiopian Eunuch: Strategies of Ambiguity in Acts* (Minneapolis: Fortress, 2013), for an investigation of the Ethiopian's sexual status. Both his blackness and his sexual status would have been in question.

11 Darrell Bock, *Acts*, Baker Exegetical Commentary on the New Testament (Grand Rapids, MI: Baker Academic, 2007), 439, says the Antioch base had no "ethnic distinctions." This is incorrect. Luke's point is exactly that there are ethnic distinctions, but they are unified through the Spirit.

12 The temptation narrative may be the moment when we are to understand he saw Satan fall as lightning from heaven (Luke 10:18).

13 There is no explicit indication of the Spirit's baptism, for example, in Acts 2:41–47; 4:4; 13:48; 16:15, even though it is assumed. On the patterns of the Spirit, see Graham H. Twelftree, *People of the Spirit: Exploring Luke's View of the Church* (Grand Rapids, MI: Baker Academic, 2009).

14 We are not told here why they need power to be witnesses (Acts 1:8). Luke had already related the purpose of the power was to overcome satanic authority (Luke 10:17–20). But he may be implying what we have concluded from prior HB reflections on the manifestation of God's power on behalf of God's children.

15 Johnson, *Acts*, 158, notes the prophetic resonances of the passage.

16 Evans, "Jesus and the Spirit," 42–43.

17 Keener, *Acts*, 1:800. For other biblical allusions, see Keener, *Acts*, 1:801–2; Parsons, *Acts*, 37; Johnson, *Acts*, 42; and Gaventa, *Acts*, 73–74.

18 With Eric Barreto, "What Happened at Pentecost?," Working Preacher, May 1, 2013, http://www.enterthebible.org/blog.aspx?post=2547, I do not think Acts depicts a complete reversal of Babel. But Luke arranges his narrative to echo the themes somewhat. It shows that God's people are unified in their diversity. Diversity is maintained, but there is a oneness found in God.

19 Of the nations listed, we should take particular note that Luke reports that Jews and proselytes from Africa were present, Egyptians and Libyan-Cyrenians (Acts 2:10).

20 Gaventa, *Acts*, 75, notes that the central location is Jerusalem. This would be so for Jewish thinkers, while this would not be so for Romans. For them, Rome was the navel of the world.

21 Niccum, "Ethiopian," 888n19.

22 Acts 2:8 suggests this as the Jews proclaimed that the languages that were spoken were *their* languages. They were speaking gentile tongues.

23 On the complexity of the notion of repentance and conversion in Luke/Acts, see Joel B. Green, *Conversion in Luke-Acts: Divine Action, Human Cognition, and the People of God* (Grand Rapids, MI: Baker Academic, 2015).

24 Again, the allusion here to Deuteronomy 32:5 is consistent with Jesus's condemnation of the generation, which is also echoed in Luke 9:41. The combined effect may indicate that Luke expected his readers to strongly consider the divine childship status of Israel to be in a fraught state.

25　Verse 37 appears in the Textus Receptus but is deemed to have weak textual support: "εἶπεν δὲ ὁ Φίλιππος Εἰ πιστεύεις ἐξ ὅλης τῆς καρδίας, ἔξεστιν ἀποκριθεὶς δὲ εἶπεν Πιστεύω τὸν υἱὸν τοῦ Θεοῦ εἶναι τὸν Ἰησοῦν Χριστόν." What purpose does this verse serve? Johnson, *Acts*, 157, 159, suggests that verse 37 would have served well for early Christian baptismal ceremonies. It is possible that a scribe would have expected a statement of faith as part of baptism.

26　Again, see Wilson, *Unmanly*, 128–30; and Lee, "Distracting," 66–67.

27　John T. Squires, "The Function of Acts 8.4–12.25," *NTS* 44 (1998): 608–17, argues that the narrative function of this section (Acts 8:4–12:25) is to show the turn to the gentiles. Scholars all generally agree with this narrative function of this larger section and the narrative of the Ethiopian in particular. See Bruce, *Acts*, 190; and Marshall, *Acts*, 160. But we can say more than this. The narrative features of Acts 8:26–40, understood in their context, suggest that the mission of the gentiles is victorious in and through the eunuch's conversion.

28　John and Peter preached among other Samaritan villages as well (Acts 8:25).

29　Luke is explicit that God led the mission to the Ethiopian, while he does not say the same for the Samaritans (Acts 8:5). An angel is the medium of communication in the beginning (8:26; see also 10:7). Afterward, the Spirit speaks to Philip (8:29; see also 10:19) and then snatches him away (8:39).

30　This portion of the story and many others allude reflect narrative elements of biblical narratives. On the numerous biblical literary parallels with this narrative, see Spencer F. Scott, *The Portrait of Philip in Acts: A Study of Roles and Relations*, JSOT Sup 67 (Sheffield: JSOT, 1992), 135–45.

31　Understood as the kingdom of Meroe.

32　Carl R. Holladay, "Interpreting Acts," *Interpretation* 66, no. 3 (2012): 256. See Luke 4:17–19.

33　As to the form of this narrative, Christopher Matthews, *Philip: Apostle and Evangelist*, NovT Sup (Leiden: Brill, 2002), 74–75, argues this is a "legend." Argument for this classification of the episode is also found in Martin Dibelius and Mary Ling, *Studies in Acts of the Apostles*, ed. Heinrich Greeven (New York: Scribner's Sons, 1956), 15. On his understanding of his notion of "legend," see Martin Dibelius, "Zur Formgeschichte der Evangelien," *TRu* 1, no. 3 (1929): 203–7. Pervo, *Acts*, 219, suggests that though the story is "highly legendary," "source theories are thus left up in the air." Though I am inclined to believe in the historicity of the story, offering a robust defense of it is not my goal. I am more interested in how the story functioned narratively and theologically to Luke's auditors. For discussions of the historical nature of the story and possible sources, see Keener, *Acts*, 2:1537; and Barrett, *Acts*, 422.

34　Irenaeus, *Haer.* 3.12.8; 4; 23.2; Eusebius, *Hist. eccl.* 2.1.13. Both certainly considered the Ethiopian as the first gentile to hear the gospel of Jesus.

35 Martin, "Chamberlain's Journey," 110–11; 121–22.

36 Dahl, "Nations," 62–63.

37 Hans Conzelmann, *Acts of the Apostles: A Commentary on Acts of the Apostles*, trans. James Limburg, A. Thomas Krabel, and Donald H. Juel, Hermeneia (Minneapolis: Fortress, 1987), 68.

38 Niccum, "Ethiopian," 892.

39 Johnson, *Acts*, 159.

40 Haenchen, *Acts*, 314.

41 Felder, *Race*, 143, takes a different viewpoint while also arguing that there is conflict in the narratives of the Ethiopian and Cornelius. In his view, Luke "unwittingly gives the distinct impression that Cornelius's baptism is more legitimate than that of the Ethiopian" because of the unambiguous indication that Cornelius received the Spirit. Felder, 143, says that Luke does so without intention because his inclusion of Simeon Niger suggests that he is not trying to be racist in his approach.

42 Niccum, "Ethiopian," 891, proposes he is a Jew "literally." Witherington, *Acts*, 293, suggests he is a Jew on the "fringes of Judaism." Fitzmyer, *Acts*, 410, says that he is "to be understood as a Jew or, possibly, as a Jewish proselyte." Fitzmyer, 410, explains him as a "diaspora Jew" on the premise that Luke would have perceived him through the lens of Isaiah 56, which includes eunuchs in the people of God.

43 Spencer, *Portrait*, 129, says this is indisputable. Most scholars agree that his identification as an Ethiopian suggests that he is a gentile. The question remains as to his relationship with Judaism. Gaventa, *Acts*, 142, suggests that he is a gentile who is receptive to Judaism. See also Holladay, *Acts*, 189.

44 Marshall, *Acts*, 162; Bruce, *Acts*, 188; Keener, *Acts*, 2:1567, 1569.

45 See discussions below on descriptions of African peoples in biblical literature. If Luke's aim is to exposit the fulfillment of prophecy, then discussing this man as an Ethiopian does more for him than if he were considered Jewish. He had already discussed African Jews and proselytes in Acts 2:10. Having discussed the mission to the Samaritans prior to this episode, he accomplishes more in fulfillment of Acts 1:8, if this man is a gentile convert. As I will demonstrate, Luke's emphasis on the Ethiopian's country of origin and his service seems to also suggest his gentile status. See also Spencer, *Portrait*, 129.

46 Parsons, *Acts*, 120.

47 Keener, *Acts*, 2:1571.

48 Gaventa, *Acts*, 142, and Parsons, *Acts*, 120, suggest he may have been allowed to worship in the outer court.

49 Keener, *Acts*, 2:1571–72.

50 Keener, 2:1537. We cannot be so sure if there was *one* moment Luke had in mind for the fulfillment of major prophecies. Jesus preached to a gentile (Luke

7:1–10) and a Samaritan (17:11–19), but these encounters still demanded more encounters. Indeed, Luke is clear, the apostle to the gentiles never received the Spirit through the Jerusalem apostles (Acts 9:17), and when he began his apostolic missions, the Antiochene leadership confirmed it (13:1–4). There are several pieces of evidence Luke brings to bear to establish his themes.

51 Niccum, "Ethiopian," 895, makes this text central to the whole point of the narrative. Scott Shauf, "Locating the Eunuch: Characterization and Narrative Context in Acts 8:26–40," *CBQ* 71, no. 4 (2009): 726–75, asserts that the Ethiopian's identity as a eunuch has no strong bearing on this passage. Indeed, he is a wealthy individual, not "a dry tree." Luke adds high-status markers to his description, suggesting that this man was not an outcast searching for acceptance. I do not think the situation is either/or. I think the Ethiopian had a complex, mixed social status situation. Some of his traits gave him high status, such as wealth, royal representation, and so on, and other aspects would lead to ridicule, such as his blackness and his sexual status.

52 Williams, "Acts," 226, suggests that Philip's witness to the Ethiopian continues Luke's tendency to portray Philip moving ahead of the apostles as he did with the Samaritans. The Ethiopian's salvation, in this respect, is similar to Paul's conversion, which also excluded the participation of an apostle (Acts 9:10–19).

53 See Randall C. Bailey, "Beyond Identification: The Use of Africans in Old Testament Poetry and Narratives," in *Stony the Road We Trod: African American Biblical Interpretation*, ed. Cain H. Felder (Minneapolis: Fortress, 1991), 165–84. One text of importance is Amos 9:7, which compares Israel to the land of Cush, Ethiopians. Many scholars have read this to indicate disparagement of black-skinned people, but Bailey sees it as an exaltation—that Cushites were beloved by God—being used as a norm for Israel. See also Brent Strawn, "What Is Cush Doing in Amos 9:7? The Poetics of Exodus in the Plural," *VT* 63 (2013): 99–123, who considers this text an example of the use of an "exodus" motif. Cush and the other nations listed, alongside Israel, had all participated in various exoduses.

54 J. J. M. Roberts, *First Isaiah: A Commentary*, Hermeneia (Minneapolis: Fortress, 2015), 252–54, deals with the chronological difficulties associated with this period in Israel's history. We can be persuaded, based on all of the evidence, that this passage is in reference to Egypt during the time of the Twenty-Fifth Dynasty. This dynasty marked the time when Nubia controlled Egypt and was making advances all throughout the ANE in trade and empire. 1 Kings 19 (see Isa 36–37) details the relationship Israel had with Egypt at this moment, when under Nubian suzerainty. First-century readers like Josephus certainly remembered the Nubian presence in Egypt (*Ant.* 8.12–15). This is to add to the fact that both in Jewish and Greco-Roman practice, black-skinned people

of different nations were often grouped, and their distinctions were treated with fluidity.

55 Rodney S. Sadler, *Can a Cushite Change His Skin? An Examination of Race, Ethnicity, and Othering in the Hebrew Bible* (New York: T&T Clark, 2005), 49.

56 There is a tendency within scholarship to completely separate Cush from Egypt. This tendency is most likely racial at its core and not borne by scholarship. See Tristan Samuels, "Herodotus and the Black Body: A Critical Race Theory Analysis," *Journal of Black Studies* 46, no. 7 (2015): 723–41. Scholars have had a vested interest in putting Egypt within the sphere of Western, and thereby white, society. As such, Egypt is not considered a black nation. The problem is that the biblical text certainly remembers it as a black nation and one of the children of Ham (Gen 10:6–8). See Frank Martin, "The Egyptian Ethnicity Controversy and the Sociology of Knowledge," *Journal of Black Studies* 14, no. 3 (1984): 299–306, for examples of bias against viewing Egyptians as Black. Also, see David H. Kelly, "Egyptians and Ethiopians: Color, Race, and Racism," *Classical Outlook* 68, no. 3 (1991): 77–82, who strongly argues that Egyptians should be considered a mixed-race people, with some Semitic, Caucasoid heritage. For other views that caution against seeing Egyptians as Black, see Denise E. McCoskey, *Race: Antiquity and Its Legacy* (Oxford: Oxford University Press, 2012), 61–62, 180.

57 To be sure, there is significant debate about the so-called curse of Ham and differences between rabbinic and Second Temple Jewish opinions on the status of Ham and his descendants (see discussion below). The evidence of Genesis 9:20–27 suggests that Ham was rebuked by Noah and his child Canaan was cursed thereafter. We cannot say there was a broadscale positive valuation of Ham's people within the biblical record. We can say that his Cushite descendants are generally held integral to the unfolding of the restoration of Israel.

58 For example, 2 Chronicles 12:4; 16:8; 21:16; Psalm 68:31; Isaiah 11:11; 18–20; 43:3; 45:14; Jeremiah 46:9; Ezekiel 29:10; 30:4–9; 38:5; Daniel 11:43; Nahum 3:9. The pattern of grouping of these nations betrays the sensibility that biblical writers understood them to be closely aligned, even, I would also argue, in appearance. We must note, however, that each one of these nations had its own unique history in the ancient world. In the first century, for example, Egypt had been occupied by Rome. Libya was also part of the Roman Empire. Ethiopia, which is not the same as modern Ethiopia, was called the kingdom of Meroe. Meroe had not been conquered by the Romans. The Ethiopian, in particular, was a representative of the Candace, the female ruler of the kingdom. Ancient Meroe occupies modern southern Sudan. On the history of ancient Nubia, see David N. Edwards, *The Nubian Past: An Archaeology of the Sudan* (London: Routledge, 2004); Walter Emery, *Egypt in Nubia*

(London: Hutchinson, 1965); John H. Taylor, *Egypt and Nubia* (London: British Museum Press, 1991); Miriam Ma'at-Ka-Re Monges, *Kush, the Jewel of Nubia: Reconnecting the Root System of African Civilization* (Trenton, NJ: Africa World, 1997); William Y. Adams, "The Kingdom and Civilization of Kush in Northeast Africa," in *Civilizations of the Ancient Near East*, ed. Jack Sasson (New York: Scribner, 1995), 3:775–800; Stanley Burstein, ed., *Ancient African Civilizations: Kush and Axum* (Princeton, NJ: Markus Wiener, 1998); and Jeremy Pope, *The Double Kingdom under Taharqo: Studies in the History of Kush and Egypt, C. 690–664 BC* (Leiden: Brill, 2014). On the ethnic tensions between ancient Egyptians and Cushites, see S. T. Smith, *Wretched Kush: Ethnic Identities and Boundaries in Egypt's Nubian Empire* (New York: Routledge, 2003); and William E. Gordon II, "Cultural Identity of the 25th Dynasty Rulers of Ancient Egypt in Context: Formulation, Negotiation and Expression" (PhD diss., UCLA, 2009). For a general history of African peoples and their relationship to the biblical text, see Edwin Yamauchi, *Africa and the Bible* (Grand Rapids, MI: Baker Academic, 2004).

59 Sibylline Oracles 3:156–165; 3:202–8; 3:319–20; 5:189–95; 7:16–21; 8:4–11; 11:51–55; 14:284–86; Letter of Aristeas 1:13; Ezekiel the Tragedian 1:60–67; Artapanus 3:7–10; Jubilees 7:13; 9:1; 10:28–30. I treat Josephus and Philo below. We can say that Jews would have combined African nations in the NT period.

60 This includes Jews and gentiles from African nations. Texts like Zephaniah 3:10 and Isaiah 11:11 anticipated the return of Jews from Africa would demonstrate that Israel was being restored. The same could be communicated through gentile worshippers of the God of Israel, which it seems the Ethiopian eunuch was as Psalm 68:31 would suggest.

61 If Weissenrieder is correct, "Searching," 122, then we can argue that the very image of black-skinned people bespoke a distant people. The Ethiopian eunuch and other black-skinned people would suggest, not only in terms of fulfillment of biblical prophecy and the restoration of Israel, but in Jesus's own argument in Luke 15:11–32, that God's most distant children have been brought home.

62 David M. Goldenberg, "Racism, Color Symbolism, and Color Prejudice," in *The Origins of Racism in the West*, ed. Miriam Eliav-Feldon, Benjamin Isaac, and Joseph Ziegler (Cambridge: Cambridge University Press, 2009), 88–108, makes this point in part to dismiss the notion that there was character prejudice against black-skinned people. In his view, black-skinned people were despised not because ancients associated black skin with having an evil disposition but because the color black signaled death and wickedness. He cites several texts: Scriptores Historia Augusta, *Severus* 22.6–7; Terence, *Phormio* 705–6; Appian, *Bell. civ.* 4.17.134; Florus 2.17.7–8; Plutarch, *Brutus* 48.5; Historiae Augustae,

Severus 22.4–5; and Suetonius, *Caligula* 57.4, which demonstrate that Greco-Roman thinkers merely saw black-skinned people in a negative light because their skin only reminded them of evil. We have to be careful with calling this view racist, as there was no systematic legal enforcement of oppression behind these views. But we must also be careful with dismissing ancient rhetoric as benign because oppressive mechanisms were not erected to implement these prejudices. For more on the association of black skin with death and bad omens, see Byron, *Symbolic*, 36–37; 44–45; 60–64; and Lloyd Thompson, *Romans and Blacks* (London: Routledge, 1989), 114–15.

63 Michele George, "Images of Black Slaves in the Roman Empire," *Syllecta Classica* 14 (2003): 175, explains the negativity in the perception of black-skinned people seen with respect to Egyptians as well as Ethiopians, despite possible physical and cultural differences: "This is also illustrated by the negative connotations in language, as evidenced by the use of *melas* and *niger* in Greek and Latin, and by expressions such as *Aegyptius dies* as a synonym for *dies ater*, 'a black day.'"

64 For example, Herodotus, *Hist.* 3.20, at least in this instance, can think of black-skinned people as tall and handsome.

65 Robert Hood, *Begrimed and Black* (Minneapolis: Augsburg Fortress, 1994), 32–35, discusses the color moralizations Black Africans made of themselves. White was not a negative color and, in some cases, black was. But this did not extend to association of skin color with evil.

66 Keener, *Acts*, 2:1562, 1987, notes that color was quite relative among ancients. Dark-complexioned white people could be called Black because they were not as white as others. Samuels, "Herodotus," 733, notes that the standard of color among Greeks was "pale brown" or "tan." But oftentimes, this was called white by people who were most likely tan in color (e.g., Heliodorus, *Aeth.* 1.1–2).

67 Snowden, *Blacks*, 3. Many other words were used, but these are the most applicable for this study. Each word used points toward darkness.

68 Snowden, 3.

69 Ancient science explained that black skin was the consequence of closeness to the sun and the environment: Herodotus *Hist.* 2.22; Ps. Aristotle, *Prob.* 10.66; Lucretius, *De Rerum Natura* 6.722, 1109; Vitruvius, *De Architectura* 6.1.3–4; Strabo, *Georg.* 15.1.24; Ovid, *Metam.* 2.235–36; Pliny the Elder, *Nat.* 2.80.189; Seneca, *Nat.* 4a, 2.18. See Tatius, *Leucippe and Clitophon*, 4.5, on the relationship between blackness of skin and relationship to the sun in India and Ethiopia. See Snowden, *Blacks*, 171.

70 Snowden, *Blacks*, 5.

71 See note above on the Latin phrase *Aegyptius dies*.

72 This is probably the case also with Simon of Cyrene (Luke 23:26; see also Matt 27:32; Mark 15:21) and Lucius of Cyrene (Acts 13:1). Sanders, "Simon

of Cyrene," 51–63, persuasively argues that Simon was a black-skinned man. He draws on Malina's theory of "dyadic" personalities in the Mediterranean to argue that Simon was portrayed as a person representing African peoples, thereby showing the diversity of the gospel's reach. On the dyadic theory, see Bruce Malina and Jerome Neyrey, SJ, "First Century Personality: Dyadic, Not Individual," in *The Social World of Luke-Acts*, ed. Jerome Neyrey, SJ (Peabody, MA: Hendrickson, 1991), 67–96. For another application of this theory in African biblical interpretation, see H. Wayne Merritt, "The Individual and the Group in Luke: A Study of Malina's Hypothesis of the Dyadic Personality in First-Century Mediterranean Society," in Bailey and Grant, *Recovery of Black Presence*, 65–76.

73 He lived around 384–322 BCE.

74 Frank Snowden, *Before Color Prejudice: The Ancient View of Blacks* (Cambridge, MA: Harvard University Press, 1983), 58–59; Snowden, *Blacks*, iii. Contra this position, see Glenn Bowersock, *Roman Arabia* (Cambridge, MA: Harvard University Press, 1983), 124, who argues there was great racial prejudice in the Roman period.

75 Sadler, "Can a Cushite Change His Skin?," 400–401.

76 John R. Clarke, "Three Uses of the Pygmy and the Aethiops at Pompeii: Decorating, 'Othering', and Warding off Demons," in *Nile into Tiber. Egypt in the Roman World: Proceedings of the IIIrd International Conference of Isis Studies, Faculty of Archaeology, Leiden University, May 11–14 2005*, ed. Laurent Bricault, Miguel J. Versluys, and Paul G. P. Meyboom (Leiden: Brill, 2007), 160.

77 Snowden, *Blacks*, 217.

78 George, "Images," 162, asserts that such views did lead to mistreatment of black-skinned people. Peter Frost, "Attitudes towards Blacks in the Early Christian Era," *Second Century* 8, no. 1 (1991): 10, suggests that "color bias" can be seen in the patristic period. This certainly occurred with the ascetic Father Moses (3–4). For prejudice against Father Moses, see Vincent Wimbush, "Ascetic Behavior and Color-ful Language: Stories about Ethiopian Moses," *Semeia* 58 (1992): 81–92.

79 Lloyd Thompson, "Roman Perceptions of Blacks," *Scholia* 2 (1993): 23.

80 Snowden (1911–2007) had a long career. He brought attention to texts about Black presence in classical literature in a time when discrimination and racism were widespread and accepted canon in America. See Frank M. Snowden Jr., "The Negro in Ancient Greece," *American Anthropologist* 50, no. 1 (1948): 31–44; and Frank M. Snowden Jr., "The Negro in Classical Italy," *American Journal of Philology* 68, no. 3 (1947): 266–92. His more recent work, "Misconceptions about African Blacks in the Ancient Mediterranean World: Specialists and Afrocentrist," *Arion: A Journal of Humanities and the Classics* 4, no. 3

(1997): 28–50, assumes that the "full" weight of discussions about Ethiopians and other black-skinned people is positive in antiquity (31–32). Any analysis that says otherwise is a "misinterpretation." Such a statement betrays bias when we have texts like Appian, *Bell. civ.* 4.17.134, which states that Blacks were considered bad luck. One cannot explain away the inherent prejudice in this concept. So even if we agree with him that most of Greco-Roman literature does not accost black skin, we have to say that at least some texts exhibit biased views.

81　See Samuels, "Herodotus," 724–28. Samuels shows that Herodotus, *Hist.* 2.104, for example, has been misinterpreted for generations because of racist inclinations that suppress the possibility that Egyptians could be Black. Again, this is the consequence of racism, perceiving Black people as incapable of civilization.

82　He lived ca. 800 BCE.

83　Also, see Homer, *Il.* 23.205–7; and Homer, *Od.* 4.81–84; 5.281–87.

84　Homer, *Il.* 1.421–25 (Murray, LCL). On the continuity of this tradition, see second-century Ps. Lucian, *Philopatr.* 4.

85　Homer, *Od.* 1.21–25 (Murray, LCL).

86　See Herodotus, *Hist.* 7.70, suggesting that there are Ethiopians from both "Libya," which he associates with ancient Nubia, and India. Though holding skin color in common, Herodotus suggests that a phenotypic difference between eastern (Indian) Ethiopians and African Ethiopians is their hair texture. The African Ethiopians have the kinkiest hair, he says. In 4.197, Herodotus describes that there are four ethnographic peoples in Libya. There are aboriginal Libyans in the north and Ethiopians in the south. The Greeks and Phoenicians, he says, settled in the region later.

87　He lived around 484–430/20 BCE.

88　He lived around 63 BCE–24 CE.

89　See Ellis, "End of the Earth," 126, for discussion of ancient conceptions of the earth's extremities.

90　523–456 BCE.

91　See Philostratus, *Imag.* 2.7. Μέλας is synonymous with Ethiopian. Similarly, its cognate term in Latin, *niger*, can also be synonymous. See Lucretius, *De Rerum Natura* 4.1160; 6.722, 1109; Manilius, *Astronomica* 1.767; and Ovid, *Metam.* 2.236.

92　Cited in Parsons, *Acts*, 119.

93　On Herodotus and his investigation of the African continent, see László Török, *Herodotus in Nubia* (Leiden: Brill, 2014).

94　I must note that this language is inherently pejorative; see Samuels, "Herodotus," 736. It assumes that Black hair texture is subnormal and closer to animal hair than the hair of people of white skin. Samuels cites A. D. Byrd and

L. L. Tharps, *Hair Story: Untangling the Roots of Black Hair in America* (New York: St. Martin's, 2001), who provide historical background for this notion arising through racist biological ideology.

95 Ethiopians and other black-skinned people are said to have come up with the practice of circumcision. See Josephus, *Ant.* 8.262; and Josephus, *Ag. Ap.* 1.169–70, who says he is unaware who learned the practice from whom. Philo, *QG* 3.48, discusses the commonality of circumcision for Jews, Egyptians, Ethiopians, and Arabians.

96 Samuels, "Herodotus," 735, considers Herodotus as not an objective observer but biased in his ethnography about black-skinned people; he was prejudiced but not racist.

97 He lived ca. first century BCE.

98 Snowden, *Before Color*, 86–87.

99 Keener, *Acts*, 2:1538.

100 Against Herodotus's view, see Aristotle, *Gen. an.* 2.2.736a.

101 Lucian, *Hermot.* 31 offers three colors for humanity: white (λευκός), yellow (ξανθός), and black (μέλας). White represents Greeks and Romans, yellow indicates central Europeans, and black suggests African peoples. Thompson, "Perception," 25.

102 See Snowden, *Blacks*, 216–17.

103 Aristotle, *Gen. an.* 5.3.782b; Ps. Aristotle, *Prob.* 14.4.909a; Polybius 4.20–21. See Snowden, *Blacks*, 172–73.

104 Herodotus, *Hist.* 2.22; Aristotle, *Gen. an.* 5.3.782b; Strabo, *Georg.* 1.1.13; Ptolemy, *Tetrabib.* 2.2.

105 Aristotle, *Gen. an.* 1.18.722a; Aristotle, *Hist. an.* 7.6.586a.

106 See Nikki Khanna, "If You're Half Black, You're Just Black: Reflected Appraisals and the Persistence of the One-Drop Rule," *Sociological Quarterly* 51, no. 1 (2010): 96–121.

107 Concerning the origins, prevalence, use, and criticism of physiognomic reasoning, see Parsons, *Body and Character*, 17–37; and Mariska Leunissen, "Physiognomy," in *Oxford Handbook of Science and Medicine in the Classical World*, ed. Paul T. Keyser and John Scarborough (Oxford: Oxford University Press, 2018), 743–64.

108 Samuels, "Herodotus," 734, interprets this passage to reflect the consequence of hegemonic perception based on setting the Hellenic standard as normative. See discussion below for how these terms apply in a reading of the Ethiopian eunuch.

109 The rationale of this comment is beyond the scope of our argument.

110 Erich S. Gruen, *Rethinking the Other in Antiquity* (Princeton, NJ: Princeton University Press, 2011), 197–202.

111 Gruen, 205.

112 Juvenal, *Sat.* 2.23 (Braund, LCL).

113 This must be stated while also recognizing that Juvenal can speak ill of Black people and the blue eyes and blond hair of Germanic people, for example (Juvenal, *Sat.* 13.162–66; see also Seneca, *Ira* 3.26.3).

114 P. Bour. 1.141–68, cited from Ronald F. Hock and Edward N. O'Neil, eds., *The Chreia and Ancient Rhetoric: Classroom Exercises*, trans. Ronald F. Hock and Edward N. O'Neil, vol. 2 (Atlanta, GA: SBL, 2002), 10.

115 For example, Juvenal, *Sat.* 13.162–66. Scholars often make this claim to dismiss prejudice against black-skinned people.

116 Agatharchides, *De Mari Erythraeo*, 16.

117 Clarke, "Three Uses of the Pygmy," 160, says the image of "Ethiopian" was perceived as being so "unbecoming" that it caused evil to flee.

118 Clarke, 160. The conception that seems to be at work is that the image of the black-skinned person is so horrific that it has the ability to scare horrible things away. It is more horrible than the attack of the evil eye. This view stands in stark contrast to Herodotus, *Hist.* 3.20, 3.114, who calls Ethiopians the tallest and most beautiful people.

119 All translations of Greek novels come from B. P. Reardon, ed., *Collected Ancient Greek Novels* (Berkeley: University of California Press, 2008). Though later than the period in which Acts was written, Greek novels provide strong evidence for the continuation of views on ethnographic thinking in regard to black-skinned people.

120 *Barbarian* (Greek: Βάρβαρος) in the ancient Greek sense did not necessarily mean what *barbaric* means today. It was a general term used to describe all foreign, non-Greek peoples. *LSJ.* Ethiopians, as earlier stated, were considered a noble kind of barbarian.

121 For discussion of racial issues in *Leucippe and Clitophon*, see Donna Shalev, "Heliodorus' Speakers: Multiculturalism and Literary Innovation in Conventions for Framing Speech," *Bulletin of the Institute of Classical Studies* 49 (2006): 184–85.

122 For interrogations of ethnicity in Heliodorus, *Aeth.*, see Tomas Hägg, "The Black Land of the Sun: Meroe in Heliodorus's Romantic Fiction," in *Parthenope: Selected Studies in Ancient Greek Fiction (1969–2004)*, ed. Lars Boje Mortensen and Tormod Eide (Copenhagen: Museum Tusculanum, 2004), 345–78; J. R. Morgan, "A Sense of the Ending: The Conclusion of Heliodorus' Aithiopika," *TAPA* 119 (1989): 299–320; and Judith Perkins, "An Ancient 'Passing' Novel: Heliodorus' Aithiopika," *Arethusa* 32, no. 2 (1999): 197–214.

123 The main character, Chariklea, responds to the surrounding bandits by thinking that they are ghosts. J. R. Morgan, "An Ethiopian Story," in Reardon, *Collected*

Ancient Greek Novels, 355n4, comments that this is because "ghosts had black faces" in Greek thinking. They were reminders of the underworld.

124 In another scene, Sisimithres speaks faltering Greek and is also described as extremely black-skinned (Heliodorus, *Aeth.* 2.30).

125 See Marcus Jerkins, "The Dynamism of Blackness in an Ethiopian Story and Acts," *PRSt* 46, no. 3 (2019): 307–26.

126 Her mother is said to have viewed an image of Andromeda, a white-skinned Ethiopian, and Chariklea became white-skinned as well (Heliodorus, *Aeth.* 4.8–9).

127 Here the Greek is "ἐπειδὴ δέ σε λευκὴν ἀπέτεκον, ἀπρόσφυλον Αἰθιόπων χροιὰν ἀπαυγάζουσαν."

128 Jerkins, "Dynamism," 320–22.

129 For example, *Gen. Rab.* 22:6; *b. Sanh. 108b*. For a broad survey of this literature, see David M. Goldenberg, *The Curse of Ham: Race and Slavery in Early Judaism, Christianity, and Islam* (Princeton, NJ: Princeton University Press, 2003). He concludes, with regard to postbiblical views, that he sees no racism in Jewish texts. He, like others, has attempted to divest seemingly prejudicial statements of their deleterious power, suggesting that these texts were never meant to demean black-skinned people, only to point out how they do not fit the norm. Against this view, see Charles B. Copher, "Three Thousand Years of Biblical Interpretation with Reference to Black Peoples," *Journal of the Interdenominational Theological Center* 13, no. 2 (1986): 225–46. On the standardization of the Jewish body, see Mira Balberg, "Rabbinic Authority, Medical Rhetoric, and Body Hermeneutics in Mishnah Negaʾim," *AJS Review* 35, no. 2 (2011): 343. Like the Greeks and Romans, in rabbinic literature, Jews considered their body color and even type to be standard.

130 For a more comprehensive perspective on Scripture and Africans, see Yamauchi, *Africa*.

131 For biblical references to Ethiopia as the southern extremity of the world, see Spencer F. Scott, *The Portrait of Philip in Acts: A Study of Roles and Relations*, JSOT Sup 67 (Sheffield: JSOT, 1992), 149; Keener, *Acts*, 2:1538; and Bailey, "Poetry," 172.

132 Hebrew: כּוּשׁ.

133 Greek: Χους. It is possible that the translators were aware of the meaning of the word χοῦς (soil; BDAG) and wanted to reference skin color.

134 The LXX first transliterates Egypt as (מִצְרַיִם) Μεσραιμ and then most other times opts for the Greek translation in the vast majority of cases Αἴγυπτος (e.g., Gen 12:10–11).

135 Genesis 2:13; Numbers 12:1–2; 2 Kings 19:9; 2 Chronicles 12:3; 14:11–12; 16:8; 21:16; Esth 8:9, 12; Psalm 68:31 (LXX 67:32); 87:4; Job 28:19; Amos

9:7; Nahum 3:9; Habakkuk 3:7; Zephaniah 2:12; 3:10; Isaiah 11:11; 18:1; 20:4; 37:9; 43:3; 45:14; Jeremiah 46:9; 36:14; Ezekiel 29:10; 30:4, 9; 38:5; Daniel 3:1; 11:43. The LXX adds Ethiopia to its translation in two places where it does not appear in the MT (LXX Ps 71:9; 73:14).

136 On Black presence, Ethiopians, Egyptians, and so on in Scripture, see Adamo, *Africa*; and Charles B. Copher, "The Black Presence in the Old Testament," in Felder, *Stony the Road We Trod*, 146–64.

137 The memory of Taharqa lasted long beyond his reign, showing up in Josephus, *Ant.* 10.17. On Taharqa, see Yamauchi, *Africa*, 107–48.

138 The memory of this Nubian also made it into Josephus's historical retelling *Ant.* 10.123.

139 Another similarity with Greco-Roman material is the belief that African peoples had great wealth (e.g., Job 28:19; Dan 11:43). See Bailey, "Poetry," 175.

140 See Sadler, "Can a Cushite Change His Skin?," 398–99; and Bailey, "Poetry," 177.

141 Sadler, *Cushite*, 91, argues this woman was tanned by the sun and not portrayed as an Ethiopian.

142 See Origen, *Comm. Cant.* 2.1, from Origen, *The Song of Songs: Commentary and Homilies*, trans. R. P. Lawson, Ancient Christian Writers 26 (New York: Newman, 1956); Byron, *Symbolic*, 70–76; and Johnson, "Blackness," 184–89.

143 Sadler, *Cushite*, 90, concludes of the biblical record, "At the same time, there also does not appear to be any clear value ascribed to skin color. . . . Though other ancient societies appear to have correlated negative themes with concepts of 'blackness' and dark skin color, such a contrast does not appear in the present instance, nor in general in the Hebrew Bible."

144 In this note, I only list texts from Qumran (other references will follow in other notes). 1QapGen ar 7:11–12; 17:19; 19:13; 4Q529 fr; 4Q454 fr; 4Qp Nah 3:11–12; 4QpsEzek^a fr; 4QpsEzek^c fr.

145 For example, Letter of Aristeas 1:13; Lives of the Prophets 1:6.

146 Sibylline Oracles 3:156–65; 3:202–8; 3:319–23; 3:516; 5:206; 5:505; 7:16–21; 8:4–11; 11:51–55; 11:61–64; 14:284–86.

147 Written ca. first to early second century.

148 John J. Collins, "Sibylline Oracles: A New Translation and Introduction," in *OTP*, 1:317–472.

149 See Heliodorus, *Aeth.*, 8, about the war with Ethiopians and Egyptians in Syene.

150 Sibylline Oracles 5:197–98, discuss Libya and Cyrene, following the pattern of mentioning other African nations along with Ethiopia and Egypt.

151 Collins, "Oracles," 390.

152 Ezekiel the Tragedian 1:60–67; Demetrius 3:3; Eupolemus 1:8; Artapanus 3:7–10. Rabbinic traditions were quite concerned with this story. See Goldenberg, *Curse*, 52–59.

153 For references to Ham and his sons, see Jubilees 4:33; 7:13; 8:10, 22, 24, 30; 9:1; 9:13; 10:28, 30; 22:21.

154 Jamal-Dominique Hopkins, "The Noahic Curse in Rabbinic Literature: Racialized Hermeneutics or Ethnocentric Exegesis," in *Re-presenting Texts: Jewish and Black Biblical Interpretation*, ed. W. David Nelson and Rivka Ulmer (Piscataway, NJ: Gorgias, 2013), 15–27, argues the rabbinic tradition and the Qumran tradition are in disagreement over the question of the significance of black skin. He presents Jubilees, which is present at Qumran, for support for this position. The disagreement over the valuation of blackness is part of other theological differences DSS community members had with later rabbinic opinions.

155 See Hopkins, "Noahic," 20.

156 See Goldenberg, *Curse*, 142–54.

157 See Snowden, *Blacks*, 171–77.

158 Balberg, "Rabbinic," 343, attests to the later notion, at least in the Mishnah, that Jews considered the body types of Blacks (Cushi) and whites (Germani) to be nonstandard.

159 Byron, *Symbolic*, 43–44, discusses the Christian use of Ethiopians as a trope for sin. See also David Brakke, "Ethiopian Demons: Male Sexuality, the Black-Skinned Other, and the Monastic Self," *Journal of the History of Sexuality* 10, nos. 3–4 (2001): 501–35. As already noted, later Christian writers easily used Ethiopians as a means to speak of sin and the devil. See Athanasius, *Vit. Ant.* 6, who says Anthony saw the devil as a "black boy."

160 See Josephus, *J. W.* 4.607–8; Josephus, *Ant.* 1.131–33 (argues that Ethiopians, Egyptians, and Libyans in his time use the biblical names given to the sons of Ham: Cush [Ethiopia], Mizraim [Egypt], and Phut [Libya]); 8.159, 165 (says that Solomon was married to an Egyptian woman and claims that the "Queen of Egypt and Ethiopia," known as the queen of Sheba in 1 Kgs 10:1–13, came to Solomon); 8.253–54 (refers to Shishak [1 Kgs 11:40; 14:25] as the king of Egypt with a great many Ethiopians and Libyans in his army); 10.4; 10.17; 10.122–23 (discusses the tradition of Ebed-Melech); 11.186 (repeats Esth 1:1; 8:9, considering Ethiopia and India as ends of Artaxerxes's empire). In *Ant.* 8.262 and *Ag. Ap.* 1.169–70, he discusses the origination of the circumcision practice among the Ethiopians from the Egyptians. See Philo, *Flacc.* 1.43, 45, 152; Philo, *Deus* 1.174; Philo, *QG* 3.48; and Philo, *Mos.* 1.99.

161 We can push Philo's reasoning beyond Cush to Ham himself. In Philo's perspective, the sons of Noah—Shem, Ham, and Japheth—can be allegorized in

the following way: Shem is what is good, Ham is what is bad, and Japheth is what is indifferent (Philo, *QG* 1.88).

162 The issue of humiliation will arise again in the next text: Philo, *Leg.* 1.68.

163 Here Philo seems to take his view from Ps. Aristotle, *Physiogn.* 812a–b.

164 Greek: ἡ ἀνδρεία.

165 Greek: ἀνδρείας.

166 Greek: ταπείνωσις.

167 Greek: ἡ δειλία.

168 Greek: δειλίᾳ.

169 C. D. Yonge, trans., *The Works of Philo Judaeus, the Contemporary of Josephus, Translated from Greek by C. D. Yonge* (London: H. G. Bohn, 1854). Though I have mostly used LCL, I used this translation, as it is more literal.

170 See David Lincicum, "Philo and the Physiognomic Tradition," *JSJ* 44 (2013): 77, who discusses Philo's link to Ps. Aristotle, *Physiogn.* 812a–b. Goldenberg, *Curse*, 51, objects to any notion that Philo was anti-Black. He argues that Philo is merely logically connecting the theological significance of colors with black-skinned people. To say he is anti-Black, in Goldenberg's view, is akin to saying he is antiraven because of his associations of evil with ravens.

171 Wilson, *Unmanly*, 129, says that Philo would have associated the Ethiopians with femininity.

172 See discussion of Nimrod above.

173 This could be because many Jews were considered black-skinned by those who considered themselves white-skinned. Tacitus, *Hist.* 5.2, held the view that Jews were of Aethiopum prolem, "Ethiopian stock." Interestingly, this translation is suppressed in the LCL (Moore, LCL). The translator has "Egyptian stock" here. He could have been conflating Egyptians and Ethiopians. But more likely, the translator is betraying a bias, since he might have considered such a claim to denigrate Jews. It is easier to say they were Egyptians, since many scholars have considered Egyptians to be white. In some cases, when scholars have marveled at Nubian culture, they have also attempted to argue that the black-skinned Nubians were not really Black or had no connection to Black Africans around them. To completely reject the observations of the totality of antiquity is to make an untenable claim.

174 Sadler, *Cushite*, 90. On the rabbinic perspectives, see Balberg, "Rabbinic," 343.

175 Mladen Popović, "Physiognomic Knowledge in Qumran and Babylonia: Form, Interdisciplinarity, and Secrecy," *DSD* 13, no. 2 (2006): 150–76; Mladen Popović, *Reading the Human Body: Physiognomics and Astrology in the Dead Sea Scrolls and Hellenistic-Early Roman Period Judaism*, Studies on the Texts of the Desert of Judah 67 (Leiden: Brill, 2007), explores other physiognomic considerations in DSS literature.

176 Parsons, *Body and Character*, 83–108, makes these characters central to his contention that Luke is subverting physiognomic reasoning. Though being "inferior human beings," Parsons says their childship status to Abraham bespeaks their true status (82). My contention is that to understand Lukan anthropology, especially as it regards the gentiles and how Luke would destroy physiognomic devaluation, we must recognize that Adam stands behind Abraham. Luke tells us that the worth of the nations rests not on their being children of Abraham but on their being children of God through Adam (Acts 17:26–29). Jesus, as the new Adam, ensures that all of the children of Adam are brought near to God. No other candidate helps Luke make this case so poignantly like one of the most distant people, an Ethiopian. To be sure, Abraham cannot be effaced from the scheme. The covenantal blessings of Abraham are still gained by the people who receive the Spirit. Thus even if Luke does not say so explicitly, gentiles who are reached by the gospel are restored children of Abraham (Acts 13:26), or they at least have fellowship with him (Luke 13:29).

177 Interestingly, the history of scholarship has proven that this view of blackness is still prevalent. Martin, "Chamberlain's Journey," 120, calls this the "politics of omission." Scholars have found this narrative in tension with Cornelius and, as a consequence, suggested that something is wrong with this narrative. Dupont, *Salvation*, 146n3, claims that this material is out of place. For this view, see Gonzalez, *Acts*, 117–18; and Barrett, *Acts*, 420.

178 Keener, *Acts*, 2:1534, lists numerous prolepses in Acts. Indeed, Acts itself is a proleptic book. Luke states at the end of the book that the gentiles will hear the gospel, even though they had not on the whole (Acts 28:28). Jervell, *Luke*, 47, notes that the gospel mission has mostly been unsuccessful with gentiles. Key for Luke is to show success in his narrative is to signify that what had happened throughout the book would pale in comparison to what God will do in the future. Thus the whole work was meant to symbolize, with the few, what God intended to do for the rest of the world. For further analysis of the proleptic emphases of Luke, see Mikeal C. Parsons, *The Departure of Jesus in Luke-Acts: The Ascension Narratives in Context*, JSNTSup (Sheffield: Sheffield Academic Press, 1987).

179 Niccum, "Ethiopian," 887.

180 Luke is most likely aware of this prediction of Jesus in Mark 13:27.

181 Against Niccum, "Ethiopian," 888, who suggests the Ethiopian's identity as an Ethiopian is "ancillary."

182 Shauf, "Characterization," 774, considers the function of this story to allow Luke to fulfill Acts 1:8 without taking emphasis away from Cornelius's conversion. As I will show, the importance of the story itself makes Cornelius's conversion only more impactful.

183 Joseph A. Grassi, "Emmaus Revisited (Luke 24, 13–35 and Acts 8, 26–40)," *CBQ* 26, no. 4 (1964): 465, claims the parallels between Luke 24:13–35 and Acts 8:26–40 suggest that Jesus is explaining the biblical text to the Ethiopian. As Jesus was revealed on the road to Emmaus, so too Jesus is revealed to the Ethiopian eunuch.

184 This is the only time this occurs in the NT and shows parallels with Elijah (2 Kgs 2).

185 Twelftree, *Spirit*, 88–89. Marshall, *Acts*, 165, maintains that the long form of verse 39 may have been original, even with weak MS evidence. Marshall explains that the text may have dropped out because of the separation of the article and the noun. I am inclined to think that this tradition may have been original but removed because some scribes had difficulty with perceiving a black-skinned person as having the Spirit before Cornelius.

186 On MS evidence, see Bruce M. Metzger, *A Textual Commentary on the Greek New Testament* (Stuttgart, Germany: Deutsche Bibelgesellschaft, 1994), 316.

187 Joy and ecstasy are often associated with the Spirit in the NT; see, for example, Luke 1:41–44; 10:21; 24:49–53; Acts 10:46; Romans 14:17; 15:13; Ephesians 5:18–19; 1 Thessalonians 1:6.

188 Smith, "Do You Understand?," 54, says, with regard to Acts 8:1b–12:25, "the whole of which illustrates the enlightening and ever-expanding power of the deity despite the increasing persecution of the church."

189 Keener, *Acts*, 2:1578.

190 The Greek is "ἐκ τῶν περάτων τῆς γῆς" (Luke 11:31). The change in language ought not to be a hindrance to this possible inference. Luke is quite capable of shifting vocabulary in statements, as he did with the promise of the baptism of the Spirit (Luke 3:16; Acts 1:5). On the afterlife of this connection to the queen of Sheba, in African tradition, see Edward Ullendorff, "Candace (Acts VIII. 27) and the Queen of Sheba," *NTS* 2, no. 1 (1955): 53–56. Yamauchi, *Africa*, 90–91, argues that Sheba is in southern Arabia. Crowder, "Luke," 171, suggests that based on Josephus (see discussion below), Luke probably thought of Sheba in Africa, related to the Ethiopians.

191 Crowder, "Luke," 171.

192 Weissenrieder, "Searching," 122.

193 Martin, "Function," viii, suggests that the gentile mission is not "formally inaugurated" until Cornelius, but even his salvation is not officially sanctioned until Acts 15.

194 Keener, *Acts*, 2:1534.

195 Gaventa, *Acts*, 75.

196 Parsons, "Unhindered," 155–56, suggests Luke has embraced the Ethiopian, with emphasis on overturning denigration of his sexual orientation. Though

he is accepted in the church, Parsons suggests it is "not as full-throated" as we would like (156). Luke does not seem to be all that concerned about the Jerusalem community's embrace of the Ethiopian, since he returns to Ethiopia rejoicing (Acts 8:40). The main point is that something has been done apocalyptically. Philip's transport to Azotus and arrival in Caesarea attest that God is working behind the scenes to destroy the barriers erected to stop the spread of the promises of God to the nations. This is why after the Ethiopian, the church expands beyond its own comfort.

197 Byron, *Symbolic*, 111. For example, Mark 12:34 and Ephesians 2:13 use the term.

198 Johnson, *Acts*, 58; Parsons, *Acts*, 47.

199 Luke's use of encomium is essential in his description of the Ethiopian. In this way, Luke's approach to the Ethiopian's blackness serves to reject whatever invective some may have considered at the very mention of a black-skinned person. Among the many economiastic descriptors Luke includes in Acts 8:26–40 are the following: he is a treasurer; he oversees the wealth of the Candace; he rides in a chariot; he is able to read; most importantly, the Spirit is the driving force behind Philip's witness. On the Lukan practices of encomium, see Mikeal C. Parsons and Michael W. Martin, *Ancient Rhetoric and the New Testament: The Influence of Elementary Greek Composition* (Waco, TX: Baylor University Press, 2018), 213–22.

200 Williams, "Acts," 226.

201 Parsons, *Body and Character*, 126–41.

202 Parsons, 136–40.

203 Parsons, 136–37.

204 Parsons, 137, cites Lucian, *Somn.* 13, which states that eunuchs are ταπεινός, "in every way."

205 Wilson, *Unmanly*, 129.

206 Keener, *Acts*, 2:1542n776, suggests Luke has framed his narrative to sequence the individual conversions of Ham (the Ethiopian), Shem (Paul), and Japheth (Cornelius) in Acts 8–10. On this reasoning, see James M. Scott, "Luke's Geographical Horizon," in *The Book of Acts in Its First Century Setting*, ed. David W. Gill and Conrad Gempf, The Book of Acts in Its Graeco-Roman Setting 2 (Grand Rapids, MI: Wm. B. Eerdmans, 2002), 544.

207 Like Philo, the text uses ταπείνωσις.

208 My translation.

209 Smith, "Do You Understand?," 63, suggests a parallel with Luke 4:16–30 and the salvation of the Ethiopian. He is part of Luke's scheme to show that Jesus embraces those maladjusted with Israel.

210 For reconciliation in the narrative, see Weissenrieder, "Searching," 123; Byron, *Symbolic*, 111; Parsons, *Body and Character*, 141; Bock, *Acts*, 347; Johnson,

Acts, 159–60; and Lee, "Distracting," 66–67. They do not necessarily advocate my divine childship view.

211 See Byron, *Symbolic*, 70–74.

212 Again, I have chosen only to discuss Simeon because I believe the strongest case can be made for him as a black-skinned person. Lucius may have also been a black-skinned Christian. See Sanders, "Simon of Cyrene," 62.

213 Again, Felder, *Waters*, 47–48, argues in favor of my proposal that Simeon is Black. He also interprets his blackness to connote that Luke was not biased against black-skinned people (see Felder, *Race*, 143). As I have tried to show, the Ethiopian's narrative accomplishes this as well.

214 Supporting this view, see Sanders, "Simon of Cyrene," 62; Keener, *Acts*, 2:1985; Felder, *Troubling*, 47–48; *Race*, 143; and Johnson, *Acts*, 220. Against this view, see Barrett, *Acts*, 603; and Marshall, *Acts*, 214.

215 As I have argued, in the ancient world, *niger* could *mean* "Ethiopian" or "Egyptian," and "Ethiopian" or "Egyptian" could *mean niger*. Keener, *Acts*, 2:1984–86, offers a detailed discussion of the possibilities. *Niger* does not have to be a nickname. It could simply be a cognomen, one of the most respectable (Keener, 2:1986). It could also speak to a dark-complexioned white person. And as Snowden cautions in *Blacks*, 12, we have to be careful drawing ethnicity from a person's name. A white person can be named Blackman in modern times. Josephus, for example, discussed a man named Niger (e.g., Josephus, *J. W.* 2.520) who was not a Black African. We can, however, conclude that *Niger* in Acts 13:1 is most likely in reference to a black-skinned person because it appears as a nickname. None of the other people in the list is given a cognomen. Simeon Niger is called *Niger* to distinguish him from another Simeon (Acts 15:14). I provide other reasons above.

216 Adamo, *Africans in the New Testament*, 33, argues that we should not leave *niger* untranslated. It is a clear reference to an African Black. From what nation does he hail? Keener, *Acts*, 2:1986, suggests that Simeon was probably a black-skinned North African. *Niger* does not necessarily have to indicate that he is an Ethiopian. Again, the definition of *black* among Greco-Roman persons was quite fluid.

217 For discussions of the social ramifications of prejudice, see George, "Images," 182; and Frost, "Attitudes," 3–4.

218 Jerkins, "Dynamism," 320, 325.

219 Williams, "Acts," 226.

Conclusion

1 On the subject of ancient constructions of race and the issues of terminology, anachronistic charges, and so on, see Sung Uk Lim, "Race and Ethnicity Discourse in Biblical Studies and Beyond," *Journal for the Study of Religions and Ideologies* 15, no. 45 (2016): 120–42; Denise K. Buell, "Anachronistic Whiteness and the Ethics of Interpretation," in *Ethnicity, Race, Religion: Identities and Ideologies in Early Jewish and Christian Texts, and in Modern Biblical Interpretation*, ed. Katherine M. Hockey and David Horrell (London: Bloomsbury T&T Clark, 2018), 149–67; and Andrew Gardner, Edward Herring, and Kathryn Lomas, eds., *Creating Ethnicities and Identities in the Roman World*, Bulletin of the Institute of Classical Studies Supp 120 (London: Institute of Classical Studies, 2013).

2 Barreto, "Ethnic Negotiations," 3.

3 Sadler, "Can a Cushite Change His Skin?," 400, calls this "racialism."

4 Against Goldenberg, "Color," 107, who suggests that antimony of blackness was purely aesthetic. The reason, he suggests, that racism developed from earlier color prejudice is because this color disdain persisted and transformed. He argues other populations who felt the sting of Greco-Roman criticism became acceptable through familiarity. Black racism arose because Blacks will always be Black.

5 Though Luke tells us that Paul was free while he was in prison, preaching the gospel unhindered (Act 28:16–31).

6 Barreto, "Ethnic Negotiations," 243.

7 W. F. Albright, "The Old Testament World," *IDB* 1:233–71.1:238. This opinion reflects its time, when the ANE and many of its civilized cultures were considered the forebearers of white people. For further exploration of the racist tones in biblical and theological scholarship, see William Dwight McKissic Sr. and Anthony T. Evans, *Beyond Roots II; If Anybody Ask You Who I Am* (Wenonah, NJ: Renaissance, 1994).

8 Albright, "Old Testament," 1:239.

9 T. G. Pinches, "Africa," *ISBE* 1:68.

10 W. S. Lasor, "Africa," *ISBE* 1:63.

11 See discussion in chapter 5 n. 173. Moore's LCL translation of Tacitus resisted calling Jews of "Ethiopian stock" and preferred "Egyptian stock." Such was much more acceptable, since they were considered by many as "white."

12 Snowden, "Misconceptions," is correct to caution against overreading the evidence of Black presence in ancient texts. But again, it is difficult to see blackness when white supremacy has dominated the discipline.

13 The consequences of which were devastating for Jewish people. See Susannah Heschel, *The Aryan Jesus: Christian Theologians and the Bible in Nazi German* (Princeton, NJ: Princeton University Press, 2008).

14 See Hockey and Horrell, *Ethnicity, Race, Religion,* for an exploration of the complex racial paradigms involved in biblical studies.

SELECTED BIBLIOGRAPHY

Ådahl, Jonatan. "The Gentiles in Adam: Adam in Amos 9:11–12 and Acts 15:16–18." In *Adam and Eve Story in the Hebrew Bible and Ancient Jewish Writings including the New Testament*, 313–339. Turku, Finland: Åbo Akademi University, 2016.

Adamo, David T. *Africa and Africans in the New Testament*. Lanham, MD: University Press of America, 2006.

———. *Africa and the Africans in the Old Testament*. San Francisco: International Scholars, 1998.

Adams, William Y. "The Kingdom and Civilization of Kush in Northeast Africa." In *Civilizations of the Ancient Near East*, edited by Jack Sasson, 775–800. Vol. 3. New York: Scribner, 1995.

Albright, W. F. "The Old Testament World." *IDB* 1:233–271.

Alexander, P. S. "The Targumim and Early Exegesis of 'Sons of God' in Genesis 6." *JJS* 23, no. 1 (1972): 60–71.

Allen, Garrick V. "Son of God in the Book of Revelation and Apocalyptic Literature." In *Son of God: Divine Sonship in Jewish and Christian Antiquity*, edited by Garrick V. Allen, Kai Akagi, Paul Sloan, and Madhavi Nevader, 53–71. University Park, PA: Eisenbrauns, 2019.

Allison, Dale C., Jr. "Behind the Temptations of Jesus: Q4:1–13 and Mark 1:12–13." In *Authenticating the Activities of Jesus*, edited by Bruce D. Chilton and Craig A. Evans, 195–213. Leiden: Brill, 1999.

Amitay, Ory. *From Alexander to Jesus*. Berkeley: University of California Press, 2010.

Anderson, H. "3 Maccabees: A New Translation and Introduction." In *OTP*, 509–529. Vol. 2. n.d.

Arndt, William. *The Gospel of St. Luke*. St. Louis, MO: Concordia, 1956.

Aus, Roger D. "Die Rückkehr des Verlorenen Sohnes: Motive aus der Jüdischen Josefüberlieferung in Lukas 15, 11–32." In *Weihnachtsgeschichte, Barmherziger Samariter, Verlorener Sohn: Studien zu Ihrem Jüdischen Hintergrund*, 126–173. Berlin: Institut Kirchen und Judentum, 1988.

———. "Luke 15:11–32 and R. Eliezer Ben Hyrcanus's Rise to Fame." *JBL* 104, no. 3 (1985): 443–469.

Bailey, Kenneth. *The Cross and the Prodigal: Luke 15 through the Eyes of Middle Eastern Peasants*. Downers Grove, IL: InterVarsity, 2005.

————. *Jacob and the Prodigal: How Jesus Retold Israel's Story*. Downers Grove, IL: InterVarsity, 2003.

Bailey, Randall C. "Beyond Identification: The Use of Africans in Old Testament Poetry and Narratives." In *Stony the Road We Trod: African American Biblical Interpretation*, edited by Cain H. Felder, 165–184. Minneapolis: Fortress, 1991.

Balberg, Mira. "Rabbinic Authority, Medical Rhetoric, and Body Hermeneutics in Mishnah Negai'm." *AJS Review* 35, no. 2 (2011): 323–346.

Balzer, Klaus. *Deutero-Isaiah: A Commentary on Isaiah 40–55*. Translated by Margaret Kohl. Minneapolis: Fortress, 2001.

Barclay, John M. G. "Paul among Diaspora Jews: Anomaly or Apostate?" *JSNT* 60 (1995): 89–120.

Barreto, Eric. "Ethnic Negotiations: The Function of Race and Ethnicity in Acts 16." PhD diss., Emory University, 2010.

————. *Ethnic Negotiations: The Function of Race and Ethnicity in Acts 16*. Tübingen, Germany: Mohr Siebeck, 2010.

————. "A Gospel on the Move: Practice, Proclamation, and Place in Luke-Acts." *Interpretation* 72, no. 2 (2018): 175–187.

Barrett, C. K. *A Critical and Exegetical Commentary on Acts of the Apostles*. ICC. Edinburgh: T&T Clark, 1994.

Bauckham, Richard. "Is 'High Human Christology' Sufficient? A Critical Response to J. R. Daniel Kirk's *A Man Attested by God*." *BBR* 27, no. 4 (2017): 503–525.

————. "James and the Gentiles (Acts 15:16–18)." In *History, Literature, and Society in the Book of Acts*, edited by Ben Witherington III, 155–184. Cambridge: Cambridge University Press, 1996.

————. "James and the Jerusalem Church." In *The Book of Acts in Its Palestinian Setting*, edited by Richard Bauckham, 415–480. The Book of Acts in Its First Century Setting 4. Grand Rapids, MI: Wm. B. Eerdmans, 1995.

Beard, Mary, John North, and Simon Price. *Religions of Rome*. Cambridge: Cambridge University Press, 1998.

Bock, Darrell. *Acts*. Baker Exegetical Commentary on the New Testament. Grand Rapids, MI: Baker Academic, 2007.

————. *Luke: 1–9:50*. Grand Rapids, MI: Baker Academic, 1994.

————. *Luke: 9:51–24:53*. Grand Rapids, MI: Baker Academic, 1996.

Bovon, François. *Luke 1: A Commentary on Luke 1:1–9:50*. Translated by Christine M. Thomas. Minneapolis: Fortress, 2002.

————. *Luke 3: A Commentary on the Gospel of Luke 19:28–24:53*. Minneapolis: Fortress, 2012.

Bowersock, Glenn. *Roman Arabia*. Cambridge, MA: Harvard University Press, 1983.

Brakke, David. "Ethiopian Demons: Male Sexuality, the Black-Skinned Other, and the Monastic Self." *Journal of the History of Sexuality* 10, nos. 3–4 (2001): 501–535.

Brand, Miryam T. *Evil Within and Without: The Source of Sin and Its Nature as Portrayed in Second Temple Literature*. JAJSup. Göttingen, Germany: Vandenhoeck & Ruprecht, 2013.

Briggs, Megan. "Eric Metaxas on His 'Ill-Considered' Jesus Was White Tweet." churchleaders.com. July 29, 2020. https://tinyurl.com/2us66vmh.

Broad, W. E. L. *Alexander or Jesus? The Origin of the Title "Son of God."* Eugene, OR: Pickwick, 2015.

Broer, Ingo. "Das Gleichnis vom Verlorenen Sohn und die Theologie des Lukas." *NTS* 20, no. 4 (1974): 453–462.

Brooke, George J. "Son of God, Sons of God, and Election in the Dead Sea Scrolls." In *Son of God: Divine Sonship in Jewish and Christian Antiquity*, edited by Garrick V. Allen, Kai Akagi, Paul Sloan, and Madhavi Nevader, 28–40. University Park, PA: Eisenbrauns, 2019.

Brown, Raymond E. *The Birth of the Messiah: A Commentary on the Infancy Narratives in Matthew and Luke*. Garden City, NY: Image, 1979.

Brown, Schuyler. *Apostasy and Perseverance in the Theology of Luke*. Rome: Pontifical Biblical Institute, 1969.

Brown, William P. *The Seven Pillars of Creation: The Bible, Science, and the Ecology of Wonder*. Oxford: Oxford University Press, 2010.

Buell, Denise K. "Anachronistic Whiteness and the Ethics of Interpretation." In *Ethnicity, Race, Religion: Identities and Ideologies in Early Jewish and Christian Texts, and in Modern Biblical Interpretation*, edited by Katherine M. Hockey and David Horrell, 149–167. London: Bloomsbury T&T Clark, 2018.

Bultmann, Rudolf. *The History of the Synoptic Tradition*. Translated by John Marsh. Oxford: Basil Blackwell, 1968.

Burke, Sean D. *Queering the Ethiopian Eunuch: Strategies of Ambiguity in Acts*. Minneapolis: Fortress, 2013.

Burke, Trevor. "The Parable of the Prodigal Father: An Interpretative Key to the Third Gospel (Luke 15:11–32)." *TynB* 64, no. 2 (2013): 217–238.

Burkert, Walter. *Greek Religion*. Translated by John Raffan. Cambridge, MA: Harvard University Press, 1985.

Burstein, Stanley, ed. *Ancient African Civilizations: Kush and Axum*. Princeton, NJ: Markus Wiener, 1998.

Byrd, A. D., and L. L. Tharps. *Hair Story: Untangling the Roots of Black Hair in America*. New York: St. Martin's, 2001.

Byrne, Brendan. *Sons of God, Seed of Abraham: A Study of the Idea of Sonship of God of All Christians in Paul against the Jewish Background*. Rome: Biblical Institute, 1979.

Byron, Gay L. *Symbolic Blackness and Ethnic Difference in Early Christian Literature*. London: Routledge, 2002.

Cadbury, Henry J. *The Making of Luke-Acts*. 2nd ed. Peabody, MA: Hendrickson, 1958.

Callon, Callie. "Adulescentes and Meretrices: The Correlation between Squandered Patrimony and Prostitutes in the Parable of the Prodigal Son." *CBQ* 75, no. 2 (2013): 259–278.

Carroll, John T. *Luke: A Commentary*. Louisville, KY: Westminster John Knox, 2012.

Clarke, John R. "Three Uses of the Pygmy and the Aethiops at Pompeii: Decorating, 'Othering', and Warding off Demons." In *Nile into Tiber. Egypt in the Roman World: Proceedings of the IIIrd International Conference of Isis Studies, Faculty of Archaeology, Leiden University, May 11–14 2005*, edited by Laurent Bricault, Miguel J. Versluys, and Paul G. P. Meyboom, 155–169. Leiden: Brill, 2007.

Collins, Adela Y. "Mark and His Readers: The Son of God among Greeks and Romans." *HTR* 93, no. 2 (2000): 85–100.

―――. "Mark and His Readers: The Son of God among Jews." *HTR* 93, no. 4 (1999): 393–408.

Collins, Adela Y., and John J. Collins. *King and Messiah as Son of God: Divine, Human, and Angelic Messianic Figures in Biblical and Related Literature*. Grand Rapids, MI: Eerdmans, 2008.

Collins, John J. "The Origin of Evil in Apocalyptic Literature and the Dead Sea Scrolls." In *Congress Volume Paris 1992*, edited by J. A. Emerton, 25–38. VTSup 61. Leiden: Brill, 1995.

―――. "Sibylline Oracles: A New Translation and Introduction." In *OTP*, 317–472. Vol. 1. n.d.

Conzelmann, Hans. *Der Mitte Der Zeit: Studien Zur Theologie Des Lukas*. Tübingen, Germany: Mohr Siebeck, 1954.

―――. *The Theology of St. Luke*. Translated by Geoffrey Burswell. New York: Harper & Row, 1961.

Cook, Johann. "The Origin of the Tradition of the of the יצר הטוב and יצר הרע." *JSJ* 38 (2007): 80–91.

Cooke, Gerald. "The Israelite King as Son of God." *ZAW* 32, no. 2 (1961): 202–225.

Copher, Charles B. "The Black Presence in the Old Testament." In *Stony the Road We Trod: African American Biblical Interpretation*, edited by Cain H. Felder, 146–164. Minneapolis: Fortress, 1991.

―――. "Three Thousand Years of Biblical Interpretation with Reference to Black Peoples." *Journal of the Interdenominational Theological Center* 13, no. 2 (1986): 225–246.

Cousland, J. R. C. "Reversal, Recidivism and Reward in 3 Maccabees: Structure and Purpose." *JSJ* 34, no. 1 (2003): 39–51.

Crowder, Stephanie B. "The Gospel of Luke." In *True to Our Native Land: An African American New Testament Commentary*, edited by Brian K. Blount, 158–185. Minneapolis: Fortress, 2007.

Crowe, Brandon. *The Last Adam: A Theology of the Obedient Life of Jesus in the Gospels*. Grand Rapids, MI: Baker Academic, 2017.

Dahl, Nils. "Nations in the New Testament." In *New Testament Christianity for Africa and the World: Essays in Honor of Harry Sawyer*, edited by Mark E. Glaswell and Edward Fashole-Luke, 54–68. London: SPCK, 1974.

Danker, Frederick. *A Commentary on the Gospel of Luke: Jesus and the New Age*. Philadelphia: Fortress, 1988.

Davies, Philip R. "The Origin of Evil in Ancient Judaism." *ABR* 50 (2002): 43–54.

Derrett, J. D. M. "Law in the New Testament: The Parable of the Prodigal Son." *NTS* 14 (1967): 56–74.

———. "The Parable of the Prodigal Son: Patristic Allegories and Jewish Midrashim." *Studia Patristica* 10 (1970): 219–224.

Dibelius, Martin. "Zur Formgeschichte der Evangelien." *TRu* 1, no. 3 (1929): 185–216.

Dibelius, Martin, and Mary Ling. *Studies in Acts of the Apostles.* Edited by Heinrich Greeven. New York: Scribner's Sons, 1956.

Donaldson, Terence L. *Judaism and the Gentiles: Jewish Patterns of Universalism (to 135 CE).* Waco, TX: Baylor University Press, 2007.

Dunn, James D. G. *Christology in the Making: A New Testament Inquiry into the Origins of the Doctrine of the Incarnation.* 2nd ed. Grand Rapids, MI: Eerdmans, 1996.

Dupont, Jacques, OSB. "Le salut des gentils et la signification théologique du livre des Actes." *NTS* 6, no. 2 (1960): 132–155.

———. *The Salvation of the Gentiles: Studies in the Acts of the Apostles.* Translated by John Keating, SJ. New York: Paulist, 1979.

Eastman, Susan. "Whose Apocalypse? The Identity of the Sons of God in Romans 8:19." *JBL* 121, no. 2 (2002): 263–277.

Edwards, David N. *The Nubian Past: An Archaeology of the Sudan.* London: Routledge, 2004.

Edwards, James R. *The Gospel according to Luke.* Grand Rapids, MI: Eerdmans, 2015.

Ellis, E. Earle. "'The End of the Earth' (Acts 1:8)." *BBR* 1 (1991): 123–132.

Embry, Brad. "The Psalms of Solomon and the New Testament: Intertextuality and the Need for a Re-evaluation." *JSP* 13, no. 2 (2002): 99–136.

Emery, Walter. *Egypt in Nubia.* London: Hutchinson, 1965.

Ernst, Josef. *Das Evangelium nach Lukas.* Regensburg, Germany: Friedrich Pustet, 1993.

Evans, Craig A. "Jesus and the Spirit: On the Origin and Ministry of the Second Son of God." In *Luke and Scripture: The Function of Sacred Tradition in Luke-Acts,* edited by Craig A. Evans and James A. Sanders, 26–45. Minneapolis: Fortress, 1993.

———. *Luke.* Peabody, MA: Hendrickson, 1990.

Evans, Craig F. *Saint Luke.* London: SCM, 2008.

Felder, Cain H. *Race, Racism, and the Biblical Narratives.* Minneapolis: Fortress, 2002.

Ferda, Tucker S. "God of the Nations: Daniel, Satan, and the Temptation of Jesus in Luke." *ZNW* 110, no. 1 (2019): 1–20.

Fitzmyer, Joseph A. *The Acts of the Apostles: A New Translation with Introduction and Commentary.* AB 31. New York: Doubleday, 1998.

———. *The Gospel according to Luke (I–IX): Introduction, Translation, and Notes.* AB 28. Garden City, NY: Doubleday, 1981.

———. *The Gospel according to Luke (X–XXIV): Introduction, Translation, and Notes.* AB 28. Garden City, NY: Doubleday, 1985.

Fletcher-Louis, Crispin H. T. *All the Glory of Adam: Liturgical Anthropology in the Dead Sea Scrolls*. Leiden: Brill, 2002.

———. *Luke-Acts: Angels, Christology, and Soteriology*. WUNT. Tübingen, Germany: Mohr Siebeck, 1997.

———. "Some Reflections on Angelomorphic Humanity Texts among the Dead Sea Scrolls." *DSD* 7, no. 3 (2000): 292–312.

———. "The Worship of Divine Humanity as God's Image and the Worship of Jesus." In *Christological Monotheism: Papers from the St. Andrews Conference on the Historical Origins of the Worship of Jesus*, edited by Carey C. Newman, James R. Davila, and Gladys S. Lewis, 112–128. Leiden: Brill, 1999.

Fohrer, G. "Υίός." *TDNT* 8:347–353.

Forbes, Greg. *The God of Old: The Role of the Lukan Parables in the Purpose of Luke's Gospel*. Sheffield: Sheffield Academic Press, 2000.

———. "Repentance and Conflict in the Parable of the Lost Son (Luke 15:11–32)." *JETS* 42, no. 2 (1999): 211–229.

Frost, Peter. "Attitudes towards Blacks in the Early Christian Era." *Second Century* 8, no. 1 (1991): 1–11.

García-Martínez, Florentino, and Eibert Tigchelaar, eds. *The Dead Sea Scrolls Study Edition*. Grand Rapids, MI: Eerdmans, 2000.

Gardner, Andrew, Edward Herring, and Kathryn Lomas, eds. *Creating Ethnicities and Identities in the Roman World*. Bulletin of the Institute of Classical Studies Supp 120. London: Institute of Classical Studies, 2013.

Gathercole, Simon. *The Preexistent Son: Recovering the Christologies of Matthew, Mark, and Luke*. Grand Rapids, MI: Eerdmans, 2006.

Gaventa, Beverly. *From Darkness to Light: Aspects of Conversion in the New Testament*. Philadelphia: Fortress, 1986.

———. *The Acts of the Apostles*. Nashville, TN: Abingdon Press, 2003.

Gealy, F. D. "Ethiopian Eunuch." *IDB* 1:177–178.

Geldenhuys, Norval. *Commentary on the Gospel of Luke*. London: Marshall, Morgan & Scott, 1952.

George, Michele. "Images of Black Slaves in the Roman Empire." *Syllecta Classica* 14 (2003): 161–185.

Glenny, W. Edward. "The Septuagint and Apostolic Hermeneutics: Amos 9 in Acts 15." *BBR* 22, no. 1 (2012): 1–26.

Godet, F. *A Commentary on the Gospel of St. Luke*. Translated by E. W. Shalders and M. D. Cusin. New York: I. K. Funk, 1881.

Goldenberg, David M. *The Curse of Ham: Race and Slavery in Early Judaism, Christianity, and Islam*. Princeton, NJ: Princeton University Press, 2003.

———. "Racism, Color Symbolism, and Color Prejudice." In *The Origins of Racism in the West*, edited by Miriam Eliav-Feldon, Benjamin Isaac, and Joseph Ziegler, 88–108. Cambridge: Cambridge University Press, 2009.

González, Justo L. *Acts: The Gospel of the Spirit*. Maryknoll, NY: Orbis, 2001.

Gordon, William E., II. "Cultural Identity of the 25th Dynasty Rulers of Ancient Egypt in Context: Formulation, Negotiation and Expression." PhD diss., UCLA, 2009.

Grabbe, Lester. " 'Better Watch Your Back, Adam': Another Adam and Eve Tradition in Second Temple Judaism." In *New Perspectives on 2 Enoch: No Longer Slavonic Only*, edited by Andrei Orlov and Gabriele Boccaccini, 273–282. Leiden: Brill, 2012.

Grassi, Joseph A. "Emmaus Revisited (Luke 24, 13–35 and Acts 8, 26–40)." *CBQ* 26, no. 4 (1964): 463–467.

Green, Joel B. *Conversion in Luke-Acts: Divine Action, Human Cognition, and the People of God*. Grand Rapids, MI: Baker Academic, 2015.

———. *The Gospel of Luke*. Grand Rapids, MI: Eerdmans, 1997.

———. *The Theology of the Gospel of Luke*. Cambridge: Cambridge University Press, 1995.

Gruen, Erich S. *Rethinking the Other in Antiquity*. Princeton, NJ: Princeton University Press, 2011.

Haag, H. "Sohn Gottes Im Alten Testament." *TQ* 154 (1974): 223–231.

———. "בֵּן." *TDOT* 1:145–158.

Haenchen, Ernst. *The Acts of the Apostles*. Philadelphia: Westminster Press, 1971.

Hägg, Tomas. "The Black Land of the Sun: Meroe in Heliodorus's Romantic Fiction." In *Parthenope: Selected Studies in Ancient Greek Fiction (1969–2004)*, edited by Lars Boje Mortensen and Tormod Eide, 345–378. Copenhagen: Museum Tusculanum, 2004.

Heinze, Matthias. " '4 Ezra' and '2 Baruch:' Literary Composition and Oral Performance in First Century Apocalyptic Literature." *JBL* 131, no. 1 (2012): 181–200.

Heiser, Michael. "Deuteronomy 32:8 and the Sons of God." *BSac* 158, no. 629 (2001): 52–74.

Hengel, Martin. *The Son of God: The Origin of Christology and the History of Jewish-Hellenistic Religion*. Philadelphia: Fortress, 1976.

Henrichs-Tarasenkova, Nina. *Luke's Christology of Divine Identity*. LNTS. London: Bloomsbury T&T Clark, 2016.

Heschel, Susannah. *The Aryan Jesus: Christian Theologians and the Bible in Nazi German*. Princeton, NJ: Princeton University Press, 2008.

Hock, Ronald F., and Edward N. O'Neil, eds. *The Chreia and Ancient Rhetoric: Classroom Exercises*. Translated by Ronald F. Hock and Edward N. O'Neil. Vol. 2. Atlanta, GA: SBL, 2002.

Hoffmeier, James K. "Son of God." *BRev* 13, no. 3 (1997): 44–49.

Holladay, Carl R. *Acts: A Commentary*. NTL. Louisville, KY: Westminster John Knox, 2016.

———. "Interpreting Acts." *Interpretation* 66, no. 3 (2012): 245–258.

Hood, Robert. *Begrimed and Black*. Minneapolis: Augsburg Fortress, 1994.

Hood, Rodney T. "The Genealogies of Jesus." In *Early Christian Origins: Studies in Honor of Harold R. Willoughby*, edited by Allen Wikgren, 1–15. Chicago: Quadrangle, 1961.

Hopkins, Jamal-Dominique. "The Noahic Curse in Rabbinic Literature: Racialized Hermeneutics or Ethnocentric Exegesis." In *Re-presenting Texts: Jewish and Black*

Biblical Interpretation, edited by W. David Nelson and Rivka Ulmer, 15–27. Piscataway, NJ: Gorgias, 2013.

Huffstetler, Joel. *Boundless Love: The Parable of the Prodigal Son and Reconciliation.* Lanham, MD: University Press of America, 2008.

Jabini, Frank. "Witness to the End of the World: A Missional Reading of Acts 8:26–40." *South African Theological Seminary* 13 (2012): 51–72.

Jeremias, Joachim. "Ἀδάμ." *TDNT* 1:141–143.

———. *The Parables of Jesus.* Rev. ed. London: SCM, 1963.

———. "Tradition and Redaktion in Lukas 15." *ZNW* 62, no. 3 (1971): 172–189.

Jerkins, Marcus. "The Dynamism of Blackness in an Ethiopian Story and Acts." *PRSt* 46, no. 3 (2019): 307–326.

Jervell, Jacob. *Luke and the People of God: A New Look at Luke-Acts.* Minneapolis: Augsburg, 1972.

Jipp, Joshua W. "Paul's Areopagus Speech of Acts 17:16–34 as Both Critique and Propaganda." *JBL* 131, no. 3 (2012): 567–588.

Johnson, Aaron. "The Blackness of Ethiopians: Classical Ethnography and Eusebius's Commentary on the Psalms." *HTR* 99, no. 2 (2006): 165–186.

Johnson, Luke Timothy. *The Acts of the Apostles.* Sacra Pagina. Collegeville, MN: Liturgical, 1992.

———. *Contested Issues in Christian Origins and the New Testament: Collected Essays.* Leiden: Brill, 2013.

———. *The Gospel of Luke.* Collegeville, MN: Liturgical, 1991.

Johnson, M. D. "Life of Adam and Eve: A New Translation and Introduction." In *OTP*, 250–283. Vol. 2. n.d.

———. *The Purpose of Biblical Genealogies: With Special Reference to the Settings of the Genealogies of Jesus.* SNTSMS. Cambridge: Cambridge University Press, 1969.

Johnson, Nathan. "Rendering David a Servant in Psalm of Solomon 17.21." *JSP* 26, no. 3 (2017): 235–250.

Joosten, Jan. "A Note on the Text of Deuteronomy Xxxii 8." *VT* 57 (2007): 548–555.

———. "Son of God in Wisdom 2:16–18: Between the Hebrew Bible and the New Testament." In *Son of God: Divine Sonship in Jewish and Christian Antiquity*, edited by Garrick V. Allen, Kai Akagi, Paul Sloan, and Madhavi Nevader, 41–52. University Park, PA: Eisenbrauns, 2019.

Kearns, Emily. *Ancient Greek Religion: A Sourcebook.* West Sussex: Wiley-Blackwell, 2010.

Keener, Craig. *Acts: An Exegetical Commentary: Introduction and 1:1–2:47.* Vol. 1. Grand Rapids, MI: Baker Academic, 2012.

———. *Acts: An Exegetical Commentary (3:1–14:28).* Vol. 2. Grand Rapids, MI: Baker Academic, 2013.

Kelly, David H. "Egyptians and Ethiopians: Color, Race, and Racism." *Classical Outlook* 68, no. 3 (1991): 77–82.

Khanna, Nikki. "If You're Half Black, You're Just Black: Reflected Appraisals and the Persistence of the One-Drop Rule." *Sociological Quarterly* 51, no. 1 (2010): 96–121.

King, Martin Luther, Jr. *Where Do We Go from Here: Chaos or Community?* Boston: Beacon, 1968.

Kirk, J. Daniel. *A Man Attested by God: The Human Jesus of the Synoptic Gospels.* Grand Rapids, MI: Eerdmans, 2016.

Kister, Menahem. "Son(s) of God: Israel and Christ: A Study of Transformation, Adaptation, and Rivalry." In *Son of God: Divine Sonship in Jewish and Christian Antiquity*, edited by Garrick V. Allen, Kai Akagi, Paul Sloan, and Madhavi Nevader, 188–224. University Park, PA: Eisenbrauns, 2019.

Kittel, Gerhard. "Ἀββᾶ." *TDNT* 1:5–6.

Klijn, A. F. J. "2 (Syriac Apocalypse of) Baruch: A New Translation and Introduction." In *OTP*, 615–652. Vol. 1. n.d.

Kochenash, Michael. "'Adam, Son of God' (Luke 3:38): Another Jesus-Augustus Parallel in Luke's Gospel." *NTS* 64 (2018): 307–325.

Kratz, Reinhard. "Son of God and Son of Man: 4Q246 in the Light of the Book of Daniel." In *Son of God: Divine Sonship in Jewish and Christian Antiquity*, edited by Garrick V. Allen, Kai Akagi, Paul Sloan, and Madhavi Nevader, 9–27. University Park, PA: Eisenbrauns, 2019.

Lagrange, P. M.-J. *Évangile Selon Saint Luc.* Paris: J. Gabalda et Cie, 1948.

———. "La Paternité de Dieu: Dans l'Ancien Testament." *RB* 5, no. 4 (1908): 481–499.

Lasor, W. S. "Africa." *ISBE* 1:63–64.

Leaney, A. R. C. *A Commentary on the Gospel of St. Luke.* 2nd ed. London: Adam, Charles & Black, 1966.

Lee, Jesse J. "On Distracting and Disappearing Joy: An Exegetical Comparison of the Ethiopian Eunuch and the Slave-Girl Rhoda in Acts." *HBT* 40 (2018): 65–77.

Leunissen, Mariska. "Physiognomy." In *Oxford Handbook of Science and Medicine in the Classical World*, edited by Paul T. Keyser and John Scarborough, 743–764. Oxford: Oxford University Press, 2018.

Levenson, Jon D. *Creation and the Persistence of Evil: The Jewish Drama of Divine Omnipotence.* San Francisco: Harper & Row, 1988.

Levine, Amy-Jill. *Short Stories by Jesus: The Enigmatic Parables of a Controversial Rabbi.* New York: HarperOne, 2014.

Lim, Sung Uk. "Race and Ethnicity Discourse in Biblical Studies and Beyond." *Journal for the Study of Religions and Ideologies* 15, no. 45 (2016): 120–142.

Lincicum, David. "Philo and the Physiognomic Tradition." *JSJ* 44 (2013): 57–86.

Livneh, Atar. "The 'Beloved Sons' of Jubilees." *Journal of Ancient Judaism* 6, no. 1 (2015): 85–96.

Ma'at-Ka-Re Monges, Miriam. *Kush, the Jewel of Nubia: Reconnection the Root System of African Civilization.* Trenton, NJ: Africa World, 1997.

Malina, Bruce, and Jerome Neyrey, SJ. "First Century Personality: Dyadic, Not Individual." In *The Social World of Luke-Acts*, edited by Jerome Neyrey, SJ, 67–96. Peabody, MA: Hendrickson, 1991.

Manson, William. *The Gospel of Luke.* London: Harper and Brothers, 1930.

Marcus, Joel. "Son of Man as Son of Adam." *RB* 110, no. 1 (2003): 38–61.

————. "Son of Man as Son of Adam: Part II: Exegesis (Continued)." *RB* 110, no. 3 (2003): 370–386.

Marshall, I. H. "The Christology of Luke's Gospel and Acts." In *Contours of Christology in the New Testament*, edited by Richard N. Longenecker, 122–147. Grand Rapids, MI: Eerdmans, 2005.

————. *The Gospel of Luke: A Commentary on the Greek Text*. 1st ed. NICGT. Grand Rapids, MI: Eerdmans, 1978.

Martin, Clarice J. "A Chamberlain's Journey and the Challenge of Interpretation for Liberation." *Semeia* 47 (1989): 105–135.

————. "The Function of Acts 8:26–40 within the Narrative Structure of the Book of Acts: The Significance of the Eunuch's Provenance for Acts 1:8c." PhD diss., Duke University, 1985.

Martin, Frank. "The Egyptian Ethnicity Controversy and the Sociology of Knowledge." *Journal of Black Studies* 14, no. 3 (1984): 295–325.

Mason, Steve, James S. McLaren, and John M. G. Barclay. "Josephus." In *Early Judaism: A Comprehensive Overview*, edited by John J. Collins and Daniel C. Harlow, 290–321. Grand Rapids, MI: Eerdmans, 2010.

Matthews, Christopher. *Philip: Apostle and Evangelist*. NovT Sup. Leiden: Brill, 2002.

McCaulley, Esau. *Reading While Black: African American Biblical Interpretation as an Exercise in Hope*. Downers Grove, IL: IVP, 2020.

McCoskey, Denise E. *Race: Antiquity and Its Legacy*. Oxford: Oxford University Press, 2012.

McKissic, William Dwight, Sr., and Anthony T. Evans. *Beyond Roots II; If Anybody Ask You Who I Am*. Wenonah, NJ: Renaissance, 1994.

Merritt, H. Wayne. "The Individual and the Group in Luke: A Study of Malina's Hypothesis of the Dyadic Personality in First-Century Mediterranean Society." In *The Recovery of Black Presence: An Interdisciplinary Exploration: Essays in Honor of Dr. Charles B. Copher*, edited by Randall C. Bailey and Jacquelyn Grant, 65–76. Nashville, TN: Abingdon, 1995.

Metzger, Bruce M. *A Textual Commentary on the Greek New Testament*. Stuttgart, Germany: Deutsche Bibelgesellschaft, 1994.

Meyer, Nicholas. *Adam's Dust and Adam's Glory in the Hodayot and the Letters of Paul: Rethinking Anthropogony and Theology*. Boston: Brill, 2016.

Middleton, Richard J. *The Liberating Image: The Imago Dei in Genesis 1*. Grand Rapids, MI: Brazos, 2005.

Minear, Paul S. "Luke's Use of the Birth Stories." In *Studies in Luke-Acts*, edited by Leander Keck and J. Louis Martyn, 111–130. Philadelphia: Fortress, 1980.

Morgan, J. R. "A Sense of the Ending: The Conclusion of Heliodorus' Aithiopika." *TAPA* 119 (1989): 299–320.

Moule, C. F. D. "The Christology of Acts." In *Studies in Luke-Acts*, edited by Leander Keck and J. Louis Martyn, 159–185. Philadelphia: Fortress, 1980.

Moxnes, H., and M. B. Kartzow. "Complex Identities: Ethnicity, Gender and Religion in the Story of the Ethiopian Eunuch (Acts 8:26–40)." *R&T* 17, nos. 3–4 (2010): 184–204.

Neyrey, Jerome, SJ. *The Passion according to Luke: A Redaction Study of Luke's Soteriology*. Eugene, OR: Wipf & Stock, 1985.

Niccum, Curt. "One Ethiopian Is Not the End of the World: The Narrative Function of Acts 8:26–40." In *A Teacher for All Generation: Essays in Honor of James C. VanderKam*, edited by Eric F. Mason, Kelley Coblentz Bautch, Angela Kim Harkins, and Daniel A. Machiela, 883–900. Leiden: Brill, 2012.

Nickelsburg, George W. E., Jr. *1 Enoch 2: A Commentary on the Book of 1 Enoch Chapters 37–82*. Hermeneia. Minneapolis: Fortress, 2012.

Nogalski, James D. "The Problematic Suffixes of Amos IX 11." *VT* 43, no. 3 (1993): 411–418.

———. "Three Faces of Hope: Amos 9:11–12 and Acts 15:12–19." *RevExp* 11, no. 2 (2015): 311–315.

Nolland, John. *Luke 1–9:20*. WBC 35A. Dallas: Word Books, 1989.

Norris, Kristopher. "Race and Resurrection: Contesting Colorblind White Supremacy with Biblical Resources." *Theology Today* 77, no. 1 (2020): 33–46.

O'Brien, Mark A., OP. *Restoring the Right Relationship: The Bible on Divine Righteousness*. Hindmarsh, South Australia: ATF Theology, 2014.

Origen. *The Song of Songs: Commentary and Homilies*. Translated by R. P. Lawson. Ancient Christian Writers 26. New York: Newman, 1956.

Park, Rohun. "Revisiting the Parable of the Prodigal Son for Decolonization: Luke's Reconfiguration of Oikos in 15:11–32." *BibInt* 17 (2009): 507–520.

Parkman, Joel W. "Adam Christological Motifs in the Synoptic Traditions." PhD diss., Baylor University, 1994.

Parsons, Mikeal C. *Acts*. Paideia Commentaries on the New Testament. Grand Rapids, MI: Baker Academic, 2008.

———. *Body and Character in Luke and Acts: The Subversion of Physiognomy in Early Christianity*. Waco, TX: Baylor University Press, 2011.

———. *The Departure of Jesus in Luke-Acts: The Ascension Narratives in Context*. JSNTSup. Sheffield: Sheffield Academic Press, 1987.

———. "The Ethiopian Eunuch Unhindered: Embodied Rhetoric in Acts 8." In *"A Temple Not Made with Hands": Essays in Honor of Naymond H. Keathley*, edited by Mikeal C. Parsons and Richard Walsh, 146–160. Eugene, OR: Pickwick, 2018.

———. *Luke*. Paideia Commentaries on the New Testament. Grand Rapids, MI: Baker Academic, 2015.

———. *Luke: Storyteller, Interpreter, Evangelist*. Waco, TX: Baylor University Press, 2014.

Parsons, Mikeal C., and Richard I. Pervo. *Rethinking the Unity of Luke and Acts*. Minneapolis: Fortress, 1993.

Peppard, Michael. "Adopted and Begotten Sons of God: Paul and John on Divine Sonship." *CBQ* 73, no. 1 (2011): 92–110.

———. "Son of God in Gentile Contexts (That Is, Almost Everywhere)." In *Son of God: Divine Sonship in Jewish and Christian Antiquity*, edited by Garrick V. Allen, Kai Akagi, Paul Sloan, and Madhavi Nevader, 135–157. University Park, PA: Eisenbrauns, 2019.

————. *The Son of God in the Roman World: Divine Sonship in Its Social and Political Context.* Oxford: Oxford University Press, 2014.

Perkins, Judith. "An Ancient 'Passing' Novel: Heliodorus' Aithiopika." *Arethusa* 32, no. 2 (1999): 197–214.

Pinches, T. G. "Africa." *ISBE* 1:68.

Plummer, A. *A Critical and Exegetical Commentary on the Gospel according to Saint Luke.* 5th ed. ICC. London: T&T Clark, 1898.

Pokorný, Petr. *Theologie der Lukanischen Schriften.* Göttingen, Germany: Vandenhoeck & Ruprecht, 1998.

Pope, Jeremy. *The Double Kingdom under Taharqo: Studies in the History of Kush and Egypt, C. 690–664 BC.* Leiden: Brill, 2014.

Popović, Mladen. "Physiognomic Knowledge in Qumran and Babylonia: Form, Interdisciplinarity, and Secrecy." *DSD* 13, no. 2 (2006): 150–176.

————. *Reading the Human Body: Physiognomics and Astrology in the Dead Sea Scrolls and Hellenistic-Early Roman Period Judaism.* Studies on the Texts of the Desert of Judah 67. Leiden: Brill, 2007.

Priest, J. "Testament of Moses: A New Translation and Introduction." In *OTP*, 919–934. Vol. 2. n.d.

Quell, G. "Πατήρ: B: 'The Father Concept in the Old Testament.'" *TDNT* 5:959–974.

Rastoin, Marc. "Le génie littéraire et théologique de Luc en Lc 15.11–32 éclairé par le parallele avec Mt 21.28–32." *NTS* 60, no. 1 (2014): 1–19.

Ravens, David. *Luke and the Restoration of Israel.* Sheffield: Sheffield Academic Press, 1995.

Reardon, B. P., ed. *Collected Ancient Greek Novels.* Berkeley: University of California Press, 2008.

Relevant Staff. "Uh, Eric Metaxas Said That Jesus Was White?" *Relevant*, July 28, 2020. https://tinyurl.com/69t8s48h.

Richardson, H. Neil. "The Old Testament Background of Jesus as Begotten of God." *BRev* 2, no. 3 (1986): 22–24, 26–27.

Ringe, Sharon. *Luke.* Louisville, KY: Westminster John Knox, 1995.

Ringren, H. "אב." *TDOT* 1:1–19.

Roberts, J. J. M. *First Isaiah: A Commentary.* Hermeneia. Minneapolis: Fortress, 2015.

Rowe, C. Kavin. "Acts 2.36 and the Continuity of Lukan Christology." *NTS* 53 (2007): 37–56.

————. *Early Narrative Christology.* ZNW. New York: Walter de Gruyter, 2006.

————. "The Grammar of Life: The Areopagus Speech and Pagan Tradition." *NTS* 57 (2010): 31–50.

Sadler, Rodney S. *Can a Cushite Change His Skin? An Examination of Race, Ethnicity, and Othering in the Hebrew Bible.* New York: T&T Clark, 2005.

————. "Can a Cushite Change His Skin? Cushites, 'Racial Othering,' and the Hebrew Bible." *Interpretation* 10, no. 6 (2006): 386–403.

Samuels, Tristan. "Herodotus and the Black Body: A Critical Race Theory Analysis." *Journal of Black Studies* 46, no. 7 (2015): 723–741.

Sanders, Jack T. "Tradition and Redaction in Luke 15:11–32." *NTS* 15, no. 4 (1969): 433–438.

Sarna, Nahum M. *Genesis: The Traditional Hebrew Text with New JPS Translation.* Philadelphia: Jewish Publication Society, 198s9.

Schlißke, Werner. *Gottessöhne und Gottessohn im Alten Testament.* Berlin: Kohlhammer, 1973.

Schweizer, Eduard. *The Good News according to Luke.* Translated by David Green. Atlanta, GA: John Knox, 1984.

Scott, James M. "Luke's Geographical Horizon." In *The Book of Acts in Its First Century Setting,* edited by David W. Gill and Conrad Gempf, 483–544. The Book of Acts in Its Graeco-Roman Setting 2. Grand Rapids, MI: Eerdmans, 2002.

Scott, Spencer F. *The Portrait of Philip in Acts: A Study of Roles and Relations.* JSOT Sup 67. Sheffield: JSOT, 1992.

Seim, Turid Karlsen. *The Double Message: Patterns of Gender in Luke-Acts.* Nashville, TN: Abingdon, 1994.

Shalev, Donna. "Heliodorus' Speakers: Multiculturalism and Literary Innovation in Conventions for Framing Speech." *Bulletin of the Institute of Classical Studies* 49 (2006): 165–191.

Shauf, Scott. "Locating the Eunuch: Characterization and Narrative Context in Acts 8:26–40." *CBQ* 71, no. 4 (2009): 726–775.

Smith, Abraham. "'Do You Understand What You Are Reading?' A Literary Critical Reading of the Ethiopian (Kushite) Episode (Acts 8:26–40)." *Journal of the Interdenominational Theological Center* 22 (1994): 48–70.

Smith, S. T. *Wretched Kush: Ethnic Identities and Boundaries in Egypt's Nubian Empire.* New York: Routledge, 2003.

Snowden, Frank M., Jr. *Before Color Prejudice: The Ancient View of Blacks.* Cambridge, MA: Harvard University Press, 1983.

———. *Blacks in Antiquity: Ethiopians in the Greco-Roman Experience.* Cambridge, MA: Belknap, 1970.

———. "Misconceptions about African Blacks in the Ancient Mediterranean World: Specialists and Afrocentrist." *Arion: A Journal of Humanities and the Classics* 4, no. 3 (1997): 28–50.

———. "The Negro in Ancient Greece." *American Anthropologist* 50, no. 1 (1948): 31–44.

———. "The Negro in Classical Italy." *American Journal of Philology* 68, no. 3 (1947): 266–292.

Squires, John T. "The Function of Acts 8.4–12.25." *NTS* 44 (1998): 608–617.

Stein, Robert H. *Luke.* New American Standard Commentary 24. Nashville, TN: Broadman & Holman, 1992.

Sterling, Greg, David T. Runia, Maren R. Niehoff, and Annewies van den Hoek. "Philo." In *Early Judaism: A Comprehensive Overview,* edited by John J. Collins and Daniel C. Harlow, 253–289. Grand Rapids, MI: Eerdmans, 2010.

Stevens, David E. "Does Deuteronomy 32:8 Refer to 'Sons of God' or 'Sons of Israel'?" *BSac* 154, no. 614 (1997): 131–141.

Stone, Michael E. *Fourth Ezra: A Commentary on the Book of Fourth Ezra.* Hermeneia. Minneapolis: Fortress, 1990.

Strauss, Mark L. *The Davidic Messiah in Luke-Acts: The Promise and Its Fulfillment in Lukan Christology.* JSNTSup 110. Sheffield: Sheffield Academic Press, 1995.

Strawn, Brent. "What Is Cush Doing in Amos 9:7? The Poetics of Exodus in the Plural." *VT* 63 (2013): 99–123.

Stuart, Streeter S. "The Exodus Tradition in Psalm 105 and the Wisdom of Solomon: Notable Similarities." *EQ* 90, no. 2 (2019): 132–141.

Stuckenbruck, Loren T. "The Book of Jubilees and the Origin of Evil." In *Enoch and the Mosaic Torah: The Evidence of Jubilees,* edited by Gabriele Boccaccini, Giovanni Ibba, Jason von Ehrenkrook, James Waddell, and Jason M. Zurawski, 294–308. Grand Rapids, MI: Eerdmans, 2009.

Sung-Ho Oh, Abraham. *That You Would Rend the Heavens and Come Down! The Eschatological Theology of Third Isaiah.* Cambridge: James Clark, 2014.

Talbert, Charles. *Reading Luke: A Literary and Theological Commentary on the Third Gospel.* New York: Crossroad, 1982.

———. *Reading Luke-Acts in Its Mediterranean Milieu.* NovT Sup. Leiden: Brill, 2003.

Tannehill, Robert. *The Narrative Unity of Luke-Acts: A Literary Interpretation.* Philadelphia: Fortress, 1986.

———. "The Story of Israel within the Lukan Narrative." In *Jesus and the Heritage of Israel: Luke's Narrative Claim upon Israel's Legacy,* edited by David P. Moessner, 325–339. Harrisburg, PA: Trinity, 2000.

Tanner, J. Paul. "James's Quotation of Amos 9 to Settle the Jerusalem Council Debate in Acts 15." *JETS* 55, no. 1 (2012): 65–85.

Taylor, John H. *Egypt and Nubia.* London: British Museum Press, 1991.

Thompson, Lloyd. "Roman Perceptions of Blacks." *Scholia* 2 (1993): 17–30.

———. *Romans and Blacks.* London: Routledge, 1989.

Tiede, David. *Luke.* Minneapolis: Augsburg, 1988.

Tigchelaar, Eibert. "The Dead Sea Scrolls." In *Early Judaism: A Comprehensive Overview,* edited by John J. Collins and Daniel C. Harlow, 204–227. Grand Rapids, MI: Eerdmans, 2010.

Török, László. *Herodotus in Nubia.* Leiden: Brill, 2014.

Twelftree, Graham H. *People of the Spirit: Exploring Luke's View of the Church.* Grand Rapids, MI: Baker Academic, 2009.

Ullendorff, Edward. "Candace (Acts VIII. 27) and the Queen of Sheba." *NTS* 2, no. 1 (1955): 53–56.

Van Unnik, W. C. "Der Ausdruck (Apostelgeschichte i 8) Und Sein Alttestamentlicher Hintergrund." In *Sparsa Collecta: The Collected Essays of W. C. Van Unnik,* 321–327. Vol. 1. NovTSup 29. Leiden: Brill, 1973.

von Martitz, Peter W. "Υἱός, Υἱοθεσία Α." *TDNT* 8:334–340.

Watts, John D. W. *Isaiah 1–33.* WBC 24. Dallas: Thomas Nelson, 2005.

———. *Isaiah 34–66.* WBC 25B. Dallas: Thomas Nelson, 2005.

Weissenrieder, Annette. "Searching for the Middle Ground from the End of the Earth: The Embodiment of Space in Acts 8:26–40." *Neotestamentica* 48, no. 1 (2014): 115–161.

Wenham, Gordon J. *Genesis 1–15*. WBC 1. Dallas: Word Books, 1987.

Wenkel, David H. "When the Apostles Became Kings: Ruling and Judging the Twelve Tribes of Israel in the Book of Acts." *BTB* 42, no. 3 (2012): 119–128.

Westermann, Claus. *Genesis 1–11: A Commentary*. Translated by John J. Scullion. Minneapolis: Augsburg Fortress, 1984.

Williams, Demetrius K. "The Acts of the Apostles." In *True to Our Native Land: An African American New Testament Commentary*, edited by Brian K. Blount, 213–248. Minneapolis: Fortress, 2007.

Wilson, Brittany E. "'Neither Male nor Female': The Ethiopian Eunuch in Acts 8.26–40." *NTS* 60, no. 3 (2014): 403–422.

———. *Unmanly Men: Refigurations of Masculinity in Luke-Acts*. New York: Oxford University Press, 2015.

Wilson, Stephen G. *The Gentiles and the Gentile Mission in Luke-Acts*. Cambridge: Cambridge University Press, 1973.

Wimbush, Vincent. "Ascetic Behavior and Color-ful Language: Stories about Ethiopian Moses." *Semeia* 58 (1992): 81–92.

Winter, Paul. "Der Begriff, 'Söhne Gottes,' im Moselied Dtn 32, 1–43." *ZAW* 67, no. 1 (1955): 40–48.

Wolff, Hans W. *A Commentary on the Book of the Prophet Hosea*. Translated by Gary Stansell. Hermeneia. Minneapolis: Fortress, 1974.

Wright, Archie T. *The Origin of Evil Spirits: The Reception of Genesis 6:1–4 in Early Jewish Literature*. Rev. ed. Minneapolis: Fortress, 2015.

Wright, N. T. *Jesus and the Victory of God*. Minneapolis: Fortress, 1996.

———. *The New Testament and the People of God*. Minneapolis: Fortress, 1992.

———. *The Resurrection of the Son of God*. Minneapolis: Fortress, 2003.

———. "Son of God and Christian Origins." In *Son of God: Divine Sonship in Jewish and Christian Antiquity*, edited by Garrick V. Allen, Kai Akagi, Paul Sloan, and Madhavi Nevader, 118–134. University Park, PA: Eisenbrauns, 2019.

Yamauchi, Edwin. *Africa and the Bible*. Grand Rapids, MI: Baker Academic, 2004.

Yonge, C. D., trans. *The Works of Philo Judaeus, the Contemporary of Josephus, Translated from Greek by C. D. Yonge*. London: H. G. Bohn, 1854.

INDEX OF MODERN AUTHORS

Martin, Clarice J., 144n23, 145n29,
146n30, 146n31, 146n32, 146n36,
157–58n107, 176n3, 177n9,
180n35, 193n177, 194n193
Martin, Frank, 182n56
Mason, Steve, James S. McLaren,
153–54n75
Matthews, Christopher, 179n33
McCaulley, Esau, 140n10
McCoskey, Denise E., 182n56
McKissic, William Dwight, Sr., 197n7
Merritt, H. Wayne, 185–86n72
Metzger, Bruce M., 151n44, 194n186
Meyer, Nicholas, 156n102
Minear, Paul S., 165n40
Morgan, J. R., 188n122
Moule, C. F. D., 166n54
Moxnes, H., 145n27, 177n10

Neyrey, Jerome, 143n12, 184–85n72
Niccum, Curt, 177n5, 177n6, 178n21,
180n38, 180n42, 181n51,
193n179, 181n193
Nickelsburg, George W. E., Jr., 151n42
Niehoff, Maren R., 153n75
Nogalski, James D., 175–76n158
Nolland, John, 141n1
Norris, Kristopher, 140n4

O'Brien, Mark A., 140n4
O'Neil, Edward N., 188n114

Parkman, Joel W., 161n7
Parsons, Mikeal C., 140n6, 140n9,
141n1, 141n2, 145n26, 145n27,
147n42, 147n45, 147n46, 160n4,
161n8, 163n20, 163n21, 163n22,
163n23, 163n25, 166n52, 167n66,
167n70, 169n83, 170n89, 170n96,
173n137, 174n141, 174n147,
175n150, 176n3, 177n10, 178n17,
180n46, 180n48, 186n92,
187n107, 193n176, 193n178,
194n196, 195n195, 195n198,

195n199, 195n201, 195n201,
195n203, 195n205, 195n210
Peppard, Michael, 144n21, 144n22,
148n2, 158n109, 159n121,
159n126, 159n128, 159n129,
159n130, 159n132, 159n133,
164n33
Perkins, Judith, 188n122
Pervo, Richard I., 141n1
Pinches, T. G., 197n9
Plummer, A., 141n2
Pokorný, Petr, 163n18, 163n19,
166n49, 174n146, 175n150
Pope, Jeremy, 183n58
Popović, Mladen, 192n175
Priest, J., 150n38

Quell, G., 147n1

Rastoin, Marc, 173n117
Ravens, David, 173n139
Reardon, B. P., 188n119, 188n123
Richardson, H. Neil, 147n1
Ringe, Sharon, 161n11
Ringren, H., 147n1
Roberts, J. J. M., 181n54
Rowe, C. Kavin, 166n54, 169n79,
175n148, 175n155
Runia, David T., 153n75

Sadler, Rodney S., 140n17, 182n55,
185n75, 190n140, 190n141,
190n143, 192n174, 197n3
Samuels, Tristan, 182n56, 184n66,
186n81, 186n94, 187n96,
187n108
Sanders, Jack T., 172n117
Sarna, Nahum M. Genesis, 154n86,
155n96
Schlißke, Werner, 142n4, 147n1,
148n7
Scott, James M., 141–42n2, 195n206
Shalev, Donna, 188n121
Shauf, Scott, 181n51, 193n182

INDEX OF SCRIPTURE

OLD TESTAMENT

THE NEW TESTAMENT

INDEX OF OTHER
ANCIENT LITERATURE

DEAD SEA SCROLLS